LOOK FOR A LETTER TOMORROW

A C...

*The Letters Home
from Wellesley College 1900–1904
of Helen Gertrude Fox, '04*

*Edited by her Daughter
Margaret Carmichael Emerson, '35*

*Freedom Press Associates, Freedom NH
2000*

Freedom Press Associates
18 Old Portland Road
Freedom NH 03836

Edited by Margaret Carmichael Emerson

Design and Typesetting by Gail H. Bickford
and Susan H. Clark

ISBN-0-945069-10-3

LOOK FOR A LETTER

TOMORROW

A College Girl's Life
100 Years Ago

For
all Helen's descendants,
those now living
and
those yet to be born

Helen Gertrude Fox

TABLE OF CONTENTS

ACKNOWLEDGEMENTS

My heartfelt thanks to all those who have helped me with publishing this book of my mother's letters. First, to my grandmother, for carefully saving these letters, so precious to her—in that old wooden Snell & Simpson Superior Biscuits box in her attic, for many long years; to my mother, for not throwing them away when she found them and for keeping them for me to find and read when the time was right.

Also, my deep thanks to my family and good friends who have encouraged me to keep at the long job of editing the letters until it was done.

My warm thanks to the New Hampshire Wellesley Club for its enthusiasm and help in publishing.

And to Donna-Belle (Nelson) Garvin, Wellesley '67, Director of Research and Publications for the New Hampshire Historical Society, for her interest, encouragement and advice.

Thanks also to Wilma Slaight, Archivist at Wellesley College Library, who took so much of her valuable time to find answers to my many questions concerning the College of 100 years ago, and who granted permission for the use of the pictures of the Wellesley girl on the cover and several of college buildings.

And to Bill Swaffield of Kingswood Press of Wolfeboro, New Hampshire and Rick Bourque, Offset Manager of the Printing Services at Wellesley for a fine job of printing, especially the Wellesley girl on the cover.

To Susann Foster Brown, Trustee of the New Hampshire Farm Museum for finding the letters of Charles Jones to Helen Fox, which I donated to the museum years ago.

And many thanks to Gail Holmgren Bickford, Wellesley '51, and Susan Clark of Freedom Press Associates for their assistance and perseverance in seeing this project through.

Margaret Carmichael Emerson, '35

EDITOR'S NOTES

The letters in this book were selected from the four hundred and forty-four letters and postals written by my mother, Helen Fox, to her family in New Hampshire during her four years at Wellesley. I have edited them with care, bypassing long pages about the weather and most comments concerning family and village affairs. There are nearly as many letters written to Helen by her family in the collection, but as most of these have little to do with college life, I have included only a few. What is left is a vibrant picture of the day-to-day life of a college girl 100 years ago; a "time capsule" that will become more valuable as the year 2000 rolls on into the next millennium.

A few things mentioned in Helen's letters are so foreign to our life today that they may need some explanation.

In 1900, automobiles were still in the experimental stage or the toys of the very wealthy. Transportation for long distances was by trains which crisscrossed the country, powered by coal-burning, powerful steam locomotives. In the more populated areas around and in cities were electric cars, called "electrics" or "cars"—later "trolleys"—which ran on tracks in the middle of the streets and roads where electricity was available. There were no motorcycles and few bicycles. Apparently they were not much in use at college, as Helen's only mention was of one belonging to a friend of her roommate Nina in Ayer, referred to as "a wheel." The long voluminous skirts and many petticoats worn by women would have made it hard to navigate on the bicycles of that day. Furthermore, most roads and streets were still dirt—and dirty—and "mud season" was long. Local transportation in 1900 still belonged to horse-drawn vehicles.

As for communication, letters were still the primary form. Mails were fast and by train. A letter mailed in New Hampshire in the early morning went out on the early "down-train" to Boston and Helen could read it in Wellesley about 3:00 P.M. that day. If she put her letter home in the morning mail collection at her dorm, her family could enjoy it at the supper table that evening. Telephoning was still very unsatisfactory, as few people had telephones in their homes. Although the dormitories had telephones, and the larger ones, an operator, the lines were so full of static that it was often impossible to put your call through at busy times. Telegrams were more dependable.

Electronic devices to make living easier and less time consuming were nonexistent; no vacuum cleaners, no electric irons, no hair dryers. Girls swept their rooms, ironed their clothing with flatirons heated on iron stove tops, and washed and dried their own long hair as best they could, curling it with metal hair curlers heated over small kerosene lamps. Each dormitory room still had a "commode" or wash stand, complete with a large earthenware pitcher and basin. Even though there were now bathrooms on every floor, they were small. The larger dorms had a basement laundry with a stove to heat the big wash boiler in which to boil underwear, sheets, etc.

Clothing, with its many layers, took an inordinate amount of time to care for, have made, or shop for. With the exception of hats from millinery shops and dresses made for her by dress-makers, the rest of Helen's clothing needs, even shoes, were purchased at wholesale prices through the family business. So, too, was everything else, from skates to fountain pens and furniture for her room.

I have not listed all of Helen's teachers and professors at college, as she did not name them all, but it is interesting that of those she did name, four were still at Wellesley in my day, 1931-1935.

Miss Ellen Fitz Pendleton, President of the College.

Miss Shackford, who taught English Literature.

Miss Agnes Abbott, whom I had in Art Lab (my minor).

Miss Sophie Chantal Hart, Head of the English Composition Department who taught us Comp. majors in our senior year.

Instead of numbered footnotes at the back of the book, for the reader's ease and so as not to break into Helen's train of thought too much, I have added my explanatory notes where needed, with my brackets [ ] right in the text, or, if too long, at the end of that letter. Helen's own comments are in parentheses ( ).

The Wellesley College Archives has the complete edited collection of Helen's letters home. The original, unedited letters themselves, both hers and those of her parents, will go to the New Hampshire Historical Society's Tuck Library in Concord, as part of their collection of the Fox Family papers. In both places they will be available to students.

All profits from the sale of this book will be given to Wellesley College.

Margaret Carmichael Emerson, '35

FAMILY AND FRIENDS
MENTIONED IN LETTERS

"Papa"—Everett Fremont Fox
"Mamma"—Caroline Belle (Ricker) Fox
"Papa Fox"—Elbridge Wood Fox
"Mama Fox"—Sarah Elizabeth (Buck) Fox
Sara Swasey—Everett's 1st cousin and member of Wellesley's 1st class of 1875
Edwina Fox - a much younger Fox cousin

Buck cousins
    Ray, Mott and Herman - brothers
    Charlie
    Grace Brackett (married Herman Buck), sister of Arthur Brackett

Ricker cousins, Aunts and Uncles
    Uncle James Ricker m. (Aunt) Ada Jones—Melrose, Mass.
        Cousins—Winnie and Clara Ricker, their daughters
    Aunt Abbie Ricker, m. (Uncle) Rev. Sullivan Atkins—Needham, Mass.
        Cousins—Edna and Beulah Atkins, their daughters
    Aunt Lydia Ricker m. (Uncle) John Larrabee, Mayor of Melrose
        Cousins—John and Helen Larrabee, their children
    Aunt Hannah Ricker m. (Uncle) Samuel Cragin, of Lowell, Mass.
        Cousins—Willa and Bert Cragin, their children
    Walter Norris m. cousin Winnie Ricker

"Aunt" Criss Mathews—old family friend
Elsie Avery—Nute High School Classmate
Arthur Thad Smith, former Headmaster at Nute—Dartmouth, Harvard Law
Frank Lee—former schoolmate at Nute H.S.—Boston
Arthur ("Artie") Dana Brackett, former schoolmate at Nute H.S.—Boston
Charles Jones, former Nute schoolmate—Cushing Academy and Harvard
Helen Lancaster—Roxbury, Mass.— family owns summer camp on Lovell
    Lake, N.H.
Miss McAllister—former teacher at Nute H.S.
Miss McClary—former teacher at Nute H.S., recent Wellesley graduate
Miss Berry—former teacher at Nute H.S.

SOME GIRLS HELEN KNEW AT WELLESLEY

Freshman Year

At Miss Whites, 13 Waban Street

Nina Hill (roommate)
Ethel Moody
Becky Ellis
Alice Sheldon
Bessie Eastman
Helen Peck
The Gladdings (?)

Muriel Windham
Bertha Long
"Only" Smith
Olive Miller
Miss Franklin
Miss Friend

Others

Edith Fox, Freshman
Grace Curtis, Freshman
Alice Dalrymple, Sophomore
Mary Emmett, Sophomore
College Hall Roommates
  Sara Marsh, Freshman
  Florence Snow, Freshman

House Big Sister: Miss Hayden, Junior ~ Miss Blackmere, Senior

Sophomore Year

At Norumbega, Mrs. Newman, Head of House

Edna Taylor, Sophomore
May Downing, Junior
Miss May Montgomery, Senior
Alice Stratton (?)
Esther H—(?)
Maude May

Clare Barnes, Senior
Mary Field (?)
Gertrude Ware, Sophomore
Mabel Gordon (?)
Louise Foster, Sophomore
Mary Riley

Junior Year

At Stone Hall

Miss Bliss, '99, a Post Grad
Jeanette Risdon (?), Jr. (?)
Mildred Franklin (possibly the "Miss" Franklin from Miss White's)
Margaret—(?)
Harriet Foss

Senior Year

At Norumbega again

Grace Mosely, Freshman in "Ville"
Katharine Macy, Senior—new, from Iowa College
Carrie—(Vt. Senior)
Helen Thomas, Senior
Ethel McTaggart

*The Milton Mills Grammar School, built in 1875.
Helen Fox is standing directly in front of the lower right
window. She is not yet sixteen, as her skirt is still short.*

FOREWORD

Helen Gertrude Fox went to Wellesley College from a small New Hampshire village in 1900 and graduated in 1904, at a time when very few young women even thought about going to college. If Helen seems unbelievably young and immature, she was. So were most girls 100 years ago, by today's standards. Because of her upbringing, however, Helen was probably more so than most.

Milton Mills, the little New Hampshire village where Helen was born and grew up, with its population of about 700 in 1900, was unusual for two reasons.

First, the Salmon Falls River, a boundary between the states of New Hampshire and Maine, with its falls, dams, mill ponds and mills, flowed down its valley right through the middle of town. Hence the village was half in the township of Milton, New Hampshire, and half in that of Acton, Maine. There were three large mills going full blast; two woolen mills on the New Hampshire side and the four storey "Shoe Shop" on the Maine side. There was a Freewill Baptist Church plus a one room school on River Street, in Maine. On the New Hampshire side was the Methodist Church and the imposing two storey grammar school with its tall bell tower, built in 1875.

Central Square, Milton Mills, NH.
Helen's home was the tree-shaded house on the right.

Central Square, the center of village business, was also on the New Hampshire side of the river. There stood the village's one hotel, Central House, frequented by transient salesmen. Also fronting on that square was the three storey, three generation family general store, proudly sporting over its wide front porch the sign "Asa Fox & Son." And right next to it was the home of Asa's son, Elbridge Fox, Helen's grandfather. Asa Fox, leaving the farm on Fox's Ridge in Acton, Maine, settled by his grandfather in the early 1780s, had crossed the river and opened his store in 1834. His son, Elbridge, having attended the New Hampton Literary Institute (now New Hampton School) joined his father as partner in the family business at age sixteen. He built his home next to the store in 1854.

Elbridge Wood Fox

It was one of the first in the area built to be heated by wood stoves instead of by fireplaces. Gas was not an option in country towns and, of course electricity was not in general use then. Kerosene street lights in the village had to be lighted individually every evening by old Mr. Applebee. Homes, too, were lighted by kerosene lamps, considered a great step up from candles and whale-oil lamps. Even when Helen went to college in 1900, electricity in country areas was still in the future. Concord, the state capital, did not get it until 1911.

Elbridge brought his bride, Sarah Buck, to his new home. She was one of nine children of Dr. Reuben Buck, who had studied medicine at Harvard College and then settled on the Maine side of the river in 1816. Everett Fox, only child of Elbridge and Sarah, was born in 1856. When he married, they could not bear to have him leave them, so he brought his young wife, Carrie Ricker, into his parents' household, where their daughter Helen Gertrude Fox was born in 1881. Helen, therefore, grew up having two sets of parents in residence— "Papa" and "Mamma" and "Papa Fox" and "Mamma Fox" as she called her grandparents.

After Everett had finished his studies at what was then Gorham Normal School in Gorham, Maine (now part of the Maine University system), because of his acute business sense, was delegated to run the family business. His father Elbridge, thus freed, pursued a life in civic affairs. He was Postmaster for many years, the office, of course, being in the store. He was also the first National

Weather Observer for the area. He was a Justice of the Peace and Notary Public, Trial Judge in the local court, Deacon of his church, President of the Board of Trustees of Nute High School (an endowed school) in Milton, from which Helen graduated. When Helen was in college, her grandfather was a New Hampshire State Senator. He was indeed, as his obituary said, "a valuable public servant and a wise counsel."

In his turn, Everett served as Treasurer for the Town of Milton and was instrumental in the founding and affairs of the village library. Besides running the family store, he dealt in lumber and shingles (buying standing timber only, never the land it stood on). Later, he added coal to his sales. The store had the first telegraph office and if not the first, one of the first telephones in the village. Everett also had a healthy mortgage and loan business, as there was no bank nearer than twenty miles away in Rochester, New Hampshire—a day's journey.

This brings us to the second reason why this village was unusual. The river ran through it, not navigable; but no main road ran through it. You didn't go through Milton Mills to get somewhere else—you went there because that was your destination. And when the railroads came north, they by-passed the town. The nearest railroad station was in Union, New Hampshire, four miles away—a long, hot and dusty ride in "the stage." This was an open carriage which could take six passengers, pulled by a team of two horses. In no way did it resemble the enclosed comfort and elegance of the old stage coaches. In the winter, an open sleigh with three hard, cold wooden seats made the trip. You provided your own warm robes. Even all the products of the busy mills had to be hauled by horsepower. On the Maine side, it was an even longer trip to the railroad station, over hills, and with worse weather, nearly fifteen miles, if you were headed east to Portland. That was a once-a-day trip. Two trips a day went to meet the train at Union.

The result of this lack of easy transportation was a village grown to be very self-sufficient by 1900; a small complete sphere of its own. That is, with the exception of those students wishing to continue their education. As the village schools on both sides of the river only went through the eighth grade, any young people wishing to go on to high school had to make that daily round trip by stage and train to Nute High School in Milton. Often, that early morning or late afternoon stage trip was impossible in winter weather, and students had to board with friends in Milton.

In Helen's day, Nute High School, although very small, was extremely fortunate in having a staff of four dedicated teachers: Arthur Thad Smith, referred to by his pupils as "Prof," a recent Dartmouth graduate, was the principal. Miss Berry was a Radcliffe graduate, Miss McAllister a Vassar graduate, and Miss McClary a recent graduate of Wellesley. They were able to instill in their young pupils a love of learning and a desire for further education.

Getting an education then, however, required an immense amount of determination. Most of the young people of Helen's age made do happily with what was at hand. There were jobs in the mills, in the woods or on the farms. People then were not accustomed to being entertained; they made their own fun together. Something was always going on, in the churches, the Grange, or the various fraternal organizations. There were singing schools, glee clubs and concerts; the Cornet Band was popular, and the Debating Club. Dancing, however, was somewhat frowned upon and almost everyone belonged to the Christian Temperance Union.

If you wanted to visit friends in the area, you walked. Most people did not keep horses. Helen's family did not. Their business kept them too busy to spend time caring for a horse. When they needed one, they rented a horse from the village livery stable, with a carriage or sleigh as the season demanded.

This was the village Helen grew up in, cossetted and overprotected by her adoring family. She was their treasure, their jewel, the center of their life. Having silver-blond hair, china-blue eyes and the pink and white complexion of a porcelain doll, and being small boned and delicately made, they thought her "frail" and treated her as if she were so. Actually, there never was any problem with Helen's health beyond the usual ailments common to all children. She was about as frail as an iron rod.

However, they would not let her go around the corner to the village school until she was eight years old. Hence she was nineteen when she went to Wellesley. It was a miracle that they let her go at all and an indication of her own perserverance. They only did so, I believe, because her father's first cousin, Sarah Swasey of Somersworth, New Hampshire, had been a member of the first graduating class in 1875. (Sarah was named for her mother's twin sister, Sarah Buck Fox, Helen's grandmother). Also, many of her mother's Ricker relatives lived in Melrose, Massachusetts, near enough to Wellesley, Helen's parents felt, in case of any emergency.

So—here is Helen Fox, on the morning down-train, munching on her peaches, chatting with her old friend Jeff, the conductor, and looking forward with joyful expectation to her new life as a Wellesley Freshman.

Let her tell you about it—

"Look for a Letter Tomorrow."

LOOK FOR A LETTER TOMORROW

FRESHMAN YEAR, 1900–1901

FIRST SEMESTER

9/20/1900. *[Postal]* Dear Papa—

Am as far as Beverly. "So far all safe." Saw the girls at Milton, also Elsie Avery, who goes to Vassar. Changing at Rochester, Charlie *[Buck]* came on, brought me two peaches and stayed till train started. Will say in advance that Uncle Sullivan met me. If he does not, you will know. Be sure, if you have not already sent check, please do, so it will be all right.

Look for a letter tomorrow.

With love, Helen

9/21. My dear Mamma & All—

I am really here at last, all safe, "no bones broken!" Uncle Sullivan met me, put me in a carriage for the Southern Union Station and in about a half hour joined me there. We arrived here about 3 P.M. Came straight to Miss White's. She is very nice, has red cheeks and parts her hair like Aunt Abbie. She seems very motherly. She gave me a choice of two rooms, second storey. I have chosen the back one because it is more roomy and has a little bay window with a couch in it—a real living room with a large dressing case, commode, two rocking chairs, two plain chairs, a what-not for my books, a large table for writing, a smaller one for books, etc. and two tiny beds. As yet, I have no roommate, but am to have a very nice one, Miss White says, a Miss Hill from Ayer, Mass. There are about eight very nice girls here; one only sixteen, three from N.Y., one from the South, and one, a Miss Friend, whom I like very much, from Maine. There is another Miss Fox in the Freshman class and I wonder if we are related. *[Edith Fox and Helen were not related.]*

College Hall

I went up to the College building *[College Hall]* all by myself to register as all the rest had gone up while I was unpacking.

Miss White has her steam on and it is very warm, so you must not worry about my getting cold. She sets a nice table—at least our supper was very good. My bag has come and is very nice. I forgot to bring writing paper, so borrowed this from Miss Friend and stamp from Miss Moody. Don't you think my pen works well, it saves so much time, not having to wet it. *[First fountain pen—they were not yet in general use.]*

Please write very soon and don't miss me too much. I know it was bitter hard to let me come and it wasn't easy for me. I will be good and careful, learn a lot and will love you all just the same and more.

Much love, Helen

Sept. 21, 1900. *[1st letter from home.]* My dear little girl—

Your postal and Uncle Sullivan's came this noon and your letter just a few moments ago. We were delighted to learn of your safe arrival and pleasant reception by Miss White. If she is kind to <u>you</u>, I shall certainly love her. I wish I could have been there to help you unpack. Yesterday was a hard day for us all, but we managed to survive. Everyone asks after you and seems quite interested in your welfare.

Be a good girl and don't be careless about your health. Don't sit by an open window and don't put on your thinnest undervest. And don't go out without taking your jacket as it blows up cool at night. Be very careful of your eyes. Don't read when it is getting dark. If you should wear your lawn dress, don't turn your undervest away at the neck.

Shall look for a letter often—

Much love, Mama

9/22. Dear Mamma & Everybody—

I am going to use my new 5¢ pencil to write as "homey" letter as I can. I am stretched out on my couch in my bay window, looking over my photographs. I forgot one of the house and Papa's tin-type. Also forgot a pair of scissors, will get one if I can ever see about my check and get my ten dollars. I went to the cashier—a queer, rather stern-looking old man—yesterday and asked if the check had come. He said "No," and I really felt entirely forgotten. This morning, I went up again and ventured to ask a second time, when he smiled and said "I was mistaken. Your check had come, but to Miss Pendleton." But then I found that in order to have it fixed, I must present my certificate of acceptance to Miss Pendleton, to get a card from her, fill it out, give it to Miss Carswell, some other "big, big," etc., etc., etc. In short, unwind about six yards of <u>red</u> <u>tape</u>. Of course, I had left my certificate at Miss White's, so shall have to go up again this afternoon. Then this evening is the Christian Assoc. reception.

[A postscript] 9/22. Two girls from R.I. near where President Hazard lives, came and they are <u>very</u> nice. This afternoon I have been up to College with two more nice Freshmen—A Miss Ellis from Maine and a Miss Franklin from N.J.—such a "sensible" sisterly girl. She has been to Normal School and has taken <u>fifteen</u> exams here, only missing one. She showed me the papers and they were <u>hard</u>. I was devoutly grateful to my dear "Prof" *[her former headmaster]* for his certificate.

Bad luck again, this afternoon. Went up <u>again</u> to see about check, but there was already a mob waiting to see Miss Pendleton, so I couldn't get in at all, as my number was 60 and only 23 had been in when closing time came. I must try again Monday.

I shall buy second hand books—except Latin which I would like to keep and shall get new. As for laundry, a woman comes to the house every Monday to take washing. Of course, collars and shirt-waists can be sent to the laundry, as she probably wouldn't do them as well as you did. Oh, I miss you all!

Love & kisses—Goodnight, Helen

9/24. Dear everybody—

Sunday at last. Had a stomach ache yesterday but it is all gone and I feel fine again. I stayed home last evening and Miss White made me a little visit and talked me blind, but I was glad to have her—made it seem more "homey." She said she wanted all her girls to feel at home. Now, when I want, I go down to the kitchen for a drink, clean towels or anything. She fixed me up last night with hot Jamaica ginger in milk and brought me her new steamer blanket lest I should be cold.

There are two girls *[maids]* Irish, of course, Maggie who is very bright and a fine cook and Mary, a decidedly "green" girl whom I really pity— she seems so stupid. I have tried to cultivate them and have succeeded very well—Maggie especially, she took special pains helping me when I felt ill. Mary, I think hardly understands—but she looked quite pleased when I said "Good morning" to her.

My roommate comes tomorrow and I am glad. It won't be half so lonely. And then we can fix our room up so much prettier with <u>two's</u> things.

9/25. I have learned now that I am "unconditional," so I have no need to see Miss Pendleton, so am hoping to get along more rapidly. Went to Chapel yesterday with Alice Sheldon, my neighbor. The text was "God is love" and when we came down to breakfast, we found tiny cards with that on them and a tiny flower stuck on one corner.

Mamma, won't you make me a laundry bag of chintz or calico? All the girls have them for their rooms. Now I know I don't tell you half of the things you want to know, so please ask me questions and I'll try to answer.

Lots of love—Good day—Helen

Sept. 24 .*[2nd letter from home..]* My dearest Helen—

Your letter came this noon and was very welcome. Sorry to hear you were not feeling well and hope you are all right now.

When you commence to study, I don't believe you will be able to go out evenings; you will have to plan to take care of yourself or you will get sick. You must remember that you can't stand what some can and act accordingly. I would try to do my studying so I could get to bed early. If you take gymnastics and if you think it injures you in the least, we want you to complain to them and let us know so we can write them we are not willing to have you continue it.

Now try to be as happy and contented as possible, as your staying will depend on your health, and take good care of your eyes. Wear your glasses and don't use your eyes when they are tired. We all send love and hope you are well and happy. If sick, let us know at once.

With very much love. Mama

9/26. Dear Papa Fox—

We had to leave very early this morning—about 7:45 to get our cards of admission to classes. Chapel after that at 8:30 and saw the Seniors come in gay in their caps and gowns. President Hazard conducts Chapel and makes it impressive. She is a grand woman, so stately, yet so sweet and queenly looking.

Then we went back to College Hall to our classes. I had three today, all in the forenoon—Geometry, Latin and Chemistry and got along all right. I like the teachers very much—the Latin one is especially fine. I never thought I could enjoy Latin so much with a lady professor. In Chemistry, she gave us each a sink with several different utensils and we are to do some work tomorrow. I bought a gingham chemistry apron for 25¢!

I have an afternoon class only once a week on Friday. Gymnastics, however, may come in the afternoon, so won't crow until I am sure of the contrary.

My roommate, Nina Hill, (who came yesterday, and who is very nice), and I have been trying to bring order out of chaos and make our room more home-like. I wish many times I <u>were</u> at home, but I am beginning at last to feel more at home here.

With love for all—Helen

9/27. Dear Mamma (and all)—

I have survived two whole days of college! Of course, it is very strange at first and I get a little discouraged, but I suppose that's to be expected. We had a few chemistry experiments today with "beakers" and "tunnels" and "evaporators." (You see I know a few of the mystic terms by name, Papa). We also had our first Biblical History Lecture. The teacher is very stately and I should judge, might be rather hard, too. Either tomorrow or next day, we have to be examined and "poked over" by a doctor—a lady I'm very glad to say.

Aunt Abbie, Uncle James and Mamma

My roommate and I are getting along very well. Nina Hill is little, dark, only seventeen and quite a genius at sewing—makes all her own clothes and has brought <u>fancy</u> <u>work</u>! So I guess I shall be all right in the way of mending.

You asked how far we have to go from here to College, but I haven't timed myself yet. Bessie Eastman, a College Hall Freshman came part way with me, but we didn't get on very fast. She kept stopping to catch grasshoppers for zoology—how glad I am I didn't elect <u>that</u>!

We had dinner at noon at first, but now as some of us have afternoon classes, we have lunch at 12:45 and dinner at 6:00. We have rising bell about 7:00 and breakfast at 7:30. We leave for Chapel a little past 8:00. I think I shall not go tomorrow as you are allowed two "cuts" a week and really, nobody can tell yet whether you are there or not as we haven't been assigned seats yet

With lots of love to all—Helen

[Oct. 1-3 Visit to Aunt Abbie in Brookline.]
Oct. 3. My dear Mamma & Mamma Fox—

I was very glad to hear from you both when I returned from Brookline. We all watch Miss White's mailbox as cats watch for rats and groan aloud when somebody gets <u>two</u> letters and we get none.

The breakfast bell has rung and I must go for I am hungry all the time, a truly fearful appetite. I now weigh 103. *[H.G.F. was 5'2."]*

Nina and I went down street and then up to College. I began to realize how beautiful the grounds are there by the lake. There is a lovely little spot called "Tupelo" where all the lovers go, but I haven't been there as yet. Think I shall have to wait till "Frankie Dear" comes out.

Tomorrow, Papa, my two weeks board is due ($14.00) so would you please send it to Miss White. The laundry did my clothes very well and only cost 75¢. I did all my handkerchiefs at Aunt Abbie's.

I've had a cold—nearly everybody has here. I guess it must be in the air. I am much better, so don't worry.

Much love and a kiss—Helen

Oct. 4. My dear Mamma—

How surprised I was yesterday to see Papa! Nina and I got hungry about 4 o'clock, as we often do, and went down to the Wellesley Tea Room to get some ice cream. We had just left for the P.O., when whom should I see walking toward us but Papa! I took him up to Miss White's and to my room. (She was out, but I was sure she would not object). Ask him if he saw a girl half dressed coming along the hall while he was there. One of the girls asked at the supper table who in world brought "<u>that</u> <u>man</u>" upstairs? Caught her just as she came to bathe after athletics!

Everett Fox, Helen's Father

I showed him around the college and walked back down to the station with him. I have felt more "contented" since he left.

Today I have had heaps of luck. My watch, which I lost off my chain while out walking—<u>where</u> I haven't the faintest idea—day before yesterday, was brought here tonight by a little boy in answer to a notice I left in the P.O.! Then, tonight, when I came home, I found a fine new dress suitcase— I suppose from Papa and for which I give him many thanks and a kiss— yes—<u>two</u>. Now it is nine o'clock and I am sleepy, so Good night.

Bushels of love—Helen

P.S. Oct. 5. Up early to study Geometry. Nina will mail this.

Oct 5. *[3rd letter from home.]*

My dear Helen—

Was very pleased with my brief visit and really feel better about you. Am very glad to know your cold is better. Don't fail to be more careful and avoid a repetition of the same. Didn't say much to your mother about it, knowing she would worry so much. I simply kept still and did the worrying myself. Take good care of your health and "stand up straight!"

Bushels of love—Papa

Oct. 7. Sunday My dear Mamma & <u>All</u>—

I suppose Papa has told you that I have kept an account of all my expenditures, and am getting on very well. Nearly all the girls do this. I was surprised to hear one of the N.Y. girls—whom I told Papa were rather "proud"—talk about spending money the other day. She said she thought it was really <u>mean</u> in a girl to be extravagant and spend money when she knew her parents had to go without to give it to her. (Please let me know if you have to "go without" meat or "German toast"!) I guess she has more sense than I thought after all. I like her better, anyway and guess in time we shall all get acquainted. Nina is a lovable child, so cute and funny. She has heaps of boy-friends and writes them lots of letters—says they have so much broader ideas than girls.

We took another walk to Tupelo. There was a pair of lovers there, one a Freshman, so we discreetly turned our backs. I told Nina we must remember the Golden Rule. I'm afraid I'll not be able to take down the right one—until I meet him.

Tomorrow the Observatory is to be opened, and there is to be quite a "fuss' about it, men coming from Harvard etc. I shall try to go. Miss Hazard said the trustees will be there too.

Our next English theme is to be a letter to a Vassar Freshman. (I shall take Elsie Avery) about our first impressions of Wellesley. I shall have to rake up some new ones, as I just got back my first theme—on that subject. It was marked "Good," which really <u>is</u> <u>good</u>, for they mark quite severely here especially in English, I think. The Vassar girls are to write to us. Quite fun.

Time to say goodnight—Love & kisses—Helen

[Helen's First Theme.]

Wellesley, Massachusetts,
October 1, 1900

Dear Mrs. March:—

Now that I have a moment's leisure I wish to thank you most sincerely for your exceedingly welcome note. In my new surroundings I felt, of course, rather strange and, perhaps, a trifle lonely, but your little greeting, coming as it did, like a bit of home itself, helped me during that first long week more than I can tell you.

Now that I am somewhat more contented and at home here, I shall be very glad, indeed, to give you "my impressions of the Wellesley girl," as you desired.

Of course, there are girls and girls, possibly seven hundred in all, here, but still among so many there seems to be a certain type peculiar to this college. As a Freshman, I have as yet seen only the more apparent, the surface characteristics of the Wellesley girl, but these alone have been so marked as to firmly convince me of the existence of still deeper traits of character to be discovered by a closer acquaintance.

In personal appearance, the Wellesley girl is naturally manifold: she may be blonde with the golden-auburn tresses of Titian's picture; she may rival Ivanhoe's Jewish Rebecca in her warm, Southern beauty; she may be tall or short, fair or plain, but she is almost certain to have an erect form, an easy carriage, a clear, ruddy complexion, and bright eyes, charm, with which she cannot but be attractive.

Nor is she charming merely because of these exterior attractions, which, you may say, any country millk-maid may acquire. There is a certain air about her of style, of good breeding, a knowledge of her own possibilities, both mental and physical, which a simple country maiden rarely possesses.

Both social and athletic duties have been necessary to her in obtaining this air, but, unlike the girls of many other colleges, she does not seem to have been harmed by either duty. She has not become proud, or self-conscious through the influence of the former, or boisterous and "mannish" through devotion to the latter. On the contrary, she has acquired a simple dignity, a quiet self-possession, which forms a fitting crown to her glorious, vigorous young-womanhood. While last, but far from least, is her admirable graciousness and hearty cordiality to verdant Freshmen, a quality, which in their eyes, proves her the superior of every other college maid, "the ideal nineteenth century woman."

These are her most easily discernable characteristics: her others I hope to learn, yes, to emulate in myself, when I too, shall become a fully acclimated "Wellesley Mädchen."

Trusting you may deem this short description worthy of an early answer,
I am yours sincerely, Helen Gertrude Fox

[Note: Helen had asked her parents' permission to attend a concert by Sousa in Boston and the answer had been "No."]

Oct. 11. My dear Mamma & All—

Your letter rec'd this afternoon and can't say I wasn't disappointed. I do want to hear Sousa ever so much and he is only to be here this week. Still, of course, if you really desire me not to, I won't go, though it <u>does</u> seem a little hard when I'm a great big girl 19 years old and in college! If I don't commence sometime to rely upon myself, I never shall learn. And if I wait for Winnie *[cousin in Melrose]* to go with me, I'll be waiting till I <u>die</u>. She doesn't care anything about it and if she did, she would expect me to pay her fare. So, if you want me to take any older person along, you'll have to give me an extra allowance to pay their fare. But I don't want you to think I am angry, for I'm not. I <u>know</u> you worry about me but it does seem rather foolish to let me come way down here alone, let me stay here alone, and then not let me go into Boston in the afternoon to a highly respectable Merchant's Fair and concert. Oh, dear, I wish that there were half-a-dozen of me, then I could go to all the Fairs I wanted, couldn't I?

With heaps of love and a kiss for each—Helen

Oct. 14. *[Melrose.]* My very dear Mamma and Everybody—

Here I am at last in dear old Melrose, which seems almost like home. Tomorrow if it is pleasant, Winnie is going into Boston with me to hear Victor Herbert who is to be at the Fair this week. So I shall not mind so much about Sousa. It would have been fearfully crowded yesterday. The Wellesley Station was just full of girls coming in (to Boston) and there was a crowd of Dana Hall girls, too, with their chaperone—a thing which <u>Wellesley</u> girls don't have to have. Miss Hurd did say, however, when I got permission to come to Melrose, that the 5:30 train from Boston was the last one I could come on <u>without</u> a chaperone.

Stacks of love and Goodnight—Helen

Oct. 18. My dear Mama—

Winnie and I had a lovely time hearing Victor Herbert. He is fine— I could listen to him all night. But, I must tell you about my purchases. I invested in a lovely <u>real</u> alligator pocket-book for $1.00; a Wellesley pin for 25¢, a pocket comb to replace one I lost, 10¢; and a stunning red tam-o-shanter, 87¢, which looks very gypsy-like and is quite becoming to my "style of beauty."

I have just come from the Lab., where we are studying water now. (I presume we shall take Hire's Root Beer next?) I find it very interesting.

Dr. Barker's physical exam yesterday wasn't bad at all, and I have the pleasure of informing you that she said she saw no reason at all why I should not be a "well, strong woman!" Isn't that lovely? I first had to answer heaps of questions—if my family had hereditary diseases, and if I had had any of a list of diseases, about a yard long, which she read off. Then she had me undress down to my waist, except my under-vest, and tried my heart (to see if I were in love?) with a funny instrument, *[stethoscope]* and made a pillow of my back, hearing me breathe, to see if my lungs were all right. They were and my back was straight. She was pleased because I was so erect and not limp and all in a heap, and that my shoulders were even.

Then she made me blow into a tank which registered the number of cubic inches my lungs held, which was 120, about average. Then she tested my eyesight and found it all right, except for a little astigmatism (that Dr. Flanders found), and examined my ears (luckily I had just washed them) and found my hearing very acute. She was much pleased that I don't wear corsets. (I have worn them only twice since I came.) She said she hoped I wouldn't. She said I had excellent habits; not eating between meals or too much candy and taking a partial cold water "splash" every morning. They all advise you here, to bathe every day, but I think if I take two hot baths in the tub a week and my "partials," I shall do very well.

I am feeling fine, eat like a pig and feel as though I had really gained a pound. I think the air here must agree with me, for I don't sneeze so often as I did at home.

We are learning to do our studying afternoons, so we get to bed before 10:00 or 10:30. Tonight, Nina, Helen P., Muriel, Betty and I are going to join the Christian Association. The fee is only $1.00 a year, and you meet many girls that way.

Finally, "brethren and sisteren," piles of love and goodnight—Helen

Oct. 21. My dear Everybody—

I had Latin yesterday and enjoy it best of all my studies. I find I know just as much as anyone there and more than some and want to get down on my knees and thank "Prof." for his teaching.

Your picture came, Papa Fox, and all the girls thought you must be my father, as you looked too young to be my grandfather! I expect they'll all tumble head over heels in love with you when you come out to see me. I shall try to protect you.

Oh, I forgot to tell you that I joined Barn Swallows, only 75¢ per year and an entertainment, etc., every other week. Last evening was the first—a drama, "Brother Against Brother: a thrilling tale of the Civil War." The parts, most of them men's, were played by girls, who made such comical men. It was a military drama, so they were in full uniform and did look quite "swell," only their

Arthur Thad Smith, "Prof"

voices were so <u>shrill</u> for soldiers. Then, in one scene, one of them who impersonated an Irishman, came on with carroty red side whiskers, but had forgotten her wig, and when she turned around her "bob" of hair at the back of her head showed very plainly. The audience (no <u>masculines</u> allowed) laughed so hard it made the actors, too, who then snickered in some of the most tragic scenes, making a very jolly affair of it—much more fun than the regular theatre.

This P.M. Nina and I went for a walk down past Dana Hall. We had quite an experience for we met as many as <u>twelve</u> <u>live</u> <u>boys</u>, by actual count! A most unheard of thing here! Then to cap it all, when we got home, we found we were to actually have a real, live one at supper, a friend of Helen Peck's, visiting with her father today. You can guess our delight when we filed one by one into the dining room and were introduced to him. He proved very jolly and nice and pretended to be <u>dreadfully</u> embarrassed by so many girls, but in reality didn't seem so at all. We all feel as though we had been in the <u>world</u> again!

You asked me if I need an evening dress, Mamma. I think I shall. The Sophomore Reception is to be Nov. 17 and I shall need something to wear. Aunt Ada is going to get samples, which I shall send to you for selection—challis, etc.

Nina is going home over Sunday and Miss White has said I may have Winnie here in her place.

With love "without end"—Helen

Oct. 25. My dear people—

I have been very lucky in the mail this week—your great family letter Monday, one from Winnie Tuesday, also a very nice <u>long</u> letter from Elsie Avery all about Vassar which she likes very much, she says. Then a letter and picture from "Frankie Dear." He called me "Helen" and said he couldn't be so formal as to say "Miss Fox" all the time. Yesterday I was greatly surprised to receive a <u>lovely</u> letter from "Prof," saying that he took great pleasure in sending me his photo, wishing me all sorts of success and asking me, if I had any leisure, would I not write him how I found my "fit" (I wonder did he mean the "fit" of my dress?) for college, etc. <u>Of course</u> I shall find leisure indeed, as I want very much to thank him for all he has done for me. Then, I received his picture, which is fine. I have given it an honored position on my dressing case now, but must get a Dartmouth frame.

The girls are waiting to go up to college, so Goodbye & love—Helen

Nov. 2. My precious "Muddie"—

We had a perfectly lovely time on Halloween night! We all went together about 7:30; I wore my black skirt and French flannel waist. (My light dress is getting so tight it is dreadfully uncomfortable). I thought at first I was going to be "out of it," for nearly all the girls here wore silk waists, but when I got there, I found all sorts of dresses—thin white ones, fancy light ones, and both silk and flannel waists, so I was all right. We took off our wraps in a cute little bedroom opening off the hall. Then after being introduced some by Miss Blackmere—a Senior and the <u>sweetest</u> girl—went down in the basement to the dining room which had been fixed like a hall with tall bamboo screens shutting off the stage.

When the play began, the stage manager announced the different acts and with another girl, drew back the screens at a signal (sometimes they didn't do it quickly enough and the actors had to improvise to fill up the wait). The play was one of the 14th century adapted from Shakespeare. The characters were King _____(a long name), his wife, daughter and two suitors, great rivals, who fought a duel with <u>feather-dusters,</u> mounted on "horses" made of <u>broom-sticks!</u> Then when the King asked one of them if his position were lofty enough, he replied "ay, sire, I am a floor-walker in Jordan Marsh & Co."

After the play, candy, nuts and apples were passed around. (I am <u>wild</u> about the delicious apples this fall, eat two or three of them a day and they don't hurt me a bit). Then we roasted marshmallows before the parlor fireplace, after which, a lot of us went down to the dining room again, turned down the gas lights, put our chairs about two feet apart and told weird ghost stories. Ten o'clock came all too soon and we all came home together, singing Wellesley songs on the way.

Yesterday, I met Aunt Ada in Boston and went straight to Hovey's, where I bought three heavy union suits, a denim laundry bag and a pair of white kid gloves.

As I was all through shopping at 5:00, I took a car (electric) to So. Station, and with some minutes to spare, thought I would look for "Frankie Dear," whom I knew should be going home to Roxbury about then, as most men in offices get out about 5:30. I found a 5:21 train to Roxbury and waited developments by the gate. The station was filled with men and I looked eagerly at every young one. Just as I had given up, whom should I see coming up in a light hat and overcoat but "Frankie Dear"! Then he saw me and we had a most <u>touching</u> greeting; that is, we merely shook hands, there were <u>so</u> many people there, you know. He was surprised to see me. I thanked him for his photo, etc. and then he walked down to my train with me (he must have missed his). I asked him to come out sometime and he said he would—so, perhaps I can take him to Tupelo after all.

With love untold—Helen

P.S. When you come down, Mamma, will you please bring my graduation underskirt and petticoat, a cake of Pear's Soap and a hot-water bag.

Nov. 5 (Sunday). My Dear Mama (and Everybody)—

We "moved" again—changed our room around, so I had to straighten out all my pictures again. Didn't go to church, and fooled away my time as I did <u>occasionally</u> at home. After dinner, I was so full that Bertha Long and I took a long walk down past the Durant and Hunnewell estates. We didn't go into the Hunnewell gardens as they were not open today, but had a good look at the house—a regular <u>mansion</u>. The lawns are beautiful now, so smooth and as green as in June. They are above an ivy-covered wall along the sidewalk. The ivy has turned bright crimson now so that the contrast is lovely. I broke off a lovely long spray of ivy for our room.

I wrote the asked-for letter to "Prof" about my "fit" here, which I am glad to say, seems quite the equal of even the Dana Hall girls. Then, of course, I thanked him for "fitting" me etc.

Now, I must study like one possessed, for this afternoon Helen, Alice, Nina and I are going on the "electric" to Natick and then this evening to the Republican Rally at the Barn, in which all the Republican Girls' Clubs are to march, with torchlights, bands, transparencies etc. The Democratic Rally was Sat. evening and we went to see the parade. There are only about 70 Democrats to 500 or more Republicans in college, so you can imagine how much better our parade will be. I really don't feel as though I knew much about the election, as there are no men here to talk it over, you see.

I have been invited to go to the Soph. Reception by Alice Dalrymple, the Rochester girl. It will seem quite "homey."

Heaps of love—Helen

Nov. 6. *[Postal.]* Dear Mama,

I shall be delighted to see you Friday after 2:30 when my recitations are up. I will try to meet you at the station, if I don't, take a carriage to Miss White's. *[13 Waban St.]* Please bring all my old essays (from last year); I can work them up. Watch the papers for the write-up of the Rally— it was simply great!

Much love—Helen

Nov. 16. Dear Folks—*[After Mother's visit.]*

I received your letter this P.M. and was disappointed that you should think of my not coming home for Thanksgiving. I know you mean it all for the best—you are afraid I will get too tired, etc. I shall have the Sunday before to rest here and only Tuesday and Weds. mornings for recitations, so don't you think if I sleep all day Sun. & Mon., I'll be quite rested? You can put me to bed early Thanksgiving night so I'll be ready for the early train next morning. So, if you leave it to me, if you really want to see me, I'll come. Truly, I have looked forward to it so much— and it seems such a long time till Christmas. There, I have followed your instructions and let you know just how I feel about it!

Gym begins next Tues. Then I shall have the pleasure (?) of going back two more afternoons—Tues. & Thurs. at 3:20 and then Fri., right after English. I think I shall like it and shall (finally) have a chance to wear that gym suit.

My new dress is lovely by lamp light—so shimmery, and a fine fit. The girls all liked it very much. I think I had better get my new winter coat soon. It is getting so cold here that I'll have to wear my jacket under my golf cape soon and I would like to keep my jacket for best.

Oh—I have been taking dancing lessons from Alice and really did very well. Tomorrow night I'll be arrayed in all my finery at The Barn. Miss White said she'd help me dress.

Heaps of love & Goodnight—Helen

[Helen's golf cape was 3/4 length, heavy gray wool with a woolen plaid lining and a hood. It survives to this day, and I have given it to the N.H. Historical Society. Why they were called "golf capes" I cannot understand, as it would be impossible to take a swing—even a putt, wearing one.]

Nov. 18. My own folks—

Here I am, cuddled up among the pillows on Alice's couch with Alice, Helen and Nina all around the table writing letters. So, you see, I have lived through the reception, without taking cold or falling in love with the orchestra, who were the only men there.

We began getting ready about <u>11:30</u> in the <u>forenoon</u>—that is, Nina and I dusted our room, picked up, etc. Then, after dinner, we went down street and bought some sardines, crackers and four oranges for breakfast this morning, so we could lie a-bed. We then laid out our clothes and "laid low" for the bathroom. Problem: if twelve girls take baths in one bathroom in one afternoon, how long a bath can each girl take and how many times will the other girls try the door in the meantime? We all got there however.

Meanwhile, mysterious paper boxes had been arriving from the florists and pretty soon one came for me and one for Nina. We both found them to contain lovely white carnations (Nina's $^1/_2$ dozen and mine one dozen) which our Sophomores had sent. We had supper at 5:30, so I only fixed my hair before—bothered and fussed with it for a good half-hour. Then, after supper I got into my dress, Alice and Helen helping me. I did <u>not</u> put on my thick union-suit, but wore my long-sleeved vest over my <u>thin</u> union-suit, then my flannel petticoat—the white one—then my "graduation" one and my underskirt. Should you think I would have been cold—I wasn't in the least!

My dress is simply lovely in the evening and very becoming and my white carnations were beautiful with it. I wore them tucked into my belt. Couldn't get them all in, it was so tight. Miss White said no wonder, over so much clothing, but I really think I am getting fatter. It is my ambition to be fat enough to wear a low-necked gown and I'm going to work for that end. I wish you could have seen the stunning gowns there last night.

My carriage came about seven and as Miss Dalrymple didn't expect me quite so early, she wasn't at the door, so, as I waited for her, I had a good chance to see them all come in. She was dressed quite simply in a pink cashmere, I should say, trimmed with black velvet. She is quite short and slender with brown hair and lovely brown eyes and a simple, cordial manner. I feel as if I had known her ever so long. She isn't in the least "stuck-up" or patronizing, but just as unaffected as a Freshman.

I should say there were about 400 at the reception—quite enough to make a jam, so that dancing wasn't much fun. I danced once (or rather skated across the floor as it was so slippery my feet slid all around) with a girl who knew about as much about it as I did. But it was great fun and the music was fine. The electric lights gave out, as they have a trick of doing at such times, so they were supplied with lamps and lanterns, which cast a "dim religious light," making it quite romantic.

Then they had delicious refreshments. I had two kinds of sherbet, orange and pineapple, that would melt in your mouth. It came half-past nine, all too soon and we all had to scamper home; but we all had to wait quite a little for a carriage, the girls taking the first one that came, not caring whose it was. Finally someone called out "Miss Fox" and I hurried down to find <u>Edith</u> Fox snugly ensconced in <u>my</u> place. Of course, I couldn't turn her out, although it <u>was</u> my carriage, so she, Nina and I and another girl all piled in. I was glad my dress wasn't muslin, or it would have been wrinkled.

This morning we didn't get up until 9:00, then went into Alice's room where we four–Nina, I, Alice and her Soph. friend, Mary Emmett feasted on our sardines, graham crackers, oranges and chocolate. We ate so much I wasn't really hungry for dinner.

Tomorrow is Field Day—tennis, golf, running, etc. And tomorrow evening a musical lecture. I may not go, since the girls here are planning a "wedding," at which I am supposed to be a bridesmaid. So—my time is quite "occupied."

One more week before I come home.

With bushels of love—Helen

THANKSGIVING RECESS

Dec. 2. My very dear Folks—

Here I am back in my "quarters" and as yet have not been half so homesick as I feared I would be.

I got to Union just in time to hand my pocket book to Ray while I stripped off my shawl, veil and hat before getting on the train *[those went back to Milton Mills on the "stage."]* We were a sleepy crowd going back. Ray got off at No. Station. He has promised to come out soon. He said he'd likely be afraid with so many girls, so I told him to bring out five Tech boys he knows. *[Ray Buck—a cousin from Milton Mills, was working in Boston.]*

I wish you could peek in a moment. I am in my kimono here at the table writing and Bertha is lying on my bed, kicking her feet and singing college songs in a slightly husky voice. Nina wants me to go home to Ayer with her overnight on the 19th. So, as I couldn't get ready to come home that afternoon without scurrying about awfully, I guess I'll go with Nina if you think best, then take the train to Boston from there on the 20th and my usual train home from No. Station.

Helen, Bertha and her Tufts College girl friend and I went up to the Biology Laboratory and the Art Building. There are some very interesting specimens in the former and some truly lovely paintings in the latter. In the evening, we all went to the "Barn" to the play—very good—nearly all singing, representing a young ladies' seminary production of "Cinderella."

This afternoon went up to Chapel to a memorial service for the late Sir Arthur Sullivan. I wish you could have heard it. It was simply <u>grand</u>.

With love—Helen

Dec. 10. Dear Mamma, (At Melrose 9:15 A.M.)

I got weighed and guess how much? Only 111! Isn't that alarming? *[She wanted to gain weight and hoped for more. This probably included clothes.]*

Winnie, Walter and I went for a walk and met his father in a dear little buggy, who invited us to go for a little ride. We turned up our collars, put our hands in Walter's pockets, had his father tuck us in with the big fur robe and put the buggy top up and away we went for about an hour.

I shall have to beg a little money for Christmas presents. I shall not get expensive ones, but you know <u>anything</u> costs money and I have only two dollars left. Can you send me what you think best as soon as possible, as I shall try to go into Boston Wednesday.

All here send love. Love, Helen

Dec. 17. My dear, dear folks—

We all talk almost continuously about "going home." Our trunks were brought up Saturday and the hall looks as though it were going on a journey with them all scattered around. Alice Dalrymple and I will go out to Ayer when I wish and we will take the morning train to Boston in time for me to get the 3:45 train up from Rochester. *[Jeff's train which she rode every school day when at Nute H.S. He was the conductor.]* So I can see all the girls from Nute.

I mustn't forget to tell you the most important thing. We have a chance now, by going to Miss Pendleton, to learn our standing. So, the other day, I summoned up my courage and knocked at her office door. She said "Come in," very pleasantly and I told her of my name and errand. Then she looked over a list of little cards and said, "Your standing is very good, Miss Fox, especially good in Latin and Math." You can guess how pleased I was; very good here means quite a little, you know. I felt like hugging "Ellen" but thought she might not understand, so merely thanked her, said I was "very glad," and backed out.

A big hunk of love for each of you—Good night—Helen

CHRISTMAS VACATION

Jan. 10, 1901. My precious Mamma and All—

Miss White came to the door to welcome me when I arrived at 13 Waban St. I was glad to be there rather than up at dreary College Hall. I unpacked my suitcase and then my trunk came and I unpacked that until dinner. How can I get it all home again, along with all I brought last fall? I shall have to begin packing in April, I guess.

I haven't spent a cent today, Papa, but tomorrow I must buy a pair of shoe strings as I forgot to bring any. Suppose I could use corset lacings, two pairs of which I did bring.

I am going to "treat" on your chocolate cake, Mamma, as soon as the girls digest their dinner, so you may look for compliments in my next.

Much love and a dozen kisses apiece—Helen

Jan. 14. My dear everybody,

Spent all last evening studying for a Geometry exam this morning which proved to be very easy. I thought how "Prof" would laugh at me— I can never help borrowing trouble over exams.

This is the first really lovely day since I came back and the sleighing is <u>fine</u>! Oh, that "Frankie Dee" would come out and take <u>me</u> out! Went to Chapel & heard Bishop Lawrence of Trinity Church. He is <u>fine</u>—so simple and direct and such a clear voice.

They say that the Dartmouth Glee Club is coming here later. Just think how many men we'll see all at once!

I am fearfully tired and must dig for my Bible paper, so will conclude— With love to all—Helen

Jan. 20. My very dear everybody—

I spent up to the last moment studying for my Algebra exam and then, as usual, it was dead easy and I got on all right.

Went to the Shakespeare Recital at 3:20, and enjoyed it very much. The play was "As You Like It" and the elocutionist, a Miss Gatchell from Emerson School of Oratory. She changed her voice and expression to suit each character. It was almost as good as a play.

After supper, we made fudge and sang, etc. Tomorrow evening, the Hoffman String Quartette is to play at College and I shall try to go. I mean to take in everything of that sort that I can. Seems a pity not to when it's about the only thing there free.

I shall be through with my exams about 11:30 Thursday—in time to get the 4:00 home—if you think best. You know I shall love dearly to see you all. On the other hand, I am quite settled and contented right here now. So, if you think it won't pay to come home for short a time, I shan't complain. Please tell me what you want me to do.

When are you going to send me my "Christmas" skates, Papa? I think the ice is safe now; it has been down to zero here. They are to have an Ice Carnival in two weeks, bonfires, colored lights and a band, all the company you want, <u>men</u> included. I shall want my skates very badly then.

Heaps of love—Helen

Jan. 23. My dear Mamma,

Grace *[a friend from home]* came out Monday and spent the day, which was a lovely one. I took her all around and she "likes it very much." We went over to Wilder, the new dormitory, to see the dining room, etc. and I am convinced that that's the place for me next year.

The Hoffman Quartette was simply superb. I just sat and dreamed through it.

Heard from Elsie at Vassar who says she has "settled down to hard work till after exams"—just as though other people <u>didn't</u>! I got a "<u>Good</u>" on my Algebra, so shall not have to take the midyears in it. Wish I could get out of all the others as easily. We had more fun in Chem. yesterday; each one had six different things and the names of them and had to fit the names to the objects. I had great luck—I may be a bright and shining light in it yet, Papa.

Oh, Papa, won't you <u>please</u> send me some <u>skates</u>. The ice is fine now and has been for several days. Carnival Night is one week from Saturday and I need to practice. I like having company and plan to invite everyone I know for the Carnival. <u>SKATES</u>, Please!!

I was a bit disappointed not to come home for the "long weekend," but it really is too short a time. It would be rather foolish, for me to chase home when I know I have so many friends here. I'll appreciate home all the more in April or March.

With love "more than the tongue can tell"—Helen

<u>Please</u> <u>SKATES</u>, Papa! *[Everything, except some school books and most clothing was bought through the family store, at wholesale prices.]*

"Asa Fox & Son," Three Generation Family Store

Jan. 27. My dear family—

I have just returned from a Memorial Service at the Chapel for Queen Victoria, and am about half asleep. We are all in the sitting-room. Nina is playing "Sunny Tennessee" on the piano and the rest are listening and eating fudge and I am at the writing desk, taking it all in.

Yesterday, after doing my washing (which I had allowed to accumulate for two weeks) I dressed for the Chemistry Reception. We Chem. students were all invited to meet Dr. Roberts, head of the department. We hated to go, as we wanted to go skating, but were very glad that we did go. It was held down in the lecture and class experimental room. Miss Penny, our teacher, met us and introduced us to Dr. Roberts who is a very pleasant, sweet-faced lady. Then we had coffee, sandwiches and wafers. The coffee was made by one of the teachers there on the experiment table in large glass flasks over the Bunsen gas burners; then passed around in little thin glass beakers, with glass rods in them to sip it through. The sugar and cream were brought around in some other chemistry dishes. It was the cutest idea and everyone enjoyed it so much because it was so unique and informal.

I wore my black dress with the pink yoke (managed to squeeze into it but don't believe I can many more times), and they all thought me very "dressed up" at dinner. Miss White asked me if I had been out on the town.

After dinner, we all went skating by moonlight. I borrowed skates, which didn't fit very well, but aside from that, it was lovely. Three girls at the house are just learning to skate and we all took turns trying to teach them. One, quite large, has weak ankles and so was continually tumbling, making us laugh. I shall be glad to get my own skates. I wrote to Ray inviting him out to the Carnival, to Winnie and Walter and to Charles Jones sending him the Wellesley pin he wanted. I

Charles Jones

imagine a letter from a girl will frighten him out of a year's growth!

I hope I am learning a little; I have tried since I came back, to study for what I <u>learned</u>, not to make a brilliant appearance in class, and mean to keep it up.

Heaps of love and kisses—Helen

[The Jones family lived on a big, old farm on Plummer's Ridge in Milton. Helen had taken piano lessons from Mrs. Jones—a six mile round trip by buggy (or sleigh). There were three boys in the family and two girls, all friends of Helen's. The youngest boy was Robert Edmund Jones, who became known in later years as "The Father of Modern Scene Design" in the theatre. He also "did" the first technicolor movie put out by Hollywood. The Jones Farm is now the New Hampshire Farm Museum.]

Jan. 30. Dear "Muddie" and "Daddie" and All.

One exam through and that not very hard, either! I feel like singing and dancing or writing or anything but <u>studying</u>! And tomorrow is a holiday, being "The Day of Prayer," and my next exam isn't until Friday afternoon. I am having a holiday today. Yes, I received the skates all O.K. and they are little beauties. *[A letter from home stated that they cost $1.50 wholesale and therefore must be <u>very</u> good ones!]* I tried them twice. We Freshmen are all obligated to take an hour's exercise each day during midyears, so I shall make mine skating, if the ice holds good. I'm afraid it isn't going to be very fine for Saturday, as it is all cut up, so many have been skating, and this P.M. it snowed a little and looks like more. I shall hope for the best. Winnie and Walter and Ray are all coming, so I shall have plenty of company and what's best—someone to put on my skates!

It is creeping towards bed-time and I am usually sleepy during exam time, so–Lots and lots of love—Helen

Feb. 3. My dear Family—   *"Sunday Gossip"*

Now for our cozy weekly chat. I can see you all around the sitting room table; Papa Fox in the big black chair reading the Biddeford paper, Mamma Fox dozing away over next Sunday's lesson, Papa with the Portland "Transcript," and Mamma on the lounge napping before starting my letter.

Now, don't you want a peek at me? I am all alone in my room, nearly all the girls are going up to Chapel, except Nina, poor child, who has to take an Algebra exam she failed tomorrow, and is in Helen P.'s room, cramming. I am sitting at my table which is littered with my "company" writing paper which I have just been using in a letter.

And now that you can see me (can't you?), I'll begin with yesterday's history. I got up early, studied Chemistry a little and went to my "doom"— to take the Chem. exam—a pretty stiff one, too; long and not extra easy. But I wrote all I knew and I guess got through all right. We don't find out for certain till March, isn't that horrid!

We had planned quite a nice surprise for our Carnival guests—to have a little lunch for them in our rooms (Helen P.'s and ours) before going up to the lake. Of course, we wouldn't be allowed to in College Hall, but we thought as it was mostly a "cousin" affair, it would be all "proper" enough. So we moved our washstand into the closet, and with our beds made into couches with pillows, you would hardly know you were in a sleeping room. Howard came about 5 o'clock and as Nina was too bashful to take him down to supper, she left him to watch the chafing dish in which the chocolate was to be made.

Helen P. & I went to the train together. We thought it would never come, we were so excited. And when it did, I thought I'd never find my people. Such a crowd of men, all with skates, as got off! I looked in vain at both ends of the train, but couldn't see any of them. Then Ray found me and in a moment, Winnie and Walter came up. I took them up to the house and introduced them all around. We had "lunch" though nobody was very hungry, showed off our rooms and went up to the lake, pointing out points of interest along the way.

A big bonfire blazed on the shore, which sent up a stream of sparks and around which the Bands were gathered, with a hurdy-gurdy near by. There were tall calcium lights with big reflectors all around on the edge of the ice. Out on the lake, men were stationed to set off fireworks, which they did all evening—big, lovely sky-rockets and all sorts of pretty things.

The ice was the worst part, rather cut and cracked on top from so much use. About the first thing Ray and I did was to skate into a crack and tumble—without any damage, however. Ray and Walter are both fine skaters and I enjoyed skating with them very much. It is so much nicer skating with a man!

As they had to get the 9:48 to Boston, we left the Carnival about 9:00 P.M. and walked to the station with our guests.

After "our men" had gone, we all went into "Only" Smith's room to Muriel Windham's birthday spread. She lives nearby and her folks had sent her three large baskets full of fruit, candy, nuts, cakes, tarts and everything. The "girl" at her home made her a birthday cake with her name and age on it—only she put <u>fifteen</u> instead of <u>seventeen</u>. We all ate until we couldn't eat any more. Miss White had said we could keep the lights on until 10:30 as it was an unusual occasion, which I suppose was a hint for us to retire then, but we didn't. We had to keep pretty quiet for fear she would hear us. Such is a "<u>Spread</u>," which we indulge in very rarely.

I made up my sleep this morning, however—didn't get up until after 10:00. Felt quite like a heathen, staying home from church. This afternoon, however, Nina, Helen P. and I went to the Wellesley town hall to hear Rev. <u>Edward Everett Hale</u>. I didn't think he was so very wonderful. He is quite an old man with a long beard. His voice seems very strong and he emphasizes very queerly and whistles a little when he speaks. It made me nervous at first, but I got used to it and should have enjoyed him only I was rather sleepy.

Now, with lots of love, goodnight, your sleepy girl—Helen

Feb. 6. My dear own Muddie—

I have taken one more exam—Bible—this forenoon and am not dead yet! Guess I'll hold out for Latin now. Was glad of your very welcome letter and Papa's very welcome check yesterday.

I try to be very careful about taking cold; have to now—my ankles and skirts get wet so easily. I have discovered that gaiters and bloomers pulled down to meet them are fine. I wonder what I ever did without bloomers *[gym costume.]* I wear them skating and walking in the snow— may take to them entirely. Another heavy snowstorm—windy and drifting. We all rode up this morning, but walked home and got so wet we had to change our skirts. *[Skirts all swept the ground—except for one "rainy day" walking skirt about 3 inches off, lined with buckram around the bottom hem, inside.]*

Yesterday, we bundled up and went to walk in the snow storm, then came home and changed our clothes and felt fine. I think Miss White will be glad when exams are over as our appetites are simply ferocious. Haven't been weighed since I came back, but shall try to gain five pounds in Melrose.

Shall now study for Latin and then pack.

Love to everybody—your "baby," Helen

SECOND SEMESTER, 1901

Feb. 13. My dear Muddie—

Just a word before I say goodnight. We begin Trigonometry tomorrow and I have been trying to see some sense in it, but can't say I've found much yet.

It has been a cold, windy day here. Our hands nearly froze going up to college this A.M. Not quite so cold this P.M., and about 4:30 I took a little walk alone and admired the sunset, which was lovely. I am just getting settled in again after my vacation—felt like a cat in a strange garrett yesterday. Oh! I am happy! The "flunk notes" are said to be all out and I didn't get any, so must have passed everything. One girl here, Muriel, got two—English and Math. She must feel rather discouraged.

Can you send me some money for books. I need one for Trig, for which Nina will pay $^1/_2$ and a new Latin book. I am quite proud of my account since I've been back—it has balanced perfectly so far. I have tried to be economical; hope you will think I have succeeded.

Must say goodnight, for the girls (I am in Helen and Alice's room) want to go to bed.

With much love, Helen

Feb. 19. My dear Papa,

I received so many letters from home that I hardly know which to answer first. However, as yours is partly business, and my time is too limited for a "gossipy" letter, I'll take yours. Very many thanks for the check. Miss White is going to get it cashed for me today, so I shall be able to get my Latin book. Miss Walton, our teacher, told us to bring them to class one day last week. As I didn't have any money, I couldn't get one, so I told her before class started that I was "poverty stricken" and therefor had no book. She laughed and said that that was rather awkward, but would be all right.

I am going to Chapel this morning, so must close.

Much love to all, "Girl Goldie"

[The following letter is from Charles Jones, who had asked her to send him a Wellesley pin, which she had sent him. At this time Charles was a Senior at Nute.]

Feb. 19, 1901 Dearest Helen:—

You said that Wellesley pins were rare down there. Well, mine is the talk of the school and the place from which it came and the one who sent it are current topics. We are just over Founders' Day. I was intending to send you a program, but my mother got in her fine work and gave them all away.

I have been leading the school since you and Elsie left. We are not having much excitement now, except that we are all kicking because we must get onto our jobs now. I consented to learn to dance on my mother's solemn promise not to tell anyone, but it wasn't a week before one of the girls asked me how I was getting along.

The undersigned sincerely regrets that he has allowed so much time to elapse before answering Miss Fox's letter, and sincerely hopes that she will not retaliate in kind, but will answer by return mail, if possible. Which reminds me that you can't answer this letter until you get it, so I must stop now, in time for tomorrow morning's mail.

Charles Jones

Feb. 22. My dear family—

We are going to have company this week, Olive's sister is coming, also Alice's and her friend. Then the Gladdings expect <u>their</u> sister. Dear me— all the girls here seem to have more <u>sisters</u> than <u>brothers</u>!

This morning, heard Lyman Abbot at Chapel and liked him immensely. His text was "Thy Kingdom come, Thy will be done on earth as it is in Heaven." And his sermon was fine. He told how we should try first to make His kingdom come in our own homes, until I wanted so much to get home and love you all! This makes the fourth really <u>big</u> preacher I have heard; Bishop Lawrence, Dr. Lorimer and Edward Everett Hale being the others. I think I like Lyman Abbot and Bishop Lawrence the best.

I had a present yesterday from Miss White. I iron quite a number of handkerchiefs in the kitchen and the holders for the hot irons always seem to be gone when I need them. Last night, Miss White brought me out a nice new one which she had bought for my very own! I told her that I would use it when I went to housekeeping for myself!

One important thing, Nina and I have been changed from one division to another in Math, and are heartbroken. Our Math teacher was the sweetest, dearest one in college—a Miss Merrill, and so good to everybody. And now we have <u>Miss Dennis</u>, who isn't <u>noted</u> for her sweetness or goodness to <u>stupid</u> people (and they are quite numerous in Math, you know). We are trying to be reconciled, especially as we have plenty of company—about half of our division, among them our particular bright star—(the most self-satisfied appearing girl you ever saw). By the fact that she was changed too, we concluded that we must be reckoned bright, too, though I'm afraid they've made a mistake.

So—with love, love and love—Helen

Feb. 25. (Sunday) My dear folks—

I must tell you about Friday evening. I didn't expect to go until Thursday and did not have a ticket; but one of the girls had two extra so I got one. I was glad, as it is the "swellest" event of the year and I didn't want to miss it. So I did my Saturday's work in the afternoon and about 5 o'clock proceeded to array myself in my very finest "finery," namely my challis. I really looked very pretty, "considering."

When we got up to College, the corridors and center were just packed with men in dress suits and girls in beautiful evening gowns. On the second floor, all the available college flags—Harvard, Yale, Princeton and even two or three little Dartmouth ones were suspended from the railing in the center. Then, in the corners, they had placed ferns and plants and cozy seats. Oh, it was so pretty! Then the concert was fine. I tried to find an extra program, but didn't succeed. However, you can see mine when I get home—that is, whatever is left of it. I brought it home in my teeth, as my hands were full holding up my dress.

Oh, I must rejoice with you! Saturday noon I got my report card and found to my joy, that I had got "credit," which is more than just "passed," in every single thing! Some of the other girls did not and a good many didn't even pass in some things. I have certainly tried very hard for it.

But—I am getting sleepy—With a dozen kisses apiece—

Goodnight—your "little girl" Helen

March 1. Dear Mamma—

I was prevented from writing earlier this morning by a fire! Not at Miss White's, so don't worry, but over on Washington St. "Only" and I, who are the two slowest girls in the house, were just finishing breakfast about 7:45, when we heard the bell over on the fire station almost opposite us, ring. At first we thought nothing of it, as it rings for school, etc. But in a moment, it began to ring again and again. Hearing all the girls upstairs scream, I rushed into the parlor to look out. You know, that fire station is quite a joke with us, because no matter how much the bell has rung, <u>nothing</u> has ever come out.

So, we were surprised and overjoyed, I must confess, to see them leading two horses out—about <u>five</u> <u>minutes</u> after the bell rang! You see, <u>their</u> fire department is little better than ours at home, for they keep their horses in a livery stable some little ways from the station itself. It took them quite a while to get harnessed, so that by chasing across lots in the direction of the smoke, we arrived on the scene almost as soon as the department did.

The house, a lovely little gabled, shingled house, had caught fire on the roof from the chimney, while the family was at breakfast, and seemed to be burning in the attic under the high pitched roof. It took them ages to get the hose going, so that the fire got well under way. But they persisted in saying they could save the house and wouldn't let the people get their things out. It began to look doubtful, however as they <u>couldn't get at</u> the fire so they began to take the things out—pictures, <u>books</u> and <u>furniture</u> first, leaving all the clothes to get soaked. Everybody helped. Our "White Squadron" quite distinguished itself.

Finally, the other fire departments from Wellesley Hills came, and they saved the house—that is the <u>shell</u> of it. I guess it was well insured, and as the man is connected with an insurance co., he will probably get it all right. But, it seems such a pity as it was such a dear house—one of the prettiest in Wellesley. If only the men had known what to do, it seems to me they could have saved it.

We saw some of the funniest things; one little boy carefully carrying one old russet shoe to a neighboring piazza; the boy of the house rushing around dripping wet, with some pink carnations in his button hole which weren't there when the fire began; and the lady carrying a pet cat as tenderly as tho' it were a baby, to the next house.

I have decided not to get my new spring suit until after Easter, when it will be cheaper, and the styles more settled, and I should probably spoil it with mud in coming home earlier.

Now I must close and get to studying.

With very much love to all—Helen

March 6. Dear Mamma Fox,

We have been to a Student Mass meeting at College Hall this afternoon—about Student Government. You may remember that we exchanged themes with the Vassar Freshmen last Fall. Now they want us to do so again and suggested as a subject "Student Government." This form of government, as its name implies, gives the management for the greatest part of many things to the students. At Vassar, they have it in full force, while we here only the very beginnings of it, which will put us at some disadvantage in writing our themes. This afternoon, however, the whole college (students) met to discuss the subject and to take measures for its adoption. I sincerely hope we'll get it, for nearly all other colleges have it. It will make us feel more like women and less like boarding school girls.

Bushels of love, your "little one," Helen

March 8. My dear "Popsie,"

I have just finished studying my Algebra. I can't get any sense out of it. Oh, dear, it is just the bane of my life—a perfect dark cloud over me all the time! I think any girl who <u>elects</u> Math really ought to be examined for a "nail" in her brain!

I spent this P.M. studying Latin and Algebra with Sara Marsh at College Hall. She is a fine girl. Tomorrow I am going to Boston with her to help her select a flannel waist. I shall keep an eye out for silk waists and invest in some shoe lacings, as both mine have been broken since yesterday morning and look rather slack.

In less than three weeks, I shall be home. But right now I am sleepy, sleepier, sleepiest, so goodnight.

Heaps of love, "your little girl" Helen

March 12. My <u>dear</u> Mamma—

I am waiting for Howard, (Nina's friend) to go, so I can go to bed. It is his birthday and he has been spending it with Nina. Just after supper, she gave us a cobweb party in our room and Helen's. Nina, Helen and Howard arranged the "web." It was a surprise to all the rest of us. Then we had refreshments—olives, crackers w. peanut butter, and <u>strawberries</u>— real nice fresh ones which Howard brought up from town. He is very nice and Nina seems to like him very much, altho' she pretends not to.

Well, Howard is gone and I can go to bed, so guess I'll say "goodnight."
"Your little girl" Helen

March 13. My dearest Muddie—

Last evening, just as I began to study, the bridge of my glasses broke. So, as I was very tired, I didn't study at all, but went to bed about 8:00. This P.M., I went in town all by my lonesome to get them fixed at the Oculist's on Boylston St. A dear little man with big hazel-brown eyes like "Prof's" fixed them for me, trying them on me some half-dozen times. He looked into my eyes and I into his, very soulfully, tho' it was rather embarrassing. Then he gave me a brand new case. He had asked my name and address (I suppose to send them if they weren't done) and actually called me "Miss Fox." Do you think I need a chaperone? Don't worry for he was <u>really</u> a <u>nice</u> <u>man</u>.

While I'm home, I want to consult with "Prof." about my choice of courses for next year. Do you think it would be "proper" for me to write him when I expect to be there and ask him to give me a "consultation?" After all, he told me to ask him for help any time, so I think I ought to feel free to do so. What do you think? We don't have to do this until we leave in June, but I'd like to get it done now. The rising bell has rung, so I must get up.

Much love to you all, Helen

March 20. My dear Muddie—

We are all sitting in Helen Peck's room, writing letters and eating pickles. So, as I've done my share of the latter, I'll now do the former. We have had no end of company and good times lately, with visiting relatives. Monday was Nina's birthday—eighteen—and both her father and grandmother were here. They brought Nina no end of good things; cake, corn cakes, candy, etc. She had some lovely presents, too—a gold watch and chain from her father and mother and a lovely opal ring from her grandmother. The girls gave her roses and violets and I gave her a sofa-pillow cover.

In the evening, we had a progressive "peanut party," which was fun, and ate considerable of the good things. I slept in Bertha's room so Mrs. Hill could have my bed.

Love & kisses for all—Helen

March 23. My dear Papa,

I have just waked up and must study again for that horrid Algebra test this morning. Oh, they just crowd tests by the wholesale on us before vacation! This is my last one, thank goodness.

Nina stayed with Bertha last night and I had Sara Marsh down from College Hall to study Algebra with me and spend the night. We are very gay here now. Tonight is the Freshman play at the Barn. Tomorrow evening there will be an Easter Vespers service and Monday afternoon, comes the Junior play. I am going to ask Ray to come out for tonight—rather late in the day, but I didn't learn until late yesterday, that men were allowed, so I guess he won't mind. Tuesday, I am going to <u>pack</u> and Wednesday sees me <u>home</u>, if nothing else happens.

I can get my trunk checked right through from here, so won't have to bother with it in Boston. Think I'll start it Tuesday night.

Oh, we are way ahead of you in Spring—the snow is gone and it's very dry and the grass is beginning to green.

Love to all—Helen

March 25. My dear "hearers,"

I got all muddled up in the Algebra exam this morning and am almost sure I flunked it. I didn't do it all and didn't get all that I did do right, I'm sure, so I'm mortally afraid of the result. Please don't be alarmed, for I imagine a lot of the girls are in the same boat. Only, I've always been lucky and shall feel it to flunk for the first time.

After the Junior play tomorrow, Criss wants me to come see Dr. Estes in town. My foot has been troubling me quite a little lately. We have had a lot of foot-work in Gym. Maybe I strained or sprained it some way. I spoke to Miss Randall about it and she is anxious for me to see Dr. Lovett, a specialist in town. Criss says I really ought to see <u>someone</u>, but thinks Dr. Estes would do very well for me and not charge "all outdoors," either, so I'll try to get in there tomorrow. *[Chriss, an old family friend, was a homeopathic nurse.]* It feels better today as I haven't any boots on.

I wrote "Prof" and had a note from him this morning. He will be very glad to help me however he can. My Latin teacher, Miss Walton, strongly advises me to keep on with my Latin next year. The other things, we'll discuss later. I will bring a new catalogue home.

"Cords and cords" of love to you all—Helen

P.S. What is the matter with the mail service? My paper came all right, but your letter postmarked <u>Monday</u> 8:00 <u>A.M.</u> didn't reach me till <u>Tues.</u>, postmarked rec'd here at 7:00 A.M. <u>Tues.</u> You'll have to mail things a week early if they're delayed like that! *[Note: Letters mailed from home at*

8:00 A.M. on any day but Sunday, always reached Helen by 3:00 P.M.!]
Junior play was simply <u>grand</u>. Algebra all right after all. Have just finished packing trunk, and going down to have it checked. Will see you all tomorrow night.

Love till then—Helen

SPRING VACATION

April 10. My dear, dear Muddie & all,   Wellesley—Tues. 7:30 P.M.
     Went up to a meeting for "sports and pastimes" but it was postponed. I stayed for a mass meeting on Student Government to hear a Bryn Mawr girl speak. I am all unpacked and am going to bed early. It hardly seems possible that I've <u>had</u> my vacation at home and am back again! I saw Miss Kelsey about Papa's note. She said I should just register and needn't go to Miss Pendleton at all. Miss Pendleton had a great sorrow this vacation; both her mother and her sister died—within one week. It must be a fearful shock to her.

     Such a time we had registering this morning! The girls were packed in more closely than at the greatest fire bargain sale. I am really lame all over from being squeezed so. Helen Peck actually lost her belt in the crowd!

     Haven't seen Dr. Barker yet about my foot, but shall if possible, this P.M. It felt very much better yesterday, so it may be somewhat due to the wet weather. Hope so.

     The house is being painted and the painters seem to like watching us <u>dress</u>—so I'll have to hurry and disappoint them!

     Well, it is after 8:00 and I'd better close. Wish I could kiss you all around.

     With much love, Goodnight. Helen

April 15. My dear Dad: Monday 8:05 A.M.
     Had a short story to write for English, so had to put off writing to you. First of all—about my foot. I saw Dr. Barker Saturday P.M. She looked at my foot and stroked it and patted it and punched it for sometime, expressing her opinion all the time and asking me questions— "had anything ever fallen on it?" I told her not to my knowledge. She said there seemed to be nothing out of place or broken, but it seemed like a bruise,

rather than a sprain as it is slightly black & blue. She thought it might be due to overwork of the foot in gym and said if my ankles were weak, it was a wonder it hadn't troubled me before. She said my instep is so high and my ankle so small that I should be very careful of turning it. I did turn it quite badly the other day and she thought it swollen from that. She suggested seeing a specialist, but it was not absolutely necessary. The alcohol and salt bath is good and I should use hot water too, and be very careful to lace up my shoes <u>very</u> loosely. Lacing them too tight <u>might</u> have caused it. She suggested ankle supports—cost about $3.00 and to let her know if I want her to order them. I feel very much better now that I've seen her and found nothing <u>serious</u> is the matter.

Love to all—Helen

April 19. My dear Muddie,   Friday Evening—
It is really Spring here, now. The grass is lovely; the buds are swelling and we can hear the frogs "sing" every evening.

The Harvard Glee Club comes here next week and the Mandolin Club, too, which Nina and I plan to go to. Today, April 19, is a holiday. No classes. Bertha, Helen, Alice & I went for a long walk this morning and this afternoon I took a tennis lesson. We have all bought a tennis net together and are going to have a tennis club of our own.

I was invited to a "fudge, cracker and chocolate" party in "Only's" room and am now writing from there so if my letters gets a little "fudgy"— that's why.

The "Annual Circus" takes place at the Barn tomorrow night, then a week from tomorrow is the Harvard Concert. This week has just skipped by.

Love & kisses—Your little girl—Helen

April 21. My dears—
Well, I went to the Circus and it was a circus! I don't believe even Barnum's could beat it. They had the regulation sawdust-sprinkled ring in the center of the Barn, with peanut and lemonade booths down the side and the side shows on the stage. There was a Wild Man from Borneo, (who screamed and tumbled around in a cage, until I should think <u>she</u> would be hoarse—and black & blue today). They had a Zulu Princess, clad in a black union suit with a feather fringe about her waist, a dwarf, an albino, a fat woman, a 3-headed monster, a snake charmer who twirled

fake snakes about herself, (she really is fond of snakes and kept them—real ones—in her room last year, till one night she found one she supposed was lost—in her bed)! Then there were clowns, a tight-rope walker (rope on the floor) bare-back riders on broom stick horses, Indian, Chinese and Japanese "jugglers," a policeman who strutted around and kept people off the "ring," trained monkeys, a band, two "chariots" of four "horses" each (one of four girls from our house). And animals—lions with wonderful manes & tails, ostriches, elephants, giraffes, etc. and the dearest (real) poodle placarded "This is a bear."

I don't know when I have laughed so much—till I could hardly stand. There was a grand parade, with all the animals making their various noises—a perfect pandemonium.

Miss Kelsey called me in the other day, to see if I wanted to move up to College Hall, if there was a chance. I think Dr. Barker may have suggested it, because of my foot. I told her I was well settled in the village and didn't care to change so late in the year. I really think half the trouble with that foot is rheumatism—it certainly is worse this wet weather. Perhaps when it finds it is not going to be petted and humored, it will stop "sulking." I agree with you, Papa, about the "anklet"—if I once get to rely on it, I'll have to wear it and I hate artificial supports. I will see Dr. Barker again, as she was very kind to take such interest in me.

Sleepy time now—wish you all goodnight—Love—Helen

April 25. My dear Muddie and Everybody,

I have just been down to see Dr. Barker again about my anklets. She was lying on the lounge and I guess my rap woke her, but she was very glad to see me. I told her my foot was much better and seems stronger and that I would not have the anklets for a time, which she thought wise. I like her, even if the girls do think her "old ladyish"—she takes such an interest in me.

I have been up to College all day; took my lunch because I had some reading in English to do during the noon hour, consequently I feel hungry for dinner. I dressed in such a hurry this morning that I went off with only two hairpins in, as I afterwards discovered. Weds. I took lunch with Sara Marsh at College Hall, as one of the girls at her table was in town. The tables seem so big and bare like a Methodist supper. They had the ever-present <u>hash</u>, some tomato cooked in some mysterious fashion, white bread, graham bread and biscuits, sweet pickles, graham crackers, dry dates, milk and water. Not as bad as I expected. Sara is to room with Florence Snow, another awfully nice girl in our class, so I can't have her. I think, if I can, unless I see someone whom I like very much, I shall room alone. That reminds me, before we draw for our rooms, May 3, we must pay $10.00 registration fee, so I wish Papa would send it to me as soon as possible. I really don't know where I want to room. Nearly all the girls I like think they will go to College Hall. The rooms will be open for inspection before we draw, so I shall be able to judge better then. The rule in regard to cottages used to be that only one year could be spent in a cottage on campus, but it has been changed, so anyone can stay as long as they like if they can get in a cottage. So perhaps I may try for one.

Miss Dennis "sprang" a test on us in Algebra and when I got my paper back today it had "credit" on it. I must tell you what she said the other day. I stopped to speak with her about how mixing the different formulas which we had been writing on the board were. She said, "Yes, but they are well to know, not only in this year's work, but if one goes on in Math, as I hope you intend to do." I said I was afraid my work wouldn't warrant that, whereupon she said that my first semester's work (Credit, you know) and this were all very good except for that one test "when you got a little mixed up," and I should feel so. I thanked her and told her I'd think it over. But I shan't. If I get through with this Math, I don't think I really need any more, unless I am to teach it. "Prof" says it isn't right to spend all your time on the things you don't like when they're not necessary and I devoutly agree with him.

Well, it's 'most seven and I've studying to do so, I'll close.

With bushels of love, Helen

P.S. I've come to the conclusion that Wellesley is a lovely place and I'm a very lucky girl, for which I must thank you all.

April 29. My dear People—

I was disappointed about getting my suit. The skirt was a little too long and the jacket had to be fitted some, so I am to get it Tuesday—have it sent out. It is very pretty, and it will be billed to you for $22.50. Nina liked it, too. I said I was disappointed not to have it for the Harvard Glee Club last evening. Miss Meade (the sales lady) laughed and said, "oh, you are after the Harvard boys, are you? Well, all the Wellesley girls, or any who have any sense, like them."

My other purchases were a 10¢ <u>wash board</u>, which I think will prove its weight in gold, and a bunch of mayflowers. I do wish you'd get someone to pick some for you to send to me. Some of the girls don't know what they are.

The Harvard Glee Club concert last evening was perfectly fine. It was at the Wellesley Town Hall. We had the best seats in the house—75¢ ones, first row balcony, center, for 50¢. We were supposed to have third row seats, but just after the concert began, the dearest old gentleman (one of the half dozen in the house—the rest being college girls) told us we might as well take the front row seats which were empty. We could see all over the house. The boys weren't particularly handsome, any more than the Dartmouth boys, but they had elegant voices. Nina and I consoled each other for not being up at College Hall last night. The boys always go up there to serenade after the concert. They sang one very cute piece to the tune of "Home, Sweet Home," "were it not for the ladies, we'd all be millionaires," ending "Be they ever so humble, I love all the Girls." Right, too, I guess.

Well—I'm sleepy so I'll go to bed and finish in the morning.

8:30 A.M. A lovely morning! Some of the girls got up at 6:00 A.M. to play tennis and some are still playing. Oh, Papa, can I have a tennis racket? You can get them for $2.00 at Wright & Ditson's. I do want to learn to play.

Bushels of love—Helen

May 2. My dear precious Mamma,

I intended to write yesterday afternoon, but I had a Bible paper to write and dawdled over it till dinner, then I ironed some handkerchiefs, then wrote a letter and went to bed, thinking to write to you early this morning.

Well, I overslept and right after breakfast, went up to College to see the Seniors roll hoops, their regular May Day custom. First, they rolled them down the hill in front of College Hall to the Chapel, and looked so funny and undignified with their long black gowns flapping about. Then, after Chapel, they formed a long line taking hold of each other's hoops, came back to College Hall and marched 'round the circle in front, singing and cheering and being cheered. It was all so pretty. But this afternoon was the prettiest, the "Children's Party" up on the campus at one side of College Hall, where it slopes off. All who took part were dressed as little girls or boys. The girls with short white, pink or blue dresses, sunbonnets and long braids or curls. Honestly, they looked like children of about ten. We sat up on the hill and looked on as they "played" "Ring around the

Rosie," "London Bridge is Falling Down," etc. and then danced around a big Maypole with bright ribbons. The grass was <u>so</u> green and they did all look so pretty. I never realized how pretty it was to be a child before, and what I have lost in growing "big."

Then President Hazard and a little English Lady, who is visiting to see the college, drove along. We all cheered her, and finally she and the English lady got out and each made a short speech. The English lady said she should have to report that the average age of Wellesley girls is 13!

Then the girls formed a ring and danced around them, finally making an arch with their arms for President Hazard and her guest to pass under to their carriage. It was all just like a picture book scene.

My foot continues to improve and I haven't thought of it since I put my shoes on this morning. I don't think <u>wash</u>-<u>boards</u> are so fine, after all. As a result of using my new one yesterday, I have a lovely water-blister on the inside of one finger and skinless knuckles—sore hands in general.

It is damp and foggy today, but may be one of April's left-over crying fits. I must say goodbye now and copy my Trig. paper.

Bushels of love—Helen

May 4. My dear Mama,

I was more than surprised and pleased, early this morning one of the girls brought in not only your letter, but the lovely mayflowers! They are perfectly beautiful, kept finely and are sweeter than any New York or Mass. ones. I carried them all around for everyone to see. Thank you so much, and thank the little girl who picked them. Nina had some from home, too, and a big bunch of roses from Howard, so our room is quite fragrant and looks like a wedding.

My suit came at last, fits very nicely and is just in time for me to wear it to Melrose this weekend.

I had a surprise the other day—a nice letter from "Frankie Dear," asking forgiveness for his long silence, hoping I would be more prompt and promising to accept my invitation to come out if he could summon courage to venture among so many young ladies. He also sent his mother's love and said she would like me to call some day when in town. Nice boy, Frankie, isn't he?

Thanks for both the board-bill and the check for me. Time to study Algebra.

With much love, Helen

May 8. My dear Mamma,

It has been so warm here that I have taken off all my winter things, except my undervest, which I shall soon. I feel so much better.

I got up at 5:45 and did Trig. till breakfast time. I cut the last two hours of Chem. Lab. yesterday to go into town on the 12:17 with Nina & Mrs. Long. We went to see "Rip Van Winkle" at the Boston theatre—and such a big barn it is! It is so old that it looks rather dingy and so big! We were in the second balcony but could see perfectly. Joe Jefferson is a great actor! It was both laughable and cryable and he was good either way. He is so old—over 70, I think, tho' you would never guess it—that I may never have another chance to see him. I am very glad that I went.

Must close for more studying. Bushels of love, Helen

May 13. My dear Hearers,

I must tell you I went to a dance Saturday evening and danced nearly every dance! It was a "Hurdy-Gurdy" dance in gym-suits at the Barn and was the biggest fun; everyone was so jolly and informal. Sunday, as my foot was tired (though it really doesn't really hurt any more to dance than to walk) and I wanted a bath, so I stayed home from church.

We had a man for dinner, a Harvard Senior (just think)! our Junior "big sister" Miss Hayden's friend. He was really very nice, jolly, interesting, and not a mite conceited or forward. He kept us laughing all the time with his jokes and funny stories.

After dinner, some of the girls went for an electric car ride (tho' it's forbidden on Sunday, I believe) and some to walk, but I stayed home to write letters. And was glad I did, as about 4 o'clock who should appear but Walter and Winnie with a box of cake and candy for me!

We took a walk up to College 'round East Lodge and then down to Tupelo. Walter thought, with two girls, it was rather a difficult place to put him in! Then we went on up to College Hall. At one window, there was one girl and in another minute, six or seven girls. So, you see how we regard men as "choice specimens" here at Wellesley. Then I took them over on the hill to the Art Building and finally back home. Supper was just ready, so I had the pleasure of introducing them to everybody and for a wonder, did so without twisting names, as I expected.

We did not go up to Vespers after supper, but stayed up in our room. Alice told me afterwards how she envied me "sitting in the twilight with that splendid man!" All the girls thought him fine. Bertha declared that he "put the Harvard man all in the shade," which is quite a compliment for a College girl. So, I feel quite proud of my "cousin."

Much love and many kisses—Helen

May 16. My dear Papa,

Saturday, we pay our next year's registration fee and Monday, I believe, draw numbers for our choice of rooms. I really don't know whether I want to go to College Hall. They say the table isn't particularly good there. They say, too, it's not the best place for getting a single room, which I mean to try for; also, the first and second floors, which I suppose you would wish me to be on, are quite noisy and someone is always dropping in on you, which gets rather tiresome after a time. I really think perhaps I had best try for a cottage on the hill, if I can't get in Wilder, which I don't expect to do. What do you think? I wish you would advise me.

This afternoon, Grace Curtis, Olive Miller, Bess Hardman and I went over to Hunnewell's and down into the Italian gardens by the lake. It is a beautiful estate; a wide, winding driveway leads up from the gates and little lodge to the house, which we didn't "visit" but which is very large and somewhat old fashioned. There are lovely lawns with trees and shrubs and flowers scattered all over them, like the real country. Only they are so beautifully kept. The gardens are very odd; the trees, mostly cedar, etc., are trimmed in every conceivable shape—one like a <u>rooster</u>. They are not all pretty, but very odd and foreign-looking. There is a driveway close to the lake, 'round which is a wall with stone steps here and there, leading down to the water. Our crews happened to be rowing just then, so we stayed quite a time watching them.

I am sitting on the stairs at College Hall to finish this, so I won't have time to say what I planned about my courses. However, do you think I might keep on with Chemistry? I like it very much and next year's work promises to be very interesting.

With love to all, Helen

May 18. My dear Muddie,

Next Thursday, we draw for rooms. I do hope I get a good number. No danger of my getting in College Hall now. They say there's only one single room left, and I don't know of anyone I really hanker after for a roommate except <u>myself</u>! I really don't know whether to try for Stone, or one of the hill cottages.

I spoke to Miss Walton, my Latin teacher, as to what I should take for minors. She advised another language, such as German, and about half-dozen old "ologys" which I have never heard of more than once or twice. I have thought of going on with Chem., perhaps making a minor of that. I'll write to "Prof" and get his advice.

Heaps of Love—Helen

May 20. My dear Mamma, and Everybody—

I worked on my Latin paper—due tomorrow, until about 4:00 P.M.—and finished it. I had three letters to read, and by the time I'd read those and my dress changed, it was about "bean-time."

Afterwards, we had a fine time; we told stories and acted out charades for awhile, then (Our Junior) Miss Hayden and Grace Curtis made penuche with nuts, (delicious). Then we had a feast of crackers and cream cheese, champagne wafers, grape juice and penuche. That night I dreamed of burglars and other _nice_ things.

Today we are going up to be measured for the Tree Day gowns. They are to be violet cheese cloth in Grecian style and will probably be about $2.00.

You wrote about my continuing with Chem.—that if I do continue with it, I should postpone some other course I had planned to take next year, maybe Physics, till the _next_ year, so my work wouldn't be any harder. There is one course, "Analysis of Food, Air & Water" which I think I should like very much. I think I'll write "Prof" and get his advice.

'Most mail time—must stop and _run_ to the Post Office.

Love and kisses to All—Helen

May 23. My precious Mamma,

I had to read an old "Food Report" for my Hygiene exam and this morning studied a little for it.

It has been _hot_ here today. We had to work a good part of the time in Chem. right over the gas burners and couldn't have the windows open as it blew the flame away, so I nearly sweltered. Then we came home to a lunch of _steak_, _roast_ _potatoes_ and _hot_ _chocolate_! Don't you think it is simply fiendish to give us such hot stuff this warm weather?

I have an invitation to a reception and outdoor dance given by a

Greek Society, which is <u>very</u> select. Miss Lorenzen, Miss Mac's friend, *[former teacher at Nute]* is on the committee, so I suppose I am indebted to her for it. It is to be at the little society house. I think I shall wear my lawn.

Tomorrow forenoon we draw—oh, I hope, I'll be lucky. In the afternoon, I'm going around to look at rooms and make a list of those I think I'd like. Then, Monday morning the choices are made and I shall probably get <u>some</u> room on my list. I think I'll try for Wilder or Wood, one of the hill cottages. They say there's to be a fine set of girls at Wood next year, one of them Miss Snyder, who played the little boy in the Junior play I liked so much. And she is a member of the Greek Society, too, so maybe I'll have a chance to meet her.

I wrote to "Prof" Monday, asking his advice about continuing Chem., and expect an answer soon.

Can I have a pair of low shoes? It's getting dreadfully warm for high ones and my two year old low ones are almost worn out. My foot is <u>very</u> much better.

I enclose two more collars, Mamma. You may be sorry you offered to do them!

Heaps of love and kisses, Helen

May 25. *[Post card.]* Dear Mamma,

Drew 56—considered a very good number. They probably drop fifteen or twenty, bringing it down to about 36. Went to look at rooms and found some very good ones. Have dropped to 39. In loving haste—Helen

May 28. My precious Mamma,

I really think that Norumbega is the best I could do. Stone Hall seemed <u>so</u> cheerless when we were there, that I couldn't make up my mind to go there. And indeed, all the rooms were on the north side, which made them all worse. Freeman had some small rooms on the first floor, but the partitions are very thin and they say the housekeeper is <u>very</u> disagreeable.

Norumbega is where President Hazard's suite of rooms is, you know, so I suppose there would be as good fare as anywhere. Then, too, you needn't worry about my "cutting up," for I shall simply <u>have</u> <u>to</u> <u>behave</u> in her presence. I shall not be so dreadfully scared, though, for she comes to the table on Sundays and certain other days and beyond that, I guess, the girls don't see much of her.

I shall be up on the third floor, but I think that when <u>you</u> come to think of it, you will feel perfectly safe about it. There are good fire escapes on the cottage, and in addition to that, judging from the house-plan which Miss Kelsey showed me, I am close by the staircase. We didn't go in the room itself as the door was closed, but I shall go up again to look at it, take measurements for curtains, bed linen, etc. Won't it be fun to furnish my room next year? The house itself is on the hill just opposite College Hall—just enough distance for a nice little walk and very convenient to the Chem. Lab, if I want to take Chem. next year.

That reminds me, I found a letter from "Prof" waiting for me this morning. He thinks I ought to elect as minors, a language or "-ology" and to take Chem. as a mere "side issue." He said he supposed I should get out early enough to come to Commencement and should be very glad to see me.

Supper Bell. We have horrid, nasty <u>croquettes</u>, (I never want to see another) Mondays. We actually had cold meat for a change tonight and it was very acceptable. When I come home, I think I'll live on salt fish and ripe tomatoes for a novelty. If I find things "tame" as you fear, it will be a <u>blessed</u> <u>tameness</u>.

Tell Papa and Papa Fox they must save all the funny advertisements they can for my room next year, and ask Papa Fox if he couldn't get me some book posters at the publishing houses, too.

It's getting dark and I must study a little before bed.

Tons of love and kisses for all—

Your "little girl," Helen

May 30. Dear Mamma,

Elsie wrote that she gets all through at Vassar on June 6th, is coming to Boston and will be out here to see me.

Oh—can Papa please have a pair of low shoes sent out before Monday. Black, with patent tips. You know the size, etc.—broad with <u>thick</u> soles. I need them badly.

Yours in loving haste—Helen

June 3. My dear folks at home—

It really seems as though I were going to have a good chance to talk to you once more. I am all alone in my room as Nina has gone home for today, taking Helen P. with her and all the other girls are out on the piazza or gone to church.

When I found Nina was going home, I wrote Beulah to come out, prepared to stay overnight. She came about 11:30 on the electric from Needham, and stayed until 5:00 this afternoon. Soon after lunch yesterday, I took her up to College and showed her all the "curiosities." We went up on the 5th floor to the Zoological Laboratory, and had great fun looking at the birds, pictured and stuffed. I do wish I could take "birdology"—it must be so interesting; only in the beginning, you have to work with bugs; catch them and analyse them. You know I love(?) them too well to pull them to pieces. We also looked at the specimens of minerals. That science I mean to study. It includes Mineralogy and Advanced Geography and is, they say, very hard, but it must be very interesting and instructive. Next year, however, I want to keep on with Chem. as a science. I want to know more about it than I can learn in one year's work. It will be just the time for me to take it, too, as the Lab. is so near Norumbega.

After meeting Bertha and watching the Freshman Crew row awhile, we went over to Norumbega to look at my room. The girl who has it this year is a Senior and was very nice. It is a very pleasant room—quite large, with one window (very few single rooms have more), which is in a corner of one wall. The roof comes down on one side a little, but not as much so as in my own room at home.

The furniture is that ugly old black stuff, which they have everywhere, save at Wilder. I should say that the girl who has it now is either in somewhat limited circumstances or hasn't much taste about fixing a room. The latter, I should say, for it wasn't fixed up half as pretty as it might have been I think, with a comfortable rocker or Morris-chair, which I hope Papa will give me; my desk and a tea-table, which I mean to get myself, with Aunt Criss' chafing-dish and my cups and saucers on it, and some sofa pillows, which I mean to make this summer, on the bed—it will be a very cozy den. There is no closet, but a large wardrobe.

As regards to the fire-escape, etc. It is directly opposite the stairs. Just under the window there is a roof built out over the driveway, which comes up to the second floor. The girl there has a "rope" to use in case of fire, hanging by the window; I say "rope," but it is really some kind of patent "fire-escape." I think with a rope like that and a pair of thick gloves to slide down with, I should be perfectly safe. I might take a fire "distinguisher," too. I quite forgot to notice the method of heating or lighting. I think, however, all the houses have electricity and of course, steam and a furnace.

You asked where Nina is to be. She and Bertha are both to have singles in Stone Hall. I wish in some ways I were going with them, if I could have had a room near. It <u>will</u> be a little hard, going in with all new girls but since you want me in a cottage, and I really think I'd prefer it myself, I'll stick to Norumbega. Olive Miller is to be next door in Freeman and Alice Dalrymple in Wilder, just across a little grass plot, so if I'm lonely, I can run in to see them. But I'm <u>not</u> <u>going</u> to be lonely. Yes, indeed, Nina and I have gotten along very well, and will part good friends. I imagine we shall both miss each other next year, even though we both want to room alone.

Beulah and I went to a "Barn Swallow" play—"The Adventures of Lady Ursula" and it was <u>fine</u>, almost as good as the Junior Play. This morning, we went to Chapel, so she had quite a variety of Wellesley entertainments.

My exams are from June 13 to June 19. Latin in the morning, that last day, and <u>Hygiene</u> at 2:00 P.M. in the afternoon. I went to Miss Sherrard to see if I could take the Hygiene some other day or even begin it an hour earlier. She was very nice, said she was very sorry, but it was not allowed—even in case of illness—and she had no authority to allow me to do it. She said I might speak to Miss Pendleton about it, but was afraid it would be of no use. And of course, it wouldn't. Miss P. has a heart of <u>ice</u>. I should get frowned at and calmly refused, and that's all.

I could <u>cut</u> the exam, which would "condition" me in that subject; come back and take the exam in the Fall, but I hate to get a "condition," even that way.

There is a train for Boston leaving Newton Lower Falls at 3:09; it's barely possible that if I get through half of the exam—enough to pass it—I can go by the electric to the "Falls" and get that train, which would get me in town in time for my "up" train to Milton. But I can't give up hope for a miracle to get me to Nute Graduation on time.

I have asked Aunt Ada to meet me Tuesday P.M. in town, to get a new shirtwaist for me and one for you, Mama Fox. I guess between us we can get you "something fit to wear." Oh, <u>clothes</u>! What a nuisance they are! I sometimes think how nice it would be if Eve had never eaten that apple!

I'm afraid I've got to make another appeal for more money. I try to be economical, but with my Tree Day costume and my Latin books, about $4.00 of my allowance is "eaten up." Just by way of comparison I must tell you that two girls in the house have spent over $200 each since Easter, so they say, and not for board, either. Of course, that is simply outrageous, but it just shows what can be spent. Time to close—

Lots of love and kisses for you all, Your "little girl" Helen

June 5. My dear "Mudder"—

Well, to begin. I went last evening to the Greek Society party. Wore my lawn and didn't catch cold a mite. It was a lovely evening. The house looked very pretty and the grounds were lighted with Japanese Lanterns; there were settees and chairs about and the music was <u>fine</u>! The platform was too small for the number of guests, so the dancing wasn't much fun, but pretty to watch.

I had good luck shopping with Aunt Ada. We found a pretty white lawn shirtwaist for Mamma Fox and a lawn dressing sack, which I hope she will like. I bought two waists for myself; a plain blue chambray for $1.75 and a really fine green and white striped gingham for only 98¢! But it is too small and I shall have to exchange it for a size 34—which I am very proud of. Then I bought a 10¢ copy of that picture "Pharaoh's Horses" which I gave you for Christmas, Mamma. It is two feet square, just the thing for my room next year. Also, a 25¢ nightgown to cut the sleeves out of and wear under my Grecian costume for Tree Day, so I'll be graceful and <u>limp</u>. *[No corsets.]*

Oh, shoes! I would prefer black; they are worn more this year. My old brown ones resoled will do for common. Many thanks for the money—it has <u>clothed</u> me!

Bushels of love—Helen

June 12, Thursday. My dear Mamma,

Tomorrow is Tree Day and if it is pleasant we are to dress in our Grecian gowns and <u>look</u> <u>pretty</u>. Some have to dance, but the majority merely to <u>look</u> which is quite enough for such weather. We are to part our hair in the center and wear it in "sicky" knots, as someone said. *[Psyche?]*

Only three more days before exams and I am <u>so</u> glad! The teachers are all coaching us up now, which, of course, serves to frighten us out of our wits. They say, however, that the finals aren't nearly as bad as midyears.

(Later) I have dressed, combed my flying locks, and feel enormously better here on the cool piazza. Do hope Miss White has something cool for supper.

(Later again) Have had dinner—fish, greens, strawberry short-cake and <u>water</u>. We were all so thirsty and the water pitcher went dry. We are all out on the piazza now, writing letters and "squabbling." Alice S.'s friend, a fine singer, is going to sing for us this evening. With the parlor windows open, we can hear her beautifully out here. We stayed out on the piazza all evening. Nina went to sleep in the hammock, the rest of us listened to the music. Then a young man, a school friend of Nina's, dropped by. Alice made some fruit punch and we talked and joked until he went home at 10:00. It seemed so good to see anything masculine again, we were in high spirits.

June 13—6 A.M. It was too late then to write more so I decided to wait until after Tree Day. I wish you could have seen me in my "Greecy" robe with a little gilt belt and wonderful violet scarf draped over my shoulders, and my hair parted and in a "sicky" knot. All our class assembled at Wilder where a funny red-headed masculine artist added the last touches to our drapery. Then we marched single file down the hill and over the campus.

The hillside below College Hall was crowded with the teachers, alumnae and some spectators, for though they are very strict and have policemen to watch (we had to give our names and a password to one, who proceeded to look us up in the catalogue)—a great many get in. Bess Hardman's mother was with us, and she walked right up to the young man who was helping the policeman, when he looked enquiringly at her. "My name is Mrs. Hardman," she said, "but you won't find it in that book." He smiled and said, "All right, Madame, you may go in." We all softly applauded.

All the other classes marched in ahead of us; the Seniors in caps and gowns, the Juniors in white with yellow ribbons and armfuls of buttercups and daisies, and the Sophomores as Robin Hoods, friars, monks, nuns, foresters and milkmaids. When we were all seated in places marked off by ribbons, the exercises began. First the Senior president made everyone welcome, then Pearl Randall, another Senior, the most beautiful girl I ever saw, made the address to undergraduates—full of laughs, but really sincere and lovely. It will seem so queer to come back next year and not see some of the Seniors I know—merely by sight, but "worship" from afar.

Then came the Senior dancers. The band, behind some trees, began to play, and down the hill came nymphs in lovely green robes with palest green gauze veils about their heads and shoulders which they floated all about as they danced—like leaves blown about by the wind. Then six or seven girls dressed in bright colors to represent flowers came dancing down. They danced in front of the leaves and then a third company—fireflies with lovely jeweled wings and huge butterflies of all colors, came flitting down. Then they all danced together. Beautiful!

Just as they finished it, it began to shower and away they flitted. Some people put up umbrellas, but we poor "Greecy" maidens skipped for a tree. It didn't last long and when it stopped, we all marched in winding lines to a little below the Seniors' place, where our dance was to be. Then, after the Tree Day spade had been presented and the class oration given, our dance began. All except our dancers formed two long lines, one behind the other, in a semicircle, and just swayed to and fro while they danced. It was very pretty and very simple. Our dancers were dressed in short crepe dresses of all colors and carried large evergreen hoops. Then led by our dancers, we all ran to our class tree, everybody following with great curiosity. The tree is a secret until that moment, and not even the prying Sophs. found it out. We all gathered around it, sang our class song, and every class cheered.

Then—we had our class picture taken; it had been a succession of drizzles and it drizzled then worse than ever, so you can imagine what a wet drabbled crowd we were. The minute it was over, everyone made a grand rush for home. We changed all our clothes and Miss White had plenty of hot chocolate waiting, so I guess none of us took cold. I, for one don't feel any worse.

With tons of love for all—As ever—Helen

June 14. My dear Papa,

I am delighted to think that you are coming down Monday. Can't you plan to be here for Float Night Tuesday evening? I am planning to come home on the 4:15 Wednesday, doing what I can of my Hygiene exam before I catch the car. I had English yesterday and it was very easy, so I'm hoping the others will be. The Hygiene couldn't be hard, only fussy.

I think I shall want an extension, if you can bring it. Then I can pack my trunk, send it home on your ticket and bring the extension on my own. (One has to pay for more than one trunk here.) I shall carry my suitcase, with the dress I will wear that evening.

Well, I must do some washing and study for my Chem. exam. I'm so glad you are coming. Let me know when, so I can walk down to the station to meet you. And I hope you can stay for Float. Please do.

Love to All, your own girl, Helen

June 16. My dear family,

This is my last Sunday in Wellesley for one long time! I could turn a dozen <u>somersaults</u>! I am going to pack my trunk in the morning. I have taken down my pictures and piled things up generally.

Everybody's mother and father and sisters and brothers are here now, for Float Night. It seems quite festive. The exams are most over. Chem. was long and pretty hard, but I guess I more than passed. Trig., most of the girls thought was awful. It was pretty hard. I did the first 4 parts very readily, but the 5th and the 6th I couldn't do at all. Very few got both and a good many, neither, so I feel all right about that. Bible was <u>fearfully</u> long—my hand aches, still—but quite easy. Weds. comes Latin and, of course, Hygiene and then—home. You ask if I will be glad to get home. If I was ever glad of anything in my life—<u>Yes</u>! I'm tired, dirty, hungry and thirsty for home!

Good bye till Weds.

With <u>tons</u> and <u>acres</u> of love for everybody, Helen

SO ENDS HELEN'S FRESHMAN YEAR

SOPHOMORE YEAR, 1901-1902

FIRST SEMESTER

Sept. 22, 1901, Sunday. My dear "hearers"—

It is all a dream and haven't I been home at all? If it were not for the bareness of my room and a feeling that I'd seen you all not long ago, I should be quite sure that I have been here ever since last June.

A group of us came out on the 2:15 train and all rode up to College together. I was in such a hurry to get off for Norumbega, that I quite forgot to pay Sam, the driver. His question, "Do you want it charged?" recalled me to myself.

A maid met me in the hall, I gave her my name and my room number and she took me up to it. I was really surprised at its size for it is much larger than I had thought. An inventory of the furniture. One bed—whose width I've not yet measured; one wardrobe, tall and grim; one washstand with pitcher, bowl, mug, and soapdish; one bureau with "side boxes" on top; one table without any cover; one bookcase—no special characteristics; two chairs—one common chamber-set chair, the other a somewhat worn "willow" chair, but not a rocker; two rugs, one large, one small; "and lastly my brethren," one fire escape rope with full directions for using.

I think now that I'm going to like Norumbega very much. I found another Soph. stranded here, so we adopted each other. Nearly all the girls here are Juniors and Seniors, some Post Grads, too. Although they are all quite reserved, they are very pleasant. Mrs. Newman, our Head of House, is a very sweet little old lady. Everything is very neat and clean; the dining room especially is a relief from Miss White's—it is a large pleasant room with four tables for eight, with ferns and other plants, and flowers on a sideboard and the tables.

Everything at the table is served in courses and it is all very formal. It

Norumbega—Helen's Sophomore Year Dorm

seems a wee bit queer at first, but it is just what I need to hurry me up a little. Then I watch the others, so don't disgrace myself by blunders. The fare is <u>very</u> good, everything is beautifully cooked and served. This noon, we had roast beef—(some white soup first) mashed creamed potatoes, succotash, bread, tomato salad and crackers and finally, cake and delicious chocolate ice-cream.

President Hazard ate at the Faculty table. Directly after dinner she and Mrs. Newman led the way to Mrs. Newman's apartment. Then Mrs. N. introduced us all to Miss Hazard, and we all had after dinner coffee. I was quite favored, as Miss Hazard asked me to pass the coffee, put her arm around me and took me to Prof. Brown to introduce me and let me serve her with coffee. Then she showed us photos, talked, and was just as sweet as she could be. She is a lovely woman and I am glad to be in the house with her. I'm sure I can't help but learn from her.

I have settled with the cashier, registered, and bought a Post Office key, so shall spend tomorrow getting settled.

Here's a goodnight kiss for you all, Your "little girl" Helen

Sept. 24. My dear Muddie Dee—

I got my schedule yesterday and then came home and unpacked until 3:00 P.M. Helen Peck, Muriel and Nina all stopped in to see me and I gave them each a photo, which they thought very good. Directly after dinner, I went to see Olive, but she was out, so I went to Alice's room, which is perfectly <u>dear</u>. She came back with me to see mine.

This morning, College opened with Chapel, when all the Seniors appeared for the first time in their caps and gowns. Then President Hazard read a list of last year's Freshmen who had secured "Honorable Mention," the highest rank for them and your "beautiful daughter's" name was among them and she has been receiving congratulations ever since.

I went to German today, also Latin, English and Chemistry. New teachers in every one. I think I am going to like them all. I am mourning the fact, however, that I shan't dare cut Latin—my one "diversion" last year, as Miss Hawes, my teacher, and the head of the department, is here in the house, if you please.

Helen Peck and I went down to see Miss White this P.M. and found her just the same. Her house has been newly papered and is quite fine.

I had quite an experience coming back to College. I bought a small hand lamp last year to use to curl my hair, as it looks rather "dismal" straight, and had left it at Miss White's. I had seen nothing to forbid bringing lamps here, so I brought it up with me. I hadn't gone far before I met Prof. Whitin, Head of Fiske. She stared at my lamp, asked me if I intended taking it into College Hall, and when I said, "No, Norumbega," she shook her head, said I must ask Mrs. Newman—that it wasn't allowed. I went on, but it did seem as if all the Faculty were out walking, as I kept meeting them and they all stared at my poor unoffending little lamp. One of them fairly <u>glared</u> at it and then at me, to see what manner of girl I could be to commit so deadly a sin.

It made me rather in doubt of my lamp's reception so I decided to sneak up the back way. Well, I sneaked and as I reached the piazza, there sat Mrs. Newman at the window, sewing.

I decided it was best to put on a bold front, so marched up to her and asked her about it. She said that she thought it had been forbidden, though <u>she</u> thought a kerosene lamp much safer than alcohol ones, which were allowed. Anyway, she let me bring it up, with her to fall back on. I guess I'm safe, but after all, I haven't any matches, so I guess it won't harm anyone.

After dinner, this evening, we had chocolate in the reception room, where I had a little chat with President Hazard and Miss Hawes. I am still greatly pleased with everything here, girls, fare, room, etc. I am really happy and contented.

With bushels of love for you all—Helen

Sept. 28. My dear people—

I have been in Edna Taylor's room all evening chatting and writing this letter, sitting in her Morris chair. I am drinking <u>two</u> glasses of milk every day—the maid brings it to me at the table and it is very good. Edna says they put out bread or crackers and milk every evening in the dining-room, but I haven't yet stayed up late enough to get hungry, so haven't been down.

Edna is a Sophomore. She is a tall, large girl, quite plain and quiet, but <u>very</u> nice when you get to know her. Her father is a doctor in McKeesport, Pa., very near Pittsburgh. Of course, Papa will ask, "Is he wealthy?" And I must say, I really don't know, but I should say about as much as we are. Edna has lots of clothes, but doesn't seem much interested in them. But I mustn't gossip about my neighbor. She is goodhearted and generous and I really like her. We went to Chapel yesterday. The preacher, who was from the Old (or New?) South Church in Boston, was not particularly interesting. In the afternoon, I visited with Edna and also chatted with May Downing, a Junior, in her room. She is from Worcester. In the evening we went to the Vesper Service, which was fine, with special music—a soprano with a gorgeous voice.

My Weds. and Thurs. are completely filled with Lab work. If I'd only known how much time it took, I shouldn't have taken Chem. It is very interesting, however, so I shall not mind it so much, as I would have <u>Math</u>.

Oh, I have thought of some more things for "the box" you are sending; some cold tablets, some more picture-hooks, some rags for "cold" handkerchiefs, and, if there's room, some crackers—grahams or saltines.

I will get me a large chamois bag, today, and price lace collars and jackets for you, Mama Fox.

My hair hasn't been curled yet and I'm really learning to like it straight, so the lamp still reposes in my wardrobe. I am glad you are pleased with my rank. I shall try to get as high this year.

Will Papa please get me a Waterman's fountain pen and have it sent out at once as I need it very much.

Goodnight, Love & kisses to all—Helen

Oct. 2. Dear Muddie Dee,

I have just finished breakfast of grapes, cream of wheat, fish, sweet potatoes, hot rolls and <u>milk</u>, so you see, I fare very well.

Alice and I went into town Monday. The shoes Papa had sent, were too small, so we hunted up Lamkin and Foster, where he ordered them. I had no idea $^1/_2$ size made such a difference. A nice little colored boy came to meet us and looked surprised and perplexed when I stated my case. "They didn't usually make exchanges that way," he said, "being a wholesale house, but just as it is—you say you're from <u>Wellesley</u>?—I guess we can." And he took me to Mr. Foster's office to try the new pair on, then followed us to the door to say good-day, and was very polite. I tell you, <u>Wellesley</u> is a charmed name! So my shoes are nice and comfortable—regular "college shoes."

Then I bought my shirts for 50¢ apiece in Jordan Marsh Co., and also bought myself a birthday present of a bamboo frame screen for the corner where my wash-stand is. I also got some lovely soft pink ribbon to make a corsage bow, and a lace collar—a perfect <u>beauty</u> to wear with my silk waist for only $1.50. I asked Edna to guess the cost and she said $3.00 or more. All from the birthday money you gave me. I also bought a little pocket map of Boston which would come in handy in case I ever "got lost."

The bell has rung for Chapel, so I must close.

Bushels of love, Helen

Oct. 4. My dear Mamma,

What lovely weather we have had since I came back! So different from last year when I was a poor homesick little Freshie. Now I'm a wise old Sophomore, and that very fact makes more difference than one would expect in my feelings. Then, I've been happy over two or three little things lately. At first, I was dreadfully discouraged over my German and French— the latter especially. I had forgotten practically all I ever knew of it, and Mlle. Caron (we have two teachers by that name—sisters) talked <u>so</u> fast and ran her words <u>all</u> <u>together</u>. But the last two lessons, I've picked up. (It was only natural that it should be hard at first after almost two years vacation from it.) Yesterday, I ventured to raise my hand on two or three little things which I knew and actually <u>shone</u>! It is all right about the German script. Some of the others don't know it either, and it seems they give us until Christmas to learn it.

We are seated at regular tables now in the dining room (before, there would be a great rush of ten girls for our table seating only eight). I am at the very table I wanted. Miss Montgomery, a Senior and the nicest girl, is at the head and all the others, save Edna and I are Post Graduates, Seniors and Juniors, so we feel quite honored—another of my joys.

Then, I must tell you of another very foolish one. Yesterday, as I was going up to College, I met several of the "Honoraries," among them, Miss Pendleton and she actually smiled and bowed to me. I was greatly overwhelmed, as she very seldom deigns to notice the girls in that way.

Went for a walk yesterday and picked an armful of wild fall asters. I filled my rose bowl with them.

Much love to you all—Helen

Oct. 6, P.M. My precious Mamma—

I am in Edna's room again, on her couch, with a mustard plaster burning my chest. I have caught the cold which everyone here has just now, so I went down to ask Mrs. Newman for some mustard to make a plaster. She was lovely and made me one herself. It is stinging away beautifully—so much that I shan't wear it to bed. She said I probably wouldn't be able to. Alice has an equally bad cold so we went together to see Dr. Sherrard, to her room and then to the hospital, but couldn't find her. Later, I went again to the hospital, and saw the head nurse, who gave me some tablets and told me to put on a mustard plaster, so here I am. Guess I'd better go to bed and add a few words in the morning.
(Oct. 7, A.M.)

I feel more like somebody this morning. Took a hot bath, drank some hot water and slept so soundly that I couldn't tell where I was when I woke up! Chapel bell has just rung.

So love to all, Helen

Oct. 12. My dearest only Mamma—

It was almost 10:00 P.M. when I finished studying last evening and in a question of a hot bath or writing to you, I chose the former, because I knew I couldn't get the hot water in the morning, but could probably find paper and pencil all right.

I have sent you an extension bag full of dirty clothes. *[An extension bag was like an expandable laundry case—still used today.]* I have begun to get desperate for clean clothes, though I have enough to last until you get these done. Whatever, the cost of sending them express—even $1.00, it would be cheaper, as I couldn't get them done here for twice that. Either American express or Adams—doesn't make much difference, as long as you get them.

The "box" you sent was great, but I rec'd a nice little bill of $1.00 from Bailey's Express, who brought it here without my orders—to me; 25¢ for transportation and 75¢ to Boston and Albany R.R. Now, what does that mean? That it costs 75¢ to get freight from Boston to here or that it stayed at the freight house overnight and was charged "board?" They also suggested that I put the money in a money box in College Hall, but I don't plan to without a receipt.

The "Gibson" pillow is <u>fine</u>. *[This may refer to the Gibson Wellesley girl on the cover of this book which would reliably date it—1902. The blown up poster looks as if the background is linen.]* You must have spent hours on it. I never realized the amount of work there was in it before. The box cover is very pretty, too, and goes very nicely with my room. The box is just about right for a window seat. *[I still have the box, though the cover is faded.]*

We had a most exciting class meeting yesterday for election of class president. There was a tie—81 votes apiece, and the two girls drew lots, our candidate winning. I expect there will be some great cheering after Chapel this morning.

Booker T. Washington's daughter is here.

Must close and go over to College. Heaps of love, Helen

Oct. 13. My dear family circle,

It is about 7:30 P.M. and I am sitting here at my table desk simply baking. You ask if the "steam" is on yet. It has been on all the time, I guess, but not in my room as I keep the register closed nearly all the time, as it is <u>so</u> warm. Especially evenings, with the electric light on. Contrary to my notion, they <u>do</u> make heat and plenty of it. *[This, apparently, is Helen's first experience of living with electric lights, rather than kerosene lamps, or gas, as Miss White had in the village.]*

This morning, the two PostGrads, Miss Stratton and Miss Nelson, and the Seniors, the Misses Barnes, Coughlin, McAusland and Montgomery ("my" Senior) and one or two others were in the little parlor alcove, playing the piano until church-time, and this evening, after supper one of the girls' friends played for us in the alcove. She was an exquisite player.

In the afternoon, I went over to Freeman to see Olive Miller. Her room is much smaller than mine and quite bare, as yet—worse than mine.

Then I went to Stone to see Nina, but she was out. Then to College Hall to see Helen Peck. She and her roommate, Mabel Champlin, were just going on a walk around the lake, so I went with them. I brought back an armful of lovely leaves to decorate my room and it looks quite gay.

Booker T. Washington brought his daughter here himself (Edna saw him and said he's fine looking) and she is staying down in the village with one of the "big" English teachers, Katharine Lee Bates. She is a small, quite dark girl with a very sweet face. Some of the Southern girls are inclined to resent her being here. They say that a reporter went to her and told her of the feeling against her and she felt very badly and wrote her father to come for her. Of course the girls wouldn't want to receive her with open arms, but I think they might treat her like a lady as I really think she is. It must be so hard to be black and educated: I think if I were black, I would want, for my own happiness, to stay ignorant.

Please, when you send my laundry, would you put in a cake, chocolate if you please. I'm enclosing a day's menu from Norumbega, so you can see I'm not starved; just some cake from <u>home</u> would taste <u>so</u> good. My cold is better and I have on my high neck vest.

With heaps and heaps of love—Helen

Menu for Oct. 13   <u>Breakfast</u>
    Fruit—Peaches and Grapes
    Shredded Wheat Biscuit or Cream of Wheat
    Beefsteak, Sweet Potatoes
    Hot Biscuits—Doughnuts
    Coffee—Milk

Oct. 18. My dear Muddie:—

Ring the bells and put up the flag!

I received a note from <u>Mr.</u> <u>Smith</u> yesterday morning inviting me to the <u>Dartmouth</u>-<u>Williams</u> football game at Newton Center tomorrow P.M. But, oh dear, I'd no sooner recovered from the shock than I learned the "Rules and Regulations"—that I must have a <u>chaperone</u>!

Instead of quietly ignoring that passage, registering to stay at Winnie's in Melrose, then meeting Mr. Smith downtown and "running away," I was foolish enough to go to Mrs. Newman, who confirmed my fears, but said, considering the facts of the case (his being my teacher and Nute Principal—and I didn't tell her how old, though she guessed he must be quite young, to be interested in athletics) she would speak of it at the meeting of the "House Heads" yesterday A.M. and let me know the result at noon.

Meanwhile, I did the only thing possible—wrote to Mr. Smith, telling him the circumstances under which I could go and practically leaving it with him. Of course, he'll have to say "Come" if he can get a ticket for the horrid old chaperone. If he can't, I don't know what we can do.

Last evening, Mrs. Newman told me that the decision was I must have a chaperone. I was at my wits' end, for I don't know any of the teachers who go as chaperones well enough to ask them. I asked her advice and she said she sometimes went. You can imagine how surprised I was! I almost hugged her and now she has promised to go. As long as I've got to have someone, I'd rather have her than anyone else.

Now I'm waiting to hear from "Prof." Wasn't it dear of him to ask me, and wasn't it horrid to have to write him about a chaperone? Really, it was the only thing I could do. I am so afraid it will rain, after all and spoil everything. It poured here yesterday.

Oh, I do hope it won't rain. Your excited Helen

Oct. 21. My dear Ones—

I received Mr. Smith's answer about the chaperone problem. He said the tickets were going so fast that he was obliged to ask for the refusal of two before he heard from me and when he tried to get the third, they were all gone. He wrote me a lovely note saying that he hadn't thought of a chaperone, or would "of course" have arranged for one, but that we would make it up some other time. He also asked me to let him know when I could receive callers, as he wished to come out in "the near future." So I'm going to write him tonight to come out next Saturday or Sunday. Don't you wish you could read my letters? It seems very queer not to pass them around and wait for Mamma Fox to get her "specs" out. It makes me feel quite young lady-ish.

This morning, we people on "the hill" were all invited over to Wilder for prayers led by the minister of today, President Hyde of Bowdoin. Later, Edna and I went to church to hear him. He was simply fine.

This evening, I went to College Hall for supper with Laura Hinkley and discovered that I'd got to be at the French table, with both Mlles. Carons. I managed to confine my attempts at conversation to "oui," and smile, so got on all right. It is a great way to learn a language, though and I wish we had a French table here.

Will mail this tonight so it will go out on the 6:00 A.M. tomorrow and you will get it at noon.

With piles of love—Your "little girl," Helen.

Oct. 25. My dearest Mamma.

Yesterday after finishing a Bible paper, I spent the P.M. in Chem. Lab. work. We have such nasty smells (like rotten eggs) that every one complains of us. I am getting quite used to it, however, and think if I get thro' that course, I'll be able to stand most anything in the "smell" line. The rotten egg gas turned my watch chain and good luck ring all black.

I am going out for sports now. Am taking English Field Hockey, a new game here, but one that promises to be great fun. It's mostly chasing a ball down the field with a long stick. Before, I merely walked—not very violent exercise—and I feel better already—was really not so sleepy last evening, and dandy this morning.

I look really "swell" in my new hat, which I bought in Melrose for $4.60. It is the same blue as my suit, quite large, with the brim turned up square all around, with blue silk folded about the crown and nearly covering the brim and a white and brown ostrich pom-pom in front. I like it so well I shall be glad to wear it two seasons! Mr. Smith hasn't written yet, so I hardly know whether to expect him Saturday or not.

The cake you sent in my laundry, Mamma, was beautiful and not a bit dry. I had some of the girls in after dinner and we had a <u>feast</u>.

I must study the German I couldn't last evening so I must close— Stacks of love—Helen

Oct. 26. Dear, dear "Everybody,"—

I am feeling quite at home in school now, only I don't feel as though I <u>knew</u> so much as I did when I was a Senior at Nute. "Prof.'s" letter made me feel a little smarter; he spoke of the success he knew I should have, etc. So, I feel that I <u>must</u> get it, in order not to disappoint him and <u>you</u> all. I have had <u>two</u> little compliments in Latin from Miss Walton. When I asked her after class about a word in the prose composition work, she said "That was quite a good exercise of yours, Miss Fox, did you spend much time on it?" In that bluff way quite like "Prof's." Then yesterday, she had told us our exercises were very poor and we might re-write them for today. I went up after class to ask her about some correction and she casually said, "Oh, you needn't bother to rewrite yours, Miss Fox, if you have corrected the mistakes I marked." So, I felt quite flattered.

Then, several of the girls have told me what a "stunner" I am in Geometry—so you see little New Hampshire girls aren't so very far behind after all. I had two tests today—Geometry and Chemistry, and, of course, dreaded them, but found them to be very easy.

I must close and dress up a little for dinner, as one of the girls is having guests.

Heaps of love for All—Helen

Oct. 28. My dear people,

Mr. Smith didn't come Sat. after all. In the morning mail, I got a note saying he had hoped to, but found it impossible. But he <u>could</u> come any time, Tues., Thurs. or Sunday, or Sat. evening, would I tell him when. So, as we were to have special Memorial services for King Alfred last evening, I sent a special delivery letter telling him to come out on the train reaching here at 5:56 P.M.—and <u>he</u> came!

Meanwhile, I went down and threw myself on Miss White's mercy, as we are not allowed to bring men here to meals on Sundays and the Tea Room is closed. She finally said she would save us a cup of chocolate, which we could have after her girls were through. She also promised to cash the check Papa sent me today, when she would have the money. Which reminds me—please, instead, send bills in a registered letter, as it is so hard to get checks cashed here.

After breakfast (Sunday) another girl and I walked down to Tupelo to see the lake from there. It was <u>so</u> lovely—oh, it is <u>perfect</u> here now and tho' I <u>do</u> hate to be away from you all, I am exceedingly thankful for the privilege of being here.

We went to church. The minister today is the father of one of our Norumbega Seniors, and he, his wife and daughter were here at dinner. After, we were all invited into Miss Hazard's for coffee and to meet him. I was standing talking to some of the girls, when Miss Hazard came along and said, "Miss Fox, I want you to meet Mr. Tompkins." So, she took me along, introduced me to him and his wife and left me there. I couldn't think of a blessed thing to say at first, and then we both started in at once. I discovered afterwards, that I had been especially honored, for only P.G.s and some Seniors, in short, "Honoraries," and this poor little Soph. had been presented! If I had known it then, I <u>should</u> have been scared.

After that, I arrayed myself in my new hat and jacket and went to the station to meet Mr. S. I didn't see him at first and began to fear he hadn't come, when I spied him down at the far end of the platform, looking for <u>me</u>. He appeared to be very glad to see me and asked all about college and news from home.

The new maid at Miss White's took us in one of the <u>girls' rooms</u> which used to be the sitting room, as all the girls were still in the parlor, which nearly drove the girls wild with laughter. Silly little Freshmen! It was <u>so</u> provoking of them, still I suppose I would have done the same last year. Finally, Miss White gave us a very nice supper.

I took him up by East Lodge to Chapel. He began to discuss my courses and mentioned receiving a letter from Wellesley when he was still Nute Principal, about the good work I was doing.

He enjoyed the Chapel services very much. Afterwards, we walked about the grounds (there was a lovely moon), peeped into College Hall, walked up here and sat down in the parlor until 9:30, when he had to leave for the train. I walked him down by the Chem. Lab. to start him in the right direction and got back to the house just as the warning bell rang at 9:45.

He told me all about his courses at Harvard Law and the suite of rooms, with a piano, fireplace—everything he wanted—that he shares with another Law-school man. He is also teaching school, two evenings a week—Advanced Latin—to people of all ages—some <u>old</u> men—just imagine!

I hope you're not tired of "Him." I thought you'd want full particulars. With loads of love—Helen

Nov. 4. My dear People,

We had an elegant time Hallow 'een. When we went down to dinner we found little pumpkin "menus" with silly quiz questions written on one side. One of the P.G.s got them up and we had great sport guessing them. Then, when we went out into the hall, there was a grand out-cry. Miss Nelson had bought a mask of a man's face, borrowed some of the janitor's clothes and stuffed them with pillows, etc. into a "man" whom she left reclining on the stairs as if drunk. He looked really natural in the dim light, and frightened one girl, who came down late, nearly to death.

We had invited the girls from 3 village houses up and entertained them with a very cute little play. After that, we danced, ate apples, popped corn, candy, etc. and talked. Finally ended up with a "Virginia Reel." A jolly time!

Friday, at Mrs. Newman's table for dinner, we toasted marshmallows over <u>candles</u>, as the fire in her fireplace toasted our fingers, too.

Yesterday P.M. I read for a "theme." [Source theme—Freshman year in my day.] We had to choose very formal subjects and look up a lot on them. I took "Feudalism in England" and find it such an enormous subject that I feel like a fly in a milk pan. We have done only one theme before this. I wrote on "<u>Maple</u>-<u>Sugar</u> <u>Making</u>." It pleased Miss Bates *[not Katharine Lee Bates, but another Miss Bates]* so much that I had to <u>read</u> <u>it</u> <u>in</u> <u>class</u>, and I was in my gym suit, too! This P.M., I tackled writing for my theme and have 5 pages—only about <u>half</u> thru. I pity Miss Bates almost as much as myself.

    With <u>acres</u>, <u>stacks</u> & <u>piles</u> of love, Helen

Nov. 10. My dear people,

    Well, the Reception is over, and I'm not sorry, though I had as good a time as could be expected under the circumstances. It is always crowded and so hard finding partners for yourself and your Freshman that everyone considers it rather a bore. Edna and I walked down, getting there just in time to meet our girls. At the last moment, I had another girl "thrown" at me. One of the girls here was ill, so asked me to take charge of her Freshman, too. I had never seen her. I just scurried around finding them partners and getting them frappes. Only danced twice myself. I wasn't sorry when I got them safely in a carriage and started home to Norumbega.

    Oh, Miss Hazard is to give a reception for all the Juniors and Seniors and asked me if I would like to help her some—be her little aide, run errands, etc., and if I would ask the other Sophs here, too. So—we feel quite honored.

    Chapel bell has rung, must go—

    Much love—Helen

Nov. 17. My dear people,

    I have been wicked today; after going to prayers here and a Bible class over at Freeman, I stayed home from church to write letters. After dinner, we were all in Miss Hazard's room for after dinner coffee and had a delightful time. She played for us—really beautifully and with so much expression. She always knows my name now and I feel quite flattered. And oh, I haven't told you that at the Reception for Seniors and Sophomores, I got there too late to serve, or anything, as I had two Chem. Lab periods and then had to dress. Mrs. Alice Freeman Palmer, one of our former presidents was there and Miss Hazard introduced me to her as "one of her girls." Mrs. Palmer actually asked me if I were a Senior! You can guess I felt quite flattered.

Friday P.M., Miss Jackson gave four or five of us the cutest little play she had written, "Cinderella in the Laboratory." So we learned what we could and made up what we couldn't remember. I was Cinderella, in my light lawn (over a lining) and white slippers. One of the girls—quite large—was the Prince in an up-to-date suit (she wore it all evening and didn't dare to sit down, the pants were too tight). And—Dr. Roberts, the Head of the Chem. Dept. was the fairy godmother! One of the girls was to be, but was ill at the last minute, so when Miss Roberts offered in fun to take her part, Miss Jackson took her at her word. So—I had the honor of dancing with the Secretary of the Academic Council and a lot of other dignitaries rolled into one. We had coffee made in Chem. flasks and served in little beakers with glass tubes for spoons, sandwiches and cake. Then we played games and sang some little Chem. songs which Miss J. had composed for the occasion. We really had a grand time.

With heaps of love to you all—Helen

Nov. 22. My dear Mamma:—

I have just heard from Mr. Smith again about meeting for the game. He is coming out here for me at 12:00 and we are to go on the electric by way of Newton. He said, "Be sure to wear warm clothing, for it will be very cold in the later afternoon." Wasn't that quite <u>fatherly</u> of him? He really seems a little like a big brother.

I am going to wear my thin union suit, my <u>thick</u> one over that, my lining under my white pique waist, my suit and fur and carry either my golf cape or coat and <u>red gloves,</u> so I think I won't freeze. Don't worry about my not going with a chaperone. Mary Montgomery, the House President is going to do the same thing. You are really not <u>expected</u> to have chaperones if you go to some other place after the game—home or aunt's etc. *[Helen was going to her Aunt & Uncle's in Melrose.]* I have been learning my German this evening while sewing the buttons on my gaiters, which I am also going to wear to the game.

Do you know that some of the tickets for the game, so the paper says, have gone for $15.00 <u>apiece</u>. I hope Mr. Smith didn't pay that much. I guess $1.00 is about ordinary. It is awfully good of him to ask me and I know I can't help having a glorious time. It will all be so exciting, for it is my <u>first</u> football game, just think! If it only doesn't storm.

With stacks of love—Helen Alta Lynde, the Melrose girl in my class last year, was married recently. Foolish girl!!

Nov. 25. My dear people—

"Three cheers for Harvard! Rah! Rah! Rah! Rah! Harvard!" Oh, it was a glorious game! The most exciting of <u>anything</u> I ever saw!

I'll begin at the beginning. Well, I put on my two Union suits, my lining and my suit skirt, thinking I'd take the chance of a storm. About when I got to College for German, it began to snow—the nastiest, heaviest wet snow. I decided to wear "old duds," and went home to put on my black skirt, laid out my black coat and <u>Yale</u> blue hat and waited. Mrs. Newman gave everyone who asked, an early lunch.

"Prof" was about 10 minutes late and I was all ready and had the fidgets badly. He made me take my shawl to sit on and asked if I was sure I was dressed warmly enough! We went in to Cambridge on the electric via Newton, which took over an hour, and got us there just in time for the game. Such a crowd as there was going over the bridge and in!

The large rectangular field itself is all closed in by huge tiers of seats, quite uncovered. Mr. S. says if it storms, you just buy rubber blankets and wrap yourself up as best you can. One side, the one we were on, was all one flutter of red flags; the opposite was all blue, and the two ends were a mixture, red predominating. We had fine seats and could see everything. One of the men in his house and a lady were on one side and on the other, two boys, one of whom, next to me, got so madly excited, that he punched me violently, in the ribs every time Harvard made a good play, which was often. I really wasn't a bit cold, just my toes and fingers a tiny wee bit, for I had so many wraps, then the excitement and cheering (Mr. S. had a fearful cold, so I cheered for <u>two)</u>—kept me warm. It was really easy to follow the principal plays, with his help. It was Harvard's game, almost from the start, much to our joy and surprise.

We were nearly squeezed to death getting over the bridge again and the cars were so crowded that Mr. S. said I could not get one in town for some time so we walked up to Harvard Sq. and I got a peep at the college gates and yard beyond, all decked out with crimson. Then we went to Mr. S.'s rooms, which were very near. Wouldn't the Wellesley authorities have just howled if they could have seen me all unchaperoned in a Harvard man's room! Of course, it was all proper, though; there were lots of girl guests in the other rooms and Mr. S. would not have done anything like that if it hadn't been all right.

He has a very pleasant living room, which was, of course, all I saw, with couch, Morris chair, pictures, book case, window seat and fireplace. We hadn't been there for more than a few minutes, when a Mr. Getchell popped in. Mr. S. introduced me as a "Wellesley girl." Soon his roommate came in—a Mr. Chandler, a Boston Lawyer, but a mere boy in looks. They called him "Tad" and I had to bite my tongue <u>not</u> to.

We left for the North Station about 6:00. Mr. S. would have come out to Melrose with me, but he was just about sick with that cold. I do hope he didn't take anymore. I was only a little hoarse (from cheering) yesterday.

All the folks here send love, and heaps from your "little girl," Helen

THANKSGIVING RECESS

Nov. 29. My precious Mamma—

It doesn't seem possible that last evening at this time I was really, truly home! Hard to believe only at 6:00 A.M. this morning. I'm very glad we have Christmas to look forward to.

I found a nice letter from Charles Jones waiting for me. He thanked me for my photo, thought it fine, said his roommate declared it "swell" and thought he must be lucky to have such a girl. Charles told him he wasn't quite so far gone yet, but all things pointed that way if I always looked as nice as in the photo. Charles is getting quite gallant, isn't he? *[His letter follows this one.]*

This P.M. Helen P. & Nina were over to sample my cake I brought back and pronounced it "fine." Edna has done the same—said it was the best she'd ever eaten. Now, aren't you proud? Becky Ellis, one of the Maine girls, is making chocolate "peps" in her room. They've promised to save me some as I'm going to bed now.

Heaps of the girls are being vaccinated and Miss Hazard has publicly advised it. I am going to see Dr. Estes tomorrow. I think I trust her more than the doctors here, who, moreover, charge $1.50. I shall feel much safer and am sure she will take every precaution. *[An epidemic of small pox in the Boston area.]*

Lots of love and a goodnight kiss to each, Helen

[This letter from Charles Jones, Nov. 24, follows. Evidently his mother had decided that it would be good for him to take a post-graduate year at Cushing Academy, a well-known boarding school in Massachusetts, as he writes from there.]

Dear Helen:

Thank you so much for the picture. I was abed with a cold when I received it, but was all right the next day, which shows how your likeness cures all ills of the flesh. My roommate was very much impressed, said "she's a swell girl" and said I was in luck if I had such a girl as that. I told him that I was not so far gone as all that, but the signs all point that way if you always look as well as that.

Forgive me if I have long owed you a letter, but I called on you last summer several times and you didn't come out home at all, so we're even.

I get along fairly well here; nothing to be proud or ashamed of. They won't let us dance here. I find that not many [teachers] can come up to Arthur Thad [*Smith, Principal at Nute*]. They may know as much, but they haven't the snap and quickness. I yell for N.H.S. [*Nute*] every chance I get, and indeed it gives more Latin and Greek and Math than Cushing. I hope you do the same. I may go to Dartmouth next year, but probably not.

I think it is up to you, now.

From your friend, Charles Jones [*Nute H.S. 1901, C.A. 1902.*]

Dec. 1. My dear assembled multitude—

Well, the ordeal is over and I am vaccinated! I went straight to Dr. Estes in Boston yesterday. She said by all means I should be vaccinated as it was the only safe thing to do, and seemed surprised that I had put it off so long. I asked if there was any danger and she said, "No," not with the present method," that the danger came from vaccinating from one person to another, as they used to do. She said she had vaccinated a large number— I forget how many—with no trouble at all. So I bared my arm and she scraped it with a tiny ivory-like scraper which came stuck in a little bag-like effect of the "matter" which is only used for one, put some prepared cotton over the place and then a piece of course net-like cloth, which she uses in place of a shield, and stuck this down at the edge with some liquid. It hurt, a mite, just as a scratch does, and the blood, which came because I'm thin-skinned, made me a little faint. She says it will "take" in about 3 to 7 days and wants to see me on the 9th day. She said not to be frightened if it made me sick at my stomach, headache, etc. as it nearly always did. She usually charges $2.00, she said, but as I was Criss' friend—only $1.00. I shall feel much safer now, and shall be willing to have headaches, etc. to escape the small pox. She says the number of cases increases every day and vaccination is the only thing. Don't worry about me, for I'll keep you fully informed as to my feelings.

I forgot my skates. The girls have been skating on Longfellow Pond. I am so provoked at myself! Also, will you send me an old long-sleeved flannel top to wear with the sleeve ripped in case my arm begins to swell.

It's sleepy time and I kiss you all goodnight, Helen

Dec. 3. My precious Mamma—

Latest bulletin! My vaccination is "taking" finely! Arm began to itch yesterday, fearfully! In the evening, it grew sore, as did my armpit—now decidedly sore, stiff and lame. That pretty much tells the tale. I am <u>extremely</u> glad I have been "done," for they say the length of time before it takes is akin to the ease with which you might have contracted small pox. It very seldom takes in much less than five days or a week and here mine seemed to begin in <u>two</u> days, which shows, to my mind, that I was "ripe" for small pox itself.

I had a letter from "Frankie Dear" yesterday and he has at last summoned up enough courage to come out—one week from next Saturday evening! He said he should have to take my word for it that the girls weren't dangerous, though he thought they <u>all</u> were, to a great extent. Isn't he quite a flatterer? He said he had been out to Cambridge once to see "Prof" Smith and that <u>he</u> spent Thanksgiving with them. "Frankie-Dee" has been vaccinated <u>three</u> times, but he thought it was going to take this last time. Everybody is being done here. There were so many that they had to form a line and have numbers to go in.

I went to a piano concert last evening given by William Sherwood, second only to Paderewski, someone said.

My arm is stiff, so I shall stop. With loads of love, Helen

Dec. 6. My dear Muddie—

My arm troubled me less today. Edna, as you know, is a doctor's daughter and quite a "doctor" herself. She says my vaccination is just like the daily pictures of one in her father's medical book. So I am feeling quite happy.

Yesterday was busy. To begin with, I earned 20¢ by posing as a model for $3/_4$ of an hour over at the Art Building. It was for a beginning class in sketching and the requirements for the model aren't so much beauty of form and face as the ability to sit or stand still. One of the girls in the class who finds models lives here, so that's how I got asked. Miss Abbott, the instructor laughed when she paid me and told me to go buy a stick of candy! But I shall keep the money, and hope to earn more the same way, to buy Christmas presents. It was really quite fun.

Miss Hazard was at our table for dinner last evening and afterwards, we went into her parlor and all sat around the open fire on pillows on the floor and drank coffee and talked. It is so funny how everyone here is talking of small pox and vaccination; no matter what subject they start with, they always wind up in the same way. Miss Hazard herself began it at the dinner table by asking Miss Montgomery and then me if we had been vaccinated. She and Miss Pendleton were, the same day. Miss P. nearly fainted and has been very ill since, but Miss Hazard's, it seems didn't take. You all must be quite wintry at home as we are quite so here—and I do want a sleigh ride so! I am crazy for one!

With pecks of love—Helen

Dec. 8. My dear Ones—

Went to Chapel this morning for an excellent sermon by a preacher from Newton. Visited in Alice Stratton's room, read some and then tried to cheer up Edna, who had "the blues." This evening we heard Booker T. Washington speak. He is truly a great man, refined, intelligent and a fine speaker. He told some very funny stories to illustrate his points, some of them rather hard on his own race. One was of an old darkey who longed for a turkey at Christmas and prayed for several nights, "Oh, Lord, send this darkey a turkey." Finally, as the turkey didn't appear, he prayed, "Oh, Lord, send this darkey <u>to</u> a turkey," and he got the turkey.

I am very glad to have had the chance to see and hear him and learn a little about his institute. Why, it is even larger than Wellesley, having some 1,200 students! He spoke about himself, too, how he was born in slavery and first began to long for an education. He had to work some harder for it than a certain young Miss I know, who sometimes feels she has a pretty hard time. When she stops to think, though, she realizes that she's a pretty fortunate young lady, who ought to be deeply grateful for all her opportunities and she <u>tries</u> to be so!

I went to town to see "When Knighthood was in Flower" yesterday and it was grand. Julia Marlowe is lovely and the whole play was superb. I had rather go to such a play than keep going to Castle Square to the "second rate" ones. One learns a great deal more and it is satisfying to know you have seen the top actors like Jefferson and Julia Marlowe.

My vaccination is healing, tho' still itching. I stopped in to tell Dr.

Estes how well it had taken. She was gratefully pleased and told me not to take off the cotton for some time, till it was completely healed.

Tomorrow, our Chem. class is going to visit the Iron Foundry in Watertown, which will be an interesting trip.

Tons of love, your "little one"—Helen

Dec. 11 My dear Mamma—

I shall be able to get home on the 7:00 train, Weds. evening. I was afraid I couldn't, as I had Chem. Lab until 5:00, but Miss Jackson said I could make it up beforehand, which I shall do today. I shall get my trunk packed and checked ahead, as there will be such a rush later.

My work is just piled up for the week between. I had a Bible paper of 12 pages (of which I'd written 1 $^1/_2$) due the day before I come home; a "theme" due Tuesday, and three reviews—one written—to say nothing of the extra Lab work. So—don't expect me to look very "fat" or rested when I get home. At least, I'm not sleepy evenings now, which is a great comfort.

Frankie is coming out Sat. evening. I wrote to Mr. Smith asking him out for the Christmas Vespers, which are to be exceptionally fine, I believe.

Now I must request "a few funds", as new books, the Soph. reception and the few Xmas presents I've bought have used up mine. And I <u>must</u> get a few more presents. I shan't be able to get out to Melrose, but intend to go in to town to Xmas shop Sat. or Mon.

Loads of love—Your busy girl, Helen

Dec. 13. My dear Muddie—

I have just been writing another bit on my Bible paper. I am doing this paper piecemeal, as it is a somewhat disjointed subject and I really find it much easier this way. I worked <u>five</u> $^3/_4$ periods in the Lab. yesterday, two at one time and three at another, and then almost <u>four</u> today. No more until after vacation in that line and I'm devotedly thankful. I also had an oral review—great fun—in French; and a written one, a little harder and less <u>funny</u>. I have another oral review Sat., and want to get my Xmas shopping in town done after that.

Please do get some sleighing and skating ready for me, so I can keep outdoors while I'm home. There has been a little skating here. Mr. Perkins, the <u>only</u> "man of all work" at College Hall, has put up several signs, first, that the ice was safe and next that it was <u>not</u> safe and so on. It is quite interesting to look for them.

My arm is still all right, but I shall see Dr. Estes about taking off the cotton, which begins to feel disagreeable. Alice was quite sick one day with her vaccination.

Thanks for the money order, Papa.

Edna is waiting for me to go down for some milk, so I'll close. One week from tonight, I can <u>talk</u> to you instead of writing!

Stacks of love—Helen

Dec. 15. My dear "Hearers"—

I am "all alone" this last Sunday! I think I really must be meant for an "Old Maid," for neither Frankie Dee nor Mr. Smith came out! Frankie Dee I haven't heard from, so I don't know whether it was too windy for him or whether his courage gave out at the last minute. Mr. S., I had a little note from yesterday P.M. saying he had postponed writing as long as possible as he had hoped to be able to come out, but found he could not postpone a previous engagement, much to his regret. I'm sorry he couldn't as I know he would have enjoyed the Vespers, as he loves music and it was <u>grand</u>. The Apollo Club from Boston came to sing with our regular girls. It was truly <u>divine</u>.

This morning Lyman Abbott preached and everyone wanted to hear him. It <u>poured</u>, so we all went in short skirts. He was as grand as ever. This P.M. we were all invited in Miss Hazard's to meet him. Her sister and husband, a professor at Yale were also there. Miss Hazard was busy hunting music and playing for us. But, we all gathered round Dr. Abbott and talked to him as he is very nice. When he left to go back to Harvard, we gave him the Wellesley cheer!

My Bible paper and theme are both done. Now only regular classes and <u>packing</u>! A dozen kisses apiece and <u>next</u> Sunday, I'll deliver them myself!

Stacks of love—Helen

Helen's house in Milton Mills

CHRISTMAS VACATION

Jan. 12. My dear ones—

I arrayed myself in my old rose waist to receive "Frankie-Dee" and I was disappointed again. I really didn't much expect him as I didn't send the note till Sat. morning and he probably didn't get it in time and then, it snowed hard. I really think it is quite laughable, the time I have getting a <u>man</u> out here. I guess I'm fated as regards the masculine gender.

We were all in Miss Hazard's after dinner and had a really good time. She always has so many new things to show us; books, magazines, flowers, etc.

I am quite contented to be back, and while I don't forget home by any means, I begin to settle into "college life" once more. I enclose a copy of one of the short themes which we had to write for English.

I saw her on my way to the village. She had paused and seemed to be considering which way to take. She was very tall, even at a distance, she towered far above me, and had a fine figure. Her tailor-made gown was of grayish-white with a bit of black running through it. The absolute plainness was relieved only by large black buttons down the front of the waist. She carried a muff to match and wore a large turban which also matched her dress, whose only ornament was a black strap upon the underside of its small "brim." She did not look old, yet her hair was almost white, and she had an exceptional pallor. This, with slightly heavy features gave her an almost striking appearance. But what impressed me most deeply was her air of haunting coldness. This, perhaps, was only natural, for upon taking a closer look, as I passed, I discovered that she was indeed a "snow-woman!"

Heaps of love to all, Your own Helen

Jan. 16. Dear Muddie—

We are beginning to analyse solutions in Chem. with all sorts of unknown things in them. It's quite fun, but woefully perplexing at times.

There is to be an entertainment at the Barn Sat. eve. under Mrs. Newman's auspices, the money raised to go to Aunt Dinah Pace, who has an industrial school for colored children down South. Mrs. N. wants us all to help—sell candy, flowers, etc., at a sort of fair afterwards.

The weather has been cold this week and the sleighing makes me crazy for a ride. Wish we could have had some while I was home.

With love & kisses, Helen

Jan. 17. My dear ones—

I didn't feel like getting up for breakfast especially since I'd left my bath for this morning, as it is Sunday, so I kept delaying it. When I finally crawled out, I had just time to take a cup of <u>warm</u> water (there was <u>no hot</u>) for a <u>cold</u> sponge bath, and get into my clothes for church. I didn't get anything to eat till dinner and was simply <u>ravenous</u>!

I've ordered a new pair of gym shoes which were $1.00, which I must have if I am to take gym as you wanted, Papa. My old ones, great clumsy tennis shoes and no good anyway, were left at the gym and taken by some near-sighted individual.

When I was last in town, I ordered a tea-table." And when I get my chafing-dish I shall be very cozy and "swell" in my room. It is bamboo— a little lower than an ordinary table—and secure from tipping, with a straw matting top shaped like an elongated hexagon and with a lower shelf. I got it for $1.75.

The entertainment was very good—the glee and mandolin clubs and some Negro reading from "Uncle Remus" by a Miss Newman. (No relation to our Mrs. Newman—pure coincidence). It was so cool that the ice-cream we sold didn't go very well, but we still made about $40.00.

We had a Chem. Dinner in the Chem. Library. All the dishes were Chem. things—little glass tubes, for instance, to suck up our coffee instead of teaspoons. We had creamed chicken in chafing dishes, rolls, crackers, olives, bananas, oranges and cherries sliced together, chocolate cake, candy and delicious coffee with thick cream. One of the first course dishes— <u>baked</u> <u>potatoes</u>, didn't get done till after dessert, so we had them with <u>cream</u> as a second dessert! Then came speeches, after which we all washed and put away the dishes. I'm happily surprised that we don't have a midyears' exam in Chem.—at least it is not posted on the exam list which went up yesterday.

Good night & love to you all—Helen

Jan. 21. My precious Muddie—

I went out to Melrose to try on the skirt Aunt Ada is making for me, and to stay over night. About the first thing Winnie said was, "how would you like to go sleigh-riding?" And I simply screamed and danced for joy. The young people from the church were going with one of Mr. Norris' big teams to pull. One of the girls was going with a boy from "Tech" and one of his friends, a Mr. <u>Plusick</u> (isn't his name awful?) was coming to be with me.

We started out about 7:30 P.M. I wish you could have seen me, with an extra flannel skirt, a knit jacket, overshoes, gaiters and Clara's golf cape on. The boy from Tech. couldn't come, so his friend, Susie, took Mr. P. to my delight. (He is pale and wore glasses). I was left alone for a little—that is without a man, but "Coopie," who had come with his cousin, soon came around and we got as "spoony" as two old lovers. He has grown a great deal, knows how to be as silly as a sleigh-ride demands without being sickening, as some boys are, so we really had a good time. He asked if we ever studied at Wellesley and I told him to come out and see, some Monday. Hope he will. We got home at 11:00 P.M., but didn't go to bed until 12:00.

So—goodnight, with bushels of love—Helen

Jan. 23. My precious Muddie Dee—

I have just come from College Hall, where I had dinner with one of my German class chums and stayed to study for the German exam with her. We were at the table of Fraulein Winklebach, Head of the German Department. She is so droll. She had been looking at me for some time and finally she broke out, "What a pretty little crescent pin you have, it sparkles so and is all bright." Who but a German would have said such a funny thing! Then, she looks exactly like a man, wears short hair and dark blue suits all the time. But she is perfectly good hearted in spite of her looks.

This has been a very busy week and next one bids fair to be even busier. Everyone will be glad when midyears are over. We really are to have no Chem. exam, which is a great relief.

With loads of love to you all. Your own Helen

Jan. 26. My dear ones—

Shall I ever be glad when the "fiery trial" otherwise known as midyears is over! But I'm really not having convulsions or any such dreadful thing but merely "keeping my powder dry" and studying what I can.

The Ice Carnival that was planned failed to occur, as the ice didn't form well until it was too late to invite any guests or make proper arrangements. I doubt it would have been safe for so large a crowd.

However, nearly everyone here was on the ice yesterday P.M., but I couldn't quite convince myself of its safety, so didn't go. Wasn't that noble of me? I knew you'd be dreadfully <u>angry</u> if I got drowned, so it may have been partially in fear of the consequences. Honestly, though, I felt you would worry if you knew I were on, and I don't want you to do that. I want you to trust me to do as near the safe and right thing as I know how—and really, when I have to depend on myself, I am quite cautious and wise.

Oh, forgot to tell you I finished analysing my Chem. solution and Miss Jackson said I did it very well. Then I've "shone" generally in the class questions so I think I ought to pass in that subject.

Don't look for long letters this week and pray I may do all my exams well.

Your loving little girl, Helen

Jan. 31. My precious Mamma—

Oh, what a relief—no exam tomorrow to cram for. I'm so rejoiced that I want to talk about nothing else. Can you understand how I feel? The French and German I dreaded so much were really just what I could do. Nearly everyone thought them hard, especially German, but I got along so well on them, that I feel quite proud. I feel certain that I did very well, <u>pass</u> at least, and maybe <u>credit</u>. Some way, I always seem to come out all right. They say "the Devil takes care of his own." But I think it's rather the <u>Lord</u> in this case, for I know the Devil would be sure to forget sometimes. English was long, but not especially hard. I still have studying to do for Bible and Latin.

The skating is grand now, and I'm looking forward to a delightfully lazy time. And Edna, Alice and I are going on a "Midyear's Spree," to see Maude Adams. And on Feb. 19, we may have a chance to hear Paderewsky (is that right?) for 25¢ by paying admission and just "rushing" for a seat.

Now, I'm going to bed—Love to all, Helen

Feb. 3. My dear ones—

You may have seen by the paper that we <u>did</u> finally have our Ice Carnival—or rather, <u>Snow</u> Carnival last evening, as it began snowing yesterday morning and kept up all day. The men plowed and swept off portions of the ice and lots of the girls went out with brooms.

I was so afraid that Winnie and Walter wouldn't come that about 1:15, when I found out for sure that they were going to have it, I called up; or <u>attempted</u> to call up by telephone; Walter had left his office, and wouldn't be back. It took me nearly half an hour to secure <u>that</u> information. The line was so busy, so many men from <u>Cambridge</u> wanted Wellesley, and the operator had a <u>stack</u> of messages to send. I helped her quite a little while I was waiting, listening at the phone while she sent telegrams. Finally I reached Winnie. They were planning to come anyway, and would I please meet them at the station. Miss Beaumont, the operator said she hoped I wouldn't have to wait so long next time, though I had been "real good company." I dropped into Mrs. Newman's for a cup of tea. she invited me to come any P.M. during midyears between 4:00 and 6:00 for tea and her open fire.

I left word for a carriage to go down to the station, it was so dark and wet, but it didn't come in time, so I went over to Wilder, to walk down with another girl. We got there just as the train did. My people didn't get there, after all, so I did take a carriage back. It had been raining hard in town, so they probably thought it too bad to come. I was disappointed, after walking all the way down, but it was a relief not to have to go out on the ice when it was so miserable. I looked on for a few minutes and everyone looked bedraggled; the band wouldn't come and they couldn't have the fireworks. Then it snowed even harder. No one but <u>Wellesley girls</u> would have kept going! It shows how <u>athletic</u> and unafraid of the weather we all are!

I went to church this morning to hear Dr. Albert Lyman of Brooklyn, with Alice, who came over for dinner, after which, we were invited to Miss Hazard's to meet him. We had coffee and strolled around, admiring some exquisite orchids she'd had sent to her. She asked me to pass some candy. Then she played <u>to</u> us and then played <u>for</u> us to sing German hymns.

Have you heard from Elsie recently? I really trembled when I went for my mail yesterday, for fear I should hear bad news—worse than the last time. I feel as though she will get well after all, and hope and pray so. Please let me know.

Stacks of love to you all. Your little girl, Helen

[See the Appendix. Elsie Avery, Helen's classmate at Nute who had gone to Vassar. This is her first mention of Elsie's illness.]

Feb. 10. My own dear ones—

I am being sketched! One of the art classes has to hand in a certain number of "ten minute exposures," so one of the girls has chosen me for a "victim."

Well, what do you think—I've taken dinner with Miss Hazard in my new <u>ten cent</u> waist! Won't that be quite amusing to tell my grandchildren—that Grandma dined with the <u>President</u> of <u>Wellesley College</u> in a 10¢ waist! Mrs. Newman asked me the last minute after church and I couldn't refuse. A few minutes before dinner, Esther Howe, Maude May, and I were ushered in to Miss Hazard's rooms. She was dressing, but soon appeared. We smelled the lovely carnations and orchids she had and exclaimed over their beauty. Then she showed us a souvenir book of the Yale Bicentennial which was very interesting. When we went out to dinner, we met Miss Hawes, Mrs. Newman and a lady guest of Miss Hawes in the hall. Miss Hazard introduced us, then we forward marched. We hesitated a little and Miss Hawes immediately held out her hand and said, "Come with me, Miss Fox," so I skipped along.

We had a really pleasant time at dinner. The only thing wrong was that Miss Hazard ate her cranberry sauce (it was very thick) with her fork so everyone else did and I was afraid I'd spill it on my <u>new waist</u>! And I wanted some more chocolate sauce on my ice-cream. The minister did not come to dinner and Miss Hawes' guest—a Wellesley alumna whose name I can't remember, was very interesting and asked a lot of questions, so it really wasn't too bad. I sat next to Miss Hazard. Miss Hawes waited for me again. Edna says she likes me and I'm sure to get "Credit." I should hope she wouldn't give it to me for that reason alone.

We've just come up from Miss Hazard's where we had coffee and music. I'm getting to be quite a society lady in my <u>10¢ waist</u>!

Yesterday, I went to Chapel; we have been having special music during midyears, which I've enjoyed immensely. Then I dusted & fixed up my room, using the silk handkerchief you sent as a temporary cover for my tea-table, and put my two little doilies on it, and it really looks quite "swell." The cake you sent looks awfully good. I've saved it for today, Mamma.

Thanks for sending my check early, Papa; I feel as if I'd fallen heir to a million!

This morning I ran over to get Alice for a walk. We went way down past Hunnewell's, enjoying it so much—the sky so blue, like summer and the wind in the pines. Oh, I was so glad to be alive and well. I don't think I ever appreciated it all so much before. I think I shall love Wellesley as a nun does her convent. It is so lovely and peaceful here—when there's nothing to do! Must decide soon. What do you think?

With a heart full of love for all—Helen

Feb. 13. My own dear Mamma—

My head is full of hearts, cupids and dismal attempts at sketching a Senior in cap and gown. We are to have original valentines at our table tomorrow at dinner. We drew names and I got May Montgomery's. Now I'm racking my brain for some appropriate poetry. She is tall, a Senior, fond of math and spends her summers at the shore, so this is what I've written.

> She is a stately Senior
> And goes a stately way;
> Her favorite study, it is Math.
> Her name, why that is May.
>
> But Cupid is a rascal,
> Who doth cap and gown despise.
> And mathematics, I am sure
> Will make more bright his eyes.
>
> Some day he'll aim an arrow,
> If he hasn't, by the shore.
> Then the law of sine and cosine
> Will avail her never more!

Then, I'm trying to draw a girl in cap and gown on the shore and with Cupid in the air aiming an arrow. It is so <u>funny</u>! The gown looks like a "Mother Hubbard," the cap looks like a shade hat; Cupid is a cross between a <u>cat</u> and a <u>bird</u> and the sea doesn't resemble anything.

Well, my <u>10¢</u> <u>waist</u> has now been to a college reception and met Miss Pendleton this P.M. As I wanted to walk to the "ville" afterward, I didn't want to wear a long skirt or my best waist. Miss Hazard is away and not likely to get back in time, so Miss P. received all alone. She was very sweet and gracious, indeed.

The flunk notes are out now and I've been "outrageously slighted" so I conclude I haven't flunked anything.

I'm glad you think as I do about asking Mr. S. out—it is not the right time. So I wrote to Frankie—asking him to let me know as soon as possible.

Time to say "goodnight"—Kisses for all—Your own Helen

Feb. 17. My own dear ones—

Winnie and Walter and Ray all came out last evening for our second Ice Carnival. I met them at the station and brought Winnie up to see my room, which she thought very pretty, leaving the two boys down in the alcove. We got on the ice about 7:30, which gave us two hours to skate. The ice was very smooth, with little patches of snow and hummocks only here and there. Ray and I did not repeat our last year's tumble and before we left, he was doing all sorts of fancy strokes. Ray brought some candy to eat on the ice, but I explained my Lenten vow of "<u>no</u> <u>candy</u>," so of course, they teased me, and ate it right under my nose. Winnie & Walter brought me a box of candy—Lowneys, but I told them I would keep it till after Easter. So, we had a <u>glorious</u> time and 9:30 came before we were ready for it.

I went to church this A.M. Dr. Palmer of Harvard was the preacher. We were in Miss Hazard's suite after dinner to meet him and his wife, Alice Freeman Palmer, a former president of Wellesley before her marriage. She is perfectly lovely. Miss Hazard started to introduce me as a Junior, said she always thought I was in "her" class, 1903, as she calls it because she came when <u>it</u> did. Mrs. Palmer said, "Oh, no, she is a happy Sophomore, happy because she has two more whole years ahead of her!"

And I think I am—college seems lovelier every day. Oh, why can't I be twins—one at home and one here?

With a mountain of love—Your own "Girl Goldie"

Feb. 21. Dear Muddie Dee—

Three cheers! My card came this noon. All "Credit!" It was really more than I expected; we all did such poor work in French the first few weeks, and I wasn't at all sure of my German, so—I am happily surprised. Poor Bertha, so Helen told me, flunked English <u>and</u> German! We all here got credits. The vice president of our class has flunked so much that she'll have to resign. I am decidedly happy, and proud of my credits.

I'm in a difficulty, Mamma. I wrote of an invitation to the "Colonial Ball," March 3, given by Zeta, Alpha Society, I think it came through one of the girls in the house, Anna Darby. So, I want to go for that reason, if not for the good time they always have. But you're supposed to wear colonial costumes, I don't know what I'm to do. Is there something at home, or that you could borrow for me? Alice will lend me a fichu, which will help.

You asked about Gym for this semester. I am not taking any "regular" class, as it meets Weds., when I have Chem. Lab, but Alice and I are taking "social dancing" Friday P.M. and find it great fun and quite a little exercise. Then I try to go for a walk every day.

With a heart full of love—"Girl Goldie"
P.S. Had a grand time last evening. Frank came and appeared to enjoy the concert, very much.

Feb. 25. My precious Mamma—

Frank was a wee bit bashful, when he came for the Concert, and so was I, though he got over it. He is looking well, and is going to Evening School taking engineering and says he may go to New York soon to work. His mother will miss him, if he does. He is coming out some Sunday for Chapel, he says.

Mr. S. made a name for himself here at the house for his patience. Do you know, he got here about 4:30, just 15 minutes after I went out, and waited until after 6:00! Mrs. Newman says he's the most patient man she ever saw. Most men would have left, I suppose, so I feel really much pleased by his waiting. I have certainly broken even <u>my</u> record of keeping anyone waiting, haven't I? He thought I was very pleasantly situated and ought to be happy (as I am). He seemed much pleased by my Credits, and told me I must, indeed finish my last two years. I told Mr. S. of Miss White's speaking how "literary" he looks and he laughed.

I have some reading for English, so I shall say Goodnight.

Your own little girl—Helen

Feb. 28. My precious Muddie—

How the time has flown since Xmas— I feel as if I'd lived years. Indeed, I will be very careful about taking cold, for I realize this is just the time of year to do so, and I want us all to be well and together this coming vacation. What a sad time it will be for Elsie's father and mother.

Alice has sent home for a "fichu" for me to wear to the Colonial party, so—if you can't find a dress—I shall wear my dimity with that. I want to powder my hair, but dread to. I shall wash it before, not after, as I heard one girl did—and had dough!

Love to all—Helen

March 2. My dear ones—

I went over to College Hall after church, as Mary Riley had asked me to have dinner with her. I really think I like Norumbega best. It is so noisy over there and they don't have as good things to eat (no soup or salad on Sundays) and nothing is cooked or served as nicely. I think now I may want to come back here next year.

We have a criticism of a book of essays due tomorrow and I am wading through Lowell's. I am quite learning to enjoy them now, so think my taste must have developed. I wish I could get to enjoying "real world things" instead of fiction.

Louise and I went to "Faculty Night" at the Barn last night. The faculty entertain us with dialogues, etc., "taking <u>us</u> off." They are naturally so dignified and some of them are rather old, so to see them dressed as girls with short skirts and shirt-waists, or kimonos and fancily dressed hair was immensely funny. In one scene, they acted Freshman preparation in the gym for Tree Day dancing, and in another, they showed a girl's room with a "busy" sign hung out and the girls engaged in gossiping and making <u>fudge</u>! It was <u>so</u> comical!

One week from Sat. is the French play. Mr. S. expressed the desire to be informed when something was going on. I think he might like something of the students' own "manufacture." I think I might invite him.

Will say goodnight, as usual,

With a heart full of love—Helen

March 4. My dear own Muddie—

I was a little disappointed about the dress—or rather, the <u>lack</u> of it in my laundry, but with Alice's fichu and her cameo pin which she lent me and my blue dress, gold chain, etc., I managed very well. I did not powder my hair, as I hadn't time to wash it and the powder might stick too much, without.

The Ball was <u>so</u> pretty! There were lots of girls there dressed in "half colonial" dress, like me, but the majority wore old-fashioned gowns or men's suits of silk and velvet or lace trim—hired, I suppose. It was <u>such</u> a pretty sight.

I had a letter from Frankie yesterday, thanking me for the very pleasant evening and saying he would come again, if I could put up with his "tiresome presence." For <u>your</u> sake, Mamma, I shall try to do so.

Love to you all. Your own Helen

March 6. My own dear Muddie—

I think I really need a new jacket for common wear. Have you seen the "golf jackets" they are wearing so much? They are some sort of knit, woolen & snug fitting, with silk sleeves to match. They come in red, blue and green, and are awfully popular and cute. About $5.00, I think. I could wear one a great deal this spring and summer and next fall when I come back, I think I shall buy one with my $5.00 left-over Xmas money.

We can talk it over when I am home for vacation. I should have a new silk waist, too.

I am quite flattered by a little note I had today from Miss Walton, my last year's Latin teacher, asking me to assist at a reception Monday night given for a Latin Lecturer, Prof. Kelsey of Michigan University, who is to be out here. I suppose my labors will consist of introducing people and seeing that they get <u>fed</u>. I dread it a little, yet feel tickled by the attention.

I wrote Mr. S. inviting him to the French Play. Hope he can come.

Good night, with love to all—"Girl Goldie"

March 10. My dear Mamma—

I had a note from Mr. S. Saturday, thanking me for my invitation and saying he would be glad to come. He also enquired if it would be a dress affair —I guess didn't want to get fouled as Frank did.

I dressed in my challis for the reception. It was really very nice and easy. Bertha Long and I and two other girls passed coffee and frappé and cakes. Miss Hazard helped Prof. Kelsey receive and introduced me to him as one of "our Sophomores." He said, "Indeed, I thought you must be a Senior."! I don't know whether he meant <u>old </u>or "stately" or what. Now I believe, I've been taken for everything from a Dana-Hall girl to a Post Graduate! Isn't it funny?

Went for a little bird hunt this P.M. with Louise, who is studying birds, but we didn't see any. The "pussies" are out, tho' and some maple sugar is in the market. I'll be home just in time.

Love to all—Helen

March 13. My dear <u>own</u> Mamma—

Well—the most wonderful thing has happened—I have been to <u>Grand Opera</u>! Isn't that grand? You know I have always been just crazy to go. When I found I could get a seat way back for $1.00, I resolved I would try, but didn't get to it until the tickets were gone. Well, it is also only a dollar to "rush." I thought it was my only chance, and as about half the college was going to rush, I thought I ought to be able to stand it. I was <u>wild</u> to hear "Lohengrin" yesterday.

Several of us from the house went in on the 12:17. When we got there, the actual "rush" was over, and all we had to do was pay our $1.00, walk up the stairs and find a seat. It was no more crowded or dangerous than going to Chapel mornings.

"Lohengrin" was perfectly grand. Three "big" singers—Mme. Gadilsi, DeRelse and Van Dyck *[?]* were in it and they are big! The costumes and scenery were so lovely and the music so grand that it was like one beautiful dream. I shall never forget it—my first real opera. I'd rather hear one opera than go to Castle Square a dozen times.

Isn't it exciting about the Teamsters' strike? I hope I'll not have to carry my own trunk across the city when I come home in two weeks.

Mountains of love to you all—Helen

March 16. My dear ones—

Last evening at this time, I was at the French play with Mr. S. I had dressed before dinner, gone up to my room for only a few minutes, when Maria, the maid came up to say that Mr. S. had come. He looked very fine in his dress suit, with a long coat or cape—the kind worn with dress suits, and a tall hat—one of the folding kind! I really hesitated to start out in my old golf cape, but finally did so.

When we got to the Barn, we discovered that Miss Shackford, the new "Lit." teacher, who, I guess I've told you, was in his high-school class, had a seat in front of us. So—Mr. S. went to speak to her. She didn't remember him at first—she hadn't seen him for five years—but then I heard her say—"Why, isn't it Arthur Smith?" And then ask for his family, etc. I don't know whether he told her how he happened to be here. Miss Bates, my English teacher, sat directly behind us and stared at him well. I think she must credit me with good taste.

After the play, we went up to College Hall which he had peeped at before, then came over here. The parlor was taken, so we sat out in the little hall alcove till 9:45 when the bell rang and Maria came to lock the door, so of course, he had to go. We talked of Nute and news from Milton, but not a word was said of Elsie's death. I do wish he'd say something—it must come up sometime, and time will only make it harder. He was pleased I'd been to the opera, and wondered if I recognized the "Wedding March" from "Lohengrin," as we marched in to Graduation to that.

Are you tired of "He" and "I"? Please don't think I'm silly and "Lovesick." I never felt more sensible—but I just thought you would want to know it all.

With a heart full of love—Helen

March 20. My dear Muddie—

I was at the Faculty table last night, and Miss Pierce, the library assistant and the sweetest little woman, asked me over. I went to her room afterward and had a good time talking and looking at pictures. She knew Miss McClary when she was here. It's curious how many people you meet who know other people in common with you.

Mr. S. says he isn't going to take any vacation, but stay in Cambridge and review. His comes in mid-April, I believe, so he wouldn't be home for Easter anyway. I expect he will over-work. He said he was glad to get out here away from work; that he'd been doing what he used to tell his scholars to do—("Not you," he said, "because you didn't need it!")—pitching into work.

Edna, who is all tired out has permission to go home early.

I want to see her off at 7:30 tomorrow morning—So—

Goodnight and love to all—Helen

March 24. My dear ones—

The last of my Sunday epistles for <u>three</u> <u>weeks</u>, do you realize it? Last evening, I heard the <u>frogs</u> for the first time this spring. Who says we can't have grand opera at Wellesley? Just let him listen to our frogs!

Yesterday I went "Birding" with Mary Louise and Minnie Neal and had a lovely walk, but didn't discover a single new bird.

This morning, having stayed in bed till 9:00 A.M., I went to taste a glass of milk I'd brought up last night for my breakfast and it was <u>sour</u>— so I made my meal of graham crackers. Then took a lovely walk down by the lake all by my lonesome before church. The lake was such a bright summer blue—our crews will be out soon.

I had made up my mind that the preacher, a Watertown man, would be old and pokey, so I was happily surprised; he was young, very energetic and interesting. This P.M., I read Miss Montgomery's copy of the Libretto for "Tannhauser" and wrote letters. I think of all the sadness so many of my friends have had recently. "Into each life some rain must fall, some days must be dark and dreary." I realize the truth of that more and more and sometimes, it frightens me to think how bright <u>my</u> life has always been; to think that "all the rain" must be before me.

However, I hope it doesn't come in vacation, either the poet's rain, or the real! I shall come home prepared for both kinds, however. I am afraid I shall not see Mr. S. again before vacation, and I doubt he'll ever come out again without letting me know, after the "long wait."

Thanks for your registered letter and the various "enclosures." Now I shall be able to get my trunk off and get home "O.K!" You will get this tomorrow and the next day, if nothing happens—<u>ME</u>!

Much love to all—Your own Helen

SPRING VACATION

April 11. My precious Muddie—

It was horribly dusty and windy driving to the station this morning. I was very glad to see Alice *[Dalrymple]* get on at Rochester—"misery loves company," you know, and neither of us was particularly desirous of coming back so soon, nor felt like talking, so read a little book of poetry she had, and watched it <u>rain</u>. We got a little supper, as we were both <u>starved</u>, in the station café and took the 8:20 out to Wellesley. I unpacked, made my bed up, got in it and <u>slept</u>.

I am glad to get back and shall soon feel settled, I know, but I <u>do</u> miss you all. The time <u>does</u> fly, and I mean to make every minute count this Spring, if I possibly can.

Most mail time so—I'll close. With stacks of love—Helen

April 15. My dear Muddie—

I <u>do</u> hope the question of clothes is settled for a little time now. I went in town yesterday, met Aunt Abbie and finally bought 5 yards of fine Venetian cloth in a pretty medium grey for my suit for $1.25 per yard at Jordan's. I also got the lining and silk for a waist, as the ready-made ones are so cheaply made. I did, however, buy a 98¢ waist I couldn't resist— plain, fine white, with tucks down the front and a tiny "Gibson" effect. Size 34, and none too large. I was up when the sun rose this morning to study, so will go to bed now (it's 8:00).

Goodnight to all—

With much love—Helen

April 20. My dear Ones—

Another Sunday—how the weeks do fly, don't they? Yesterday was a holiday. Edna and I went over to Hunnewell Gardens in the morning.

She had never been there before—imagine, after being here almost two years! It is lovely there now, all so fresh and green with the trees getting ready to leaf. That reminds me of the song, "Tupelo."

> "Oh thou Tupelo, thou hast the power to leaf in Spring
> To leaf in Spring is thine, love,
> To <u>leave</u> just now is mine, love—"

Rather a cute play on <u>leaf</u>, don't you think?

Edna told me something about the Gardens that I never knew; that they were built to please Mr. Hunnewell's Italian wife, who was very homesick. He even brought over a gondola for her.

In the afternoon, with Edna's help, I was rearranging my room. Everything was in the center of it, when there was a knock on the door and in walked Louise and four of her friends from home, out for the day. She had said she'd bring them over, but I'd not expected them so early! In the evening, Clare Barnes, one of the Seniors, was up, staying until "bath-time."

Today, I got hold of a book by Katharine Lee Bates, one of the—or rather, <u>the</u> Lit. teacher, and read till most church time.

Next Saturday evening is the Wellesley-Vassar Debate, which, I expect, will be intensely exciting. I <u>do</u> hope we win. If fairness of action up to now counts, we will, most assuredly. They complain at everything we do. Everyone thinks they are afraid of us now, and are trying to force us to break it off.

You'll be sending my laundry soon. Please will you send some medium-weight undervests as I have only very thin ones here.

With a heart full of love for you all—Your own "little girl" Helen

April 24. My dear Mamma—

I am pretty tired tonight. Had a Physical Exam and a written lesson in Chem. The exam was to see whether we had gained or lost physically since the Fall of our Freshman year, and was just like that exam. I was disappointed in one respect as I had gained only $5\,^1/_2$ lbs.—weighed 105 $^1/_2$. My chest girth, rib girth and lung capacity were much better. My leg power was better, but my back not quite so strong, and my ankles, tho' still "crooked" *[pronated]* were not so bad.

The mayflowers you sent in the laundry came thro' and are so sweet. I have them close beside me, on the table. And the <u>cake</u> was delicious. I have been "treating" some of the girls on this floor tonight.

I have just written a letter to "Frankie-Dee" telling him that I should be glad to "endure his painful presence" (his words) on Sat. or Sun. evening. Haven't heard from Mr. S. yet. Hope they all don't come at the same time! Haven't heard from Ray since the Ice Carnival.

Don't worry about my changing into summer things. I'll really be careful. Oceans of love—Helen

April 27. My dear ones—

[Vassar-Wellesley debate.] They won! You can't guess how disappointed we all were and are. It didn't seem true that Vassar should defeat us! Oh, it was hard to bear. I don't think I ever realized how much I love Wellesley till last night, it seemed like a purely personal grief to each of us. I felt like crying, and did see one girl with tears in her eyes. But we did <u>nobly</u> and all the Faculty say they are very proud of us; <u>our</u> arguments were strong and more forcibly put. They had more polish and style of delivery, however, which "took" with the judges, two of whom, at least were (*Boston Globe*) literary men. I really think, as do many, that had they been <u>business</u> men, the victory would have been ours. The Vassar people were really very nice about taking it, which helped out immensely. One was heard to say, "if the Wellesley girls do so well in their very first debate, what <u>will</u> they do next year."

Yesterday was a <u>very</u> busy day. The Vassar team, committee, etc. came Friday night, so were here for Chapel yesterday. Of course, everyone turned out, "spic 'n span," to show we could have a full house, even if it wasn't obligatory, as it <u>is</u> with them. The Chapel was packed.

I played "maid," too yesterday. Miss Hazard had invited 20 of the Kindergarten Assoc. out for a visit and lunch, but at the last moment, got word that <u>50</u> would come! Mrs. Newman didn't know what to do, unless some of the girls would volunteer to help her wait on them. I thought it would be great fun to be <u>thought</u> a maid, so dressed very simply in a white waist and black skirt, and "wore" a sweet, meek look, and what do you think, the very first lady I waited on blasted my hopes by enquiring very sweetly, "Are you a Wellesley student?" I don't see why!

In the P.M. there was a general reception for the Vassarites at College Hall, but I didn't care much about going, so dallied until too late to see much.

The preacher at church today was Robert Spera, not an ordained minister, but a N.Y. man connected with the Y.M.C.A., who does considerable work in mens' colleges. He is truly grand; about thirty-thirty five, tall, smooth face— "thoroughly clean looking," as Papa would say, with a deep voice and so interesting and deeply earnest. He makes it seem very desirous to be good and accomplish great things. He talked to the Christian Assoc. this P.M. and spoke at Vespers this evening. All the girls worship him and crowd to hear him when he comes once a year.

Tomorrow, after lessons in the morning, is our class social—a hurdy-gurdy shirt-waist dance at the Barn.

I sent some of my mayflowers to one of our Norumbega Seniors who had an operation for appendicitis some 10 days ago and is in the hospital getting along very nicely. I feel very proud of the care she had from the College—trained nurses, village doctors and a specialist or two from town; not much like packing her off home (as Vassar did to Elsie).

Thank you so much for the money-order, Papa. I will try to be very prudent. When I teach, as I really think I want to, now, I'll try to pay you a little back.

With seas of love to all—"Girl Goldie"

P.S. Oh—I got "<u>Excellent</u>" on my Chem. Exam!

April 29. My dear Papa—

I really think your note of condolence on the results of the debate merits an answer on my best paper. The victory was ours, truly, in everything but name! Both Vassar faculty who were here and debaters write in saying that we deserved it far more than they. So, we don't feel by any means beaten, would you? Mr. Sinclair, Pres. of the Boston Chamber of Commerce, who presided, said he didn't see how any of the judges could so decide. The fact was, they came—one of them, at least—determined to favor Vassar. Bliss Perry was so prejudiced in their favor that he actually sent <u>flowers</u> to one of their debaters!

I got my class pin at last today and it is a little beauty! A gold square with a raised blue enamel center with 1904 in gold on it; Wellesley is engraved on the side and my name on the back. The safety clasp is so good I could hardly get it off my waist just now. I'm so proud! As Mr. S. says, "You can't touch me with a 10 foot pole!"

I've just learned to make soap in Chem. Made some the other day in the Lab, so will set up a kiln when I come home and support the family. Why, I'll be as famous as <u>Pear's</u> yet, and all you'll have to do will be to ride around in your automobile!

With heaps of love to all. Your own "Girl Goldie"

May 1. My precious Mamma—

Well, I have been a "little boy," today for the May Day "Children's Party." I didn't wear my muslin dress after all. I rigged up in my gym suit with my sailor collar, long tie and my hair loose like Little Lord Fauntleroy. We all had a lovely time, playing all sorts of games, dancing around the May-pole, etc.

Mr. S., I guess has forgotten me. Frankie, ditto. Did you know today is Mr. S.'s birthday—twenty seven, I believe.

This is a poor apology for a letter, but I must get to bed so I can get up early to do German tomorrow morning.

Stacks of love to all—Your own "little boy"

May 4. My dear family—

The Chapel preacher today was Dr. Drawn of the Cambridge Theological School, who is also one of the Bible teachers here. He was very good. In the afternoon, Mary Field and I went up to the hospital to see one of the girls who sprained her knee. I took a bouquet of pansies, from a box I had bought, and Mary took her a box of candy. She has a nice, neat comfortable little private room, but was feeling a little lonely, though she says she's getting a lovely rest.

My new suit has come—so neat and simple and fits so nicely. Everyone admires it. I wore it to the Circus last night, which was very much like last year's, very funny; a band of combs, chafing dishes, bath tub drums, etc., plus the "animals," clowns, jugglers, etc.

Now I must come to the serious part of my letter. May 9, next Friday, is the time for us to pay our advance registration fee for next year. Now am I to come back or not? I know when I came, it was "wait and see," at the end of two years. I love college. I am happy here. I know I am learning and I really want to be fitted to teach when I come out. But— I know you said that when I left college, you would "get out of" the store. Now, I don't think you're exactly pinching, or going without, etc. to keep me here, but I <u>do</u> know it costs <u>something</u> and that you work harder than you ought and I don't want to stay at the expense of your health or happiness. I am willing to abide by your decision and shall look for your answer.

With a heart full of love for you all.

Your own loving "Girl Goldie"

May 7. My dear Muddie—

You asked about my underflannels. Yes, I have taken off the thick ones and am wearing the thin, short sleeve, high neck ones; I was <u>so</u> uncomfortable with the others on. I wear a lining and flannel waists when it is cool, too, and haven't taken any cold.

I had a sweet little note from "Frankie" asking if he might come out Sat. this week or next. I shall tell him to come next week. He says Mr. S. has been to their house several times, but they don't expect to see much more of him until June, as he is so busy. I think he must have quite forgotten me.

Must say goodnight, as I am trying to get to bed reasonably early so as to get <u>up</u> <u>early</u> to do my studying. It is really easier than I thought!

With a heart full of love. Your own "Girl Goldie"

May 8. My dear Mamma—

I found your letter waiting for me when I came out of Chem. Lab about 5:30, and took it down to one of the "Crow's Nests" by the lake to read. So you'll say "<u>Stay</u>." I <u>will</u>, and will try <u>never</u> to make you regret saying so.

Just as I finished reading, I heard cheering up at College Hall, announcing the returns of the next year's Senior class president elections. I ran up to share in the excitement. There was no end of it, I can tell you. The girl elected is <u>this</u> year's president, and lives in Norumbega and is <u>very</u> popular. They cheered, marched up and down with flowers and last evening serenaded her.

The day before was the election of the Student Government president, which was even more exciting because we <u>all</u> had a share in it. Today, next year's Seniors have drawn for rooms. Alice drew 143 which has dropped to 110. She is feeling very blue, as she wants to stay in Wilder. <u>We</u> draw one week from today. Pray I may have good luck. I want to get in a cottage, if I can, with Louise, Mary and some of the girls I know best. But it all depends on the draw.

I must close, but I want to tell you how glad it made me feel—your saying that you had perfect confidence in me. I will try to <u>merit</u> it. Thanks for the check; I'll pay my advance registration for next year tomorrow.

With oceans of love.

Your own little girl—Helen

May 14. My dear Mamma—

Everyone is busy now. My good times outside are over for this year, it seems. One bit of news for you—Alice has chosen her room; one on the second floor of Wood, between here and Wilder—a very nice, popular house. I draw tomorrow. (By the time you get this, my fate will be pretty well settled). I think I shall try to stay on the Hill if I possibly can—either Wilder or Wood. All the singles at College Hall are gone, now, as it is to be a Senior House almost entirely. About all my class wants to be here on the Hill, so I tremble for my fate.

Haven't heard anything from Frankie so I expect him Sat. evening. Hope it will be pleasant, so I can take him around some. I shouldn't know how to entertain a man indoors!

The warning bell has rung, so I must take this down.

Tons of love—Helen

May 18. My dear family—

I don't think there's much chance of my getting on the Hill again, with the high number I drew. I looked through Stone Hall and do you know, I really think I want to go up there! It is very pleasant; rooms large and pleasant and the food is called the best on the grounds. I know several girls there, Nina and Helen P. among them, both of whom expect to be there next year, too. Then, I think I should have one year in a large hall, and I don't care for College Hall. I don't want a roommate. We begin to draw at 8:00 A.M. tomorrow. I'll let you know by postal the result of my choice.

Frank came out about 7:30. It was so lovely, we walked over by College Hall and then down to Tupelo. (Being "immune," I didn't mind taking him there.) It seems as if we met everyone; May Montgomery, who knew I was expecting a man and had joked me about taking him to Tupelo, two other girls from Norumbega, on the way down and Nina and Helen on the way back. After taking him over to see Stone, I meant to walk over to Hunnewell's, but it is closed as old Mr. H. is very ill. So, we came back and sat down in one of the little "crow's nests" overhanging the lake. It was then lovely moonlight and almost as good as being out on the water. We had a very pleasant time, talking of all our old school friends, some of whom he sees frequently.

He wasn't nearly as bashful this time, really very nice and sensible. He is quite a man, after all. He spoke of Mr. S.—said he was such a fine fellow, so sunny and good-natured, not discouraged by anything, and so bright and jolly. Mr. S, said he had to "put his nose to the grind-stone" till June 19, Frank told me. (And I <u>do</u> want to see him so much about my next year's courses. I shall consult <u>you</u> soon). Frank invited me to go to the theatre—June 7—that an old Nute girl is playing in. And that he had enjoyed the evening very much.

I am glad to really get acquainted with him. I <u>do</u> want some good sensible men <u>friends</u> better than silly lovers, don't you think?

Hope to hear about my room tomorrow.

Love to you all—Your own Helen

May 21. My dear Mamma—

I am almost sick and horribly disappointed over the room I drew; I had just made up my mind that I <u>wouldn't</u> go to College Hall. I have applied for a single in either Wilder, Norumbega, Stone or Freeman, and think I ought to get one somewhere; if not now, certainly, this summer, when so many drop out. It won't be the worst thing, to be sure, if I have to stay in C.H., but I shall hope and pray I <u>don't</u>.

The room I got, is a double in C.H., with a girl named Gertrude Ware. She is a lovely girl, bright, but quiet and modest. I would rather room with her than most any other girl, if worse comes to worst. We took the best we could get and it is really very pleasant. It is on the south side of College Hall, looking on the lake, where it gets all the sun, and good-sized. In fact, there are two rooms, a tiny bedroom and a study. I haven't seen Gertrude since the drawing, so don't know what she has done. She is as anxious to get out as I am, and was going to apply for Stone.

With love to all—Helen

May 22. My dear Mamma—

It is only 7:15 P.M. and I'm up here in my room with my clothes off and my hair down, all ready to go to bed! You see, I had to sit up late last night to finish a "short, rather, <u>long</u> story" and get up early this morning to copy it, so I am rather tired tonight. Also—it is still so lovely <u>out</u> that the only way I could keep from going out was to take my clothes right off!

We have been told to apply again if we want a change of room, though we shan't know whether or not we are changed, until we come back next Fall. I'd write a bushel of applications, if it would do any good.

Tons of love to you—Helen

May 25. My dear ones—

I want to ask your joint advice about my next year's courses. I shall keep on with Latin, of course, as I intend to teach that. What do you think about my taking another year of German? I know you will say "Nonsense," at first, Papa, but when I explain, I think you may feel differently. In the first place, I like it, and Fraulein says I do well in it. She stopped me in the hall the other day to speak about my going on with it. I said I might like to, if she thought I knew enough to. She said, "Why, Miss Fox, how you do talk. You are one of my best girls. I had even thought you might do something extra with it." I almost fainted, it was so unexpected! Now, I don't want to be overcome by <u>flattery</u>, but I really think that with one more year's work, I could, by trying hard perhaps learn enough to teach it in High School. Then, if I take one more year of it, I shall have a "major" in it.

I am not going on with Chem., tho' I'd like to, but don't think I ought to spend any more time on it. I think I shall take Physics instead. That will complete my list of electives. For required work, I shall have Philosophy, course 1 and 6; English 15, debates, and Bible 3,4,8 & 9. I would like awfully well 4, "The Life of Christ," but Miss Locke who has it, I have had this year and she is so dry and uninteresting, I am afraid to take such a sacred subject with her, for fear she might make me <u>dislike</u> it, as I fear she has some of the Old Testament.

Now, please tell me what you think of my choices and offer any suggestions you may have. I am going to have a consultation with Miss Hawes, Head of the Latin department, in which I am taking my first major, and get her advice. How I <u>do</u> wish Mr. S. would come out so I could ask his! It would be of much more help to me than ever before.

It is getting very warm now, with this electric light on, so I guess I'll say "Goodnight."

With oceans of love to all.

Your own "little girl" Helen

May 27. My precious Mamma—

I had a letter from Frankie. He began—"Dear <u>Miss</u> Fox, It is awful to be so formal" and closed—"Yours sincerely, <u>Mr.</u> Lee." What <u>can</u> I say in reply? I don't exactly want to say "You may call me <u>Helen</u>" before he asks, tho' I know he wants to, and I'd like him to. It <u>is</u> stiff and foolish, I agree with him. He said he was over to see Mr. S. last Sunday, the day after he was out here, and found him "with his nose in close proximity to the grindstone." I guess he cares more about it than about anything else.

Frank also said he has tickets for the "Messenger Boy" on June 7th and should look for me that P.M. Of course, you haven't any objections, have you? I know you, Mamma, like "Frankie-Dee" too well!

I have just been in Miss Hawes' room to talk over my next year's courses with her, and she thinks the work I have planned is good. She says I must try to take Latin Senior year. She is to be in Europe next year.

Goodnight everybody. With oceans of love—your own—"Girl Goldie"

June 4. My dearest Mamma and all—

Taking work, heat and bees, which you don't have, I don't get any surplus sleep. You see, the windows here have no screens, only inside blinds, so all sorts of winged creatures can come in. The mosquitoes don't bother me; they never did you know, but a family of yellow-jackets has determined to take up its abode with me and won't listen to my objections. They worm their way in, between the window and the blinds about 5:30 mornings and "sing!" I couldn't stand it any longer, so I armed myself with a stiff piece of cardboard and went to work. I killed four and mean to keep on until I've "distinguished" the whole family!

I have finished my Chem. Lab. work and cleaned up, even to taking account of stock; only my breakage bill to pay and I'll be through with that.

Stacks of love to all, Helen

June 6. My dear Muddie—

Another Tree Day over. Only two more to be in. I shall always want to come back and see it! It was perfectly lovely, like a beautiful dream. (I shall tell you all about it when I get home and you will probably read about it in the papers. I didn't "dress up," after all, for I didn't get time to make my costume, so, I had a grand chance to see it all—with plenty of company.

I had just got home from Chem., when the maid brought up Aunt Abbie's card. She had cousin Edna and Beulah with her. I took them around and they were entranced with everything. They all left before dinner, tho' I invited them to stay.

We have lots of fun over at College Hall, and on the campus with the Freshmen in the evening before Tree Day— I'll tell you about it, later. After the exercises this afternoon the Seniors all came over here to supper outdoors and we all helped wait on them—then "stuffed" ourselves. At midnight, I expect to be wakened by the Senior Serenade.

I have an invitation to Melrose for next week, but can't go as I have an invitation to the Shakespeare Play here, one of the "big" times which I wouldn't miss for the world, Sat. evening, the 14th.

Oceans of love to everyone—Helen

June 9. My dear ones—

I went in town on the 12:15 yesterday. Wore my walking suit, as it looked like a shower, and my white silk waist. Frank was there to meet me, but my train came in on the wrong track, but I discovered him, so met him! He was intending to take me to lunch (had had his own, as I discovered, as he didn't work that A.M.) but I, too, had had my lunch—at Wellesley, so we went right to the theatre, only stopping to get a box of candy—and he left me in a store while he went down to his office for an umbrella, as it had started to rain.

The play was fine, light opera, and very comical, "cute fun." Flora Zabelle is certainly very handsome and graceful. We had about the best seats in the house and a really good time. Frank wanted me to go out to his home for supper or at least stay in town, but it was so nasty and sticky that I didn't feel "presentable," plus I had to get in my schedule card for next year by 8:00. So, I decided to come right out.

Frank is still a little bashful, not a "Lady's Man" by any means, but we got on very well. Nina is eager for me to go home with her to spend the night of the 18th and if I can get packed before then, I think I will. Mrs. Hill was here for Tree Day and seemed to want me.

Heaps of love to all—

Your own "little girl," Helen

June 11. My precious Muddie—

Please thank Papa for the check. They are charging us storage—in advance—25¢ an article. I shall have my Morris chair, screen, tea-table and box—$1.00 at least, which makes me disgusted. It's charge for everything at the last.

I passed in my schedule for next year, electing the Latin, German and Physics as I planned; my first one without Mr. S.'s help. One more recitation tomorrow A.M., then exams begin Thursday. I have French Thurs. P.M., German Fri. P.M., Bible Tues. P.M. and Latin Weds. P.M. I don't dread the exams so awfully—they are usually easier than midyears; still, I don't "hanker" for them. I shall do my best and let it go. Oh, Dr. Roberts told me today that she was very sorry they were going to lose me from Chem. next year. I guess she has been satisfied with my work as I have had "excellent" on two written lessons from her.

Love and kisses to all—Helen

June 12. My dear Mamma—

Only three more exams and one more week! The French exam this morning was not so very hard, but long and catchy. I think I got through all right, but won't be sure about the "Credit." Have been trying to study for German, which comes tomorrow P.M., but it has been too hot and I was too tired to do much. Shall have to "dig in" tomorrow A.M.

The die is cast, as to Float Night. I should have liked to invite Mr. S., but having heard nothing from him since he was last here, I shall invite cousin Bert instead, and Winnie and Walter plan to come, so I shall enjoy it, anyway.

Got a very pretty graduation invitation from Charles Jones, but don't plan to go as I'll be going to that at Nute on my way home.

Well, I must close and get my electric light off, or the mosquitoes will <u>devour</u> me, I'm afraid. I bragged about how they never bothered me—and didn't knock on wood when I said it!

Goodnight and tons of love—Your sleepy "Girl Goldie"

June 15. My own dear ones—

The Shakespeare play, which was simply <u>beautiful</u>—more so than Tree Day ever dreamed of being. It would take a ream of paper to describe, so I'll wait until I can <u>talk</u> to you.

Edna's father is here—came last Friday, so after dinner, I went part way with them to So. Natick, where they wanted to view a very old graveyard. He is very nice, makes me think of some "<u>Noble</u>." He is a large man and speaks in a soft drawl.

I have gone over all my rented books, erasing all marks in them, so they're ready to return. Tomorrow, after a last trip to town to get your waist, Mamma, I shall get things ready to pack and study for Bible. Had my old "school" hat retrimmed, as the silk was faded and crushed. It is trimmed now with black ribbon, a big bow and a black quill. Sounds "old," doesn't it? But it's about all they are wearing on walking suit hats now, and is very becoming.

Winnie expects to be very busy this summer as she and Walter are to be married in the Fall, tho' the day hasn't been set yet.

My Chem. breakage and storage bills were even larger that I expected. I suppose I should be glad that I haven't any message or carriage bills, as poor Mabel Gordon has. She is the one who sprained her knee over a month ago and is just beginning to walk without crutches.

Well, this is the last Sunday for writing to you! Five days at the most, and I'll be home.

With a heart full of love—

Your "little girl," Helen

June 17. *[Postal]* Dear Papa—

Just in from Float Night—Lovely! All my people came and had a very good time. One more exam and I'm thro'. I expect to go to Melrose tomorrow P.M. and leave there for home on Thursday—the 12:15 from Boston.

Please get my hammock up under the apple tree, as I plan to lie in it <u>all</u> <u>day</u>!

Much love—Helen

END OF SOPHOMORE YEAR

JUNIOR YEAR, 1902–1903

FIRST SEMESTER

Sept. 21. My dear ones—

Rejoice with me for I am in Stone Hall! I tried to telephone you about 8:00 P.M. last evening, but when I went in the operator shook her head and said it was really no use to try. The line buzzed so, owing to the rush of business, that it had been almost impossible to hear, even for the village, for several evenings. So I didn't try.

I went directly to College Hall when I got here, and after I had registered, I looked for Miss Kelsey and was told I couldn't see her until after dinner. A Miss Young helped me out, looked in a little book and told me I was transferred to "<u>32</u> <u>Stone</u>." I could have hugged her! I did give a little half

Old Stone Hall

scream of joy and then told her why. She laughed and said she was glad.

Well, my room is a very pleasant one on the 2nd floor. It is in the right wing as you look at the picture of Stone, facing somewhat east, I should say; there's not enough sun to determine very accurately. I found Mary, Louise, and several of the other girls. Helen P. and Nina haven't come yet. Nearly all the girls I know well are here and I think we shall all have a gay time together.

We all went to the Christian Assoc. reception last evening and enjoyed it, tho' it was a perfect jam. The service at Chapel this morning was fine. This A.M., I've been over on the hill to see Alice and Edna—both at Wilder as they had hoped; but they were both out. I stepped into Norumbega to see Mrs. Newman, but she had company, so I didn't go in. It made me a little homesick to come out again; seemed as if I ought to go up to room 25. However, I think I shall like it here very much—do, already, in fact, and know I shall even more when I unpack my trunks, get my "box" and get more settled.

Mary and Louise want me to go out for a little walk before supper, so I'll stop now, and post this on the way.

I miss you all very much, but I am happy to be here.

A great big lot of love for you all—Helen

Sept. 23. My precious Mamma—

I don't think I have ever been so busy in my life as I have these last two days, unpacking and settling. Why last year was nothing by comparison! Perhaps I mind it more because I'm old!

The box was as much work as both trunks. Nothing was broken in it, but the cover was split clean in two! I've had to scurry around after my text books, today, too, and recitations have begun.

This morning, things began in earnest, with the Seniors first appearance in cap and gown at Chapel. As always, it was very imposing and solemn. Just think, next year, I shall wear my cap and gown.

Heaps of love for all—Your own "little girl," Helen.

Sept. 25 My dear Mamma—

I continue to like Stone—like it better every day, in fact. Of course, so large a house seems a little queer at first after Norumbega, not nearly as home-like. However, it is very much so, considering its size. Do you know when my "homesick" time always is? When I first wake up in the morning, for the first few moments. After I am once up, however, and through with my cold bath, it is gone. In the daytime, I'm much too busy with my classes and with so many girls I know and like so well. I really think I am "right in clover" coming to Stone Hall. The fare is excellent, too, and I get milk twice a day. We have a night watchman here, Papa, so you needn't worry about fire.

I went down to the village yesterday. It looks quite the same, with the exception of the "Wellesley Inn," an old house fixed over, which is going to be fine. Shall I engage rooms for you all for the Commencement of 1904?

The college grounds are a sight, all torn up to put in a central heating system. I have met several of my old teachers (nearly all are new to me this year) and they are all very cordial. Everything in the study line seems altogether different, but I think I shall like the work.

Today, we had our first experience in Debates, and it was just my luck to be one of four chosen at random to debate extemporaneously on the subject: <u>Resolved</u>—That N.Y. proprietors of apartment houses are justified in breaking their contracts with tenants by raising rent in view of the present rise in the price of coal. Well, knowing about how much <u>I</u> know about rent contracts and the subject generally, you can guess about what a "brilliant" speech I made after the five minutes or so we had to talk it over in. I could say almost nothing and never felt so like an absolute idiot in my life! One of the girls here in the house told me this evening that I did better than the others, which is somewhat of a comfort. It was all a huge farce anyway.

Could you have a Waterman's fountain pen sent me, Papa?

Good night now, and oceans of love—Helen

Oct. 1. My dear Muzzie—

This will have to be a short letter, as I'm sleepy. Moreover, I'm turned out of house and home because my electric light bulb has just burned out and there isn't an extra one in the house! So, I am "visiting" long enough to write you in Gertrude Ware's room. She was the girl I drew for my College Hall room with, you know. She got a single in Stone, too.

One week from tonight, I shall be in Melrose for Winnie and Walter's wedding. It is in the evening, so I shall have to stay overnight, but only miss one recitation the next morning.

I have decided I must get to bed at 10:00 tonight, light or no light, as

I've had to sit up more or less this week, getting things started. Later, I'll be able to plan my work better.

I wonder if "Prof" is back. Haven't heard any news, or found him—or Frankie either—on my doorstep yet.

Well—my time is up, so Goodnight—Your loving Helen.

Oct. 6. My own dear ones—

I am here in my room, snug as a "bug in a rug," beginning to feel more at home, and Louise is here, too, writing to <u>her</u> family. She and I and two other girls decided yesterday P.M. to walk to Baker's Gardens. I'd never been there before. It is a lovely walk, about two and a half miles over these splendid, level, smooth roads; they are so different from ours at home—more tiresome on the whole, for scenery, for there's no hill to climb and look down from, just a long, level, but much less tiresome to <u>walk</u> on. We found plenty of apples, delicious ripe ones on the way, and some chestnuts, which unfortunately <u>weren't</u> ripe. *[A blight soon after this killed all the chestnut trees in New England.]*

The gardens are really worth the walk. Mr. Baker was an eccentric man and when a great deal of money came to him, it turned his head so he became almost crazy. He built these lovely gardens with tunnels opening into little rooms with queer images of Indians and idols, arches, fountains (I believe they once ran with wine), little lakes, pits for bears and other animals, and even a little chapel. But now, even tho' it is long neglected, with the little chapel in ruins and ivy running wild all over it and the ruins of the bear cages, it is interesting and picturesque. We were hungry as bears when we got back. *[Baker's Gardens were way out on Grove St.]*

At church this A.M., the preacher was Dr. Van Dyke of Princeton, a brother of the famous author, Henry Van Dyke, and we had communion. Miss Hazard was there, back at last—she has been home resting as she was so tired last June—and it seemed quite "homey" to see her face again. I have always felt as if I knew her well.

Did I tell you about the dining table system here? They assign us places at a table with a faculty head for breakfast and dinner. I am at Miss Hart's, the Head of the English Department. *[Sophie Chantal Hart was still head of the English Dept. in my day, and taught my Senior English Comp. class—my major.]* For lunch, we make up our own tables and all of us, Helen, Nina, myself and several others are together.

My room locality is very pleasant; it is down a little side corridor.

Miss Randall, one of the Physical Culture teachers, rooms just beyond. Opposite her is Miss Bliss, a Post Graduate, who was in Miss McClary's class, '99. *[Miss McClary was Helen's teacher at Nute N.S.]* She is just as sweet as can be. I wish I knew her well, but have been a little bashful about making up to her, as she is so far "above" me, but I overheard her telling Miss R. how lonely she is, how she misses the old girls, etc. So, I think I shall venture. Jeannette Risdon, a very nice girl in my class, rooms opposite me.

Dr. Bissel, a Wellesley alumna, who is a missionary in the East, spoke to us in Chapel. She was very interesting, besides being a very sweet little woman, not at all the dried-up old maid I feared to see.

I suppose this is Winnie's "last Sunday on earth" as a single woman. I shall write you all about the wedding when I return Weds. Don't worry about rules, as I am not breaking any by "cutting" my one recitation.

With heaps of love for all— "Girl Goldie"

Oct. 13. My dear Ones—

When we walked to the "ville" yesterday afternoon, we had quite a "side show." The Automobile Club, etc., that started Friday from N.Y., to speed to Boston, passed through. There were about 75 cars, I should say, a steady procession for almost a half hour—great, huge, yellow and red autos, holding six or more, all the men so dusty and wearing great goggles, looking almost like inhabitants from another planet. It was very interesting and exciting.

The minister at church today, I didn't particularly like, but he said one thing which greatly impressed me. "College culture consists, not in the study of letters in itself, but in the building up of a stronger, sweeter, nobler will." Don't you think it true?

I continue to like Stone as much if not better than ever. There is a saying here in connection with this place—"No one comes to Stone unless driven to it, and after they've been here a year, they can scarcely be driven away!"

Time to say goodnight.

With a heart full of love—"Girl Goldie"

(P.S.) Oh, I almost forgot to tell you what my German teacher told me the other day. I waited to speak to her about something and she took the occasion to remark, "Oh, Miss Fox, your composition that you passed in the other day was just <u>perfect</u>"!! Isn't that a good start?

[Letter from Charles Jones. He did not go to Dartmouth and is now a Freshman at Harvard.]

October 15, 1902 Ma chère Helène—

Je suis allé a Roxbury, et je viens à Cambridge par le train élevé, mais j'ai passé plus d'une heure chaque jour, ainsi, j'ai cherché une maison ici en Cambridge. But enough of French, as I have no dictionary and as I have not had it for awhile, my memory is faulty and I do not take it this year. I have six courses, the maximum number allowed. They are Latin, Greek, English, German, History and Physics.

My amusements are not very varied. A little tennis, gym and football games are my excitement, except a game of cards once in a while. I am waiting for the ponds to freeze over, so that the Ice Carnival on Lake Waban will come off.

I have been enquiring about Harvard pins and I can get one for somewhat less that ten dollars, or I can get one of the larger pennants for about the same or even a Harvard flag. You may take your choice and I will get it for you sometime, but only on the condition that you give me your word of honor (if you have any) that you haven't any Yale flag up in your room or are wearing any Yale pin. I don't mind your having them, but don't have Harvard ones (on display) at the same time. Please put the Yale things out of sight.

In return, I would request the favor of a letter. Since last June I have written you about 14 letters and have answers to three of them. I hope you will not make me waste any more stamps! Besides, it spoils the disposition. If you answer promptly, I shall have another favor to request and if you wait until Xmas, I shall be silent as the grave. Your curiosity ought to make you answer pretty soon. I will add that there is one more thing which might be regarded, if you consider it carefully, as a favor to both you and me. I am not sure about that yet, but the rest will go on like the brook, until I get a letter from Wellesley.

De votre ami, pas aimé, comme je crains *[from your friend, not your love, as I believe.]*

<u>Charlemagne</u>
Harvard 1906

[Helen, as she wrote home, was able to find, in Boston, a Wellesley pin for 25¢! Poor Charles! This letter arrived just at the time that "Prof" (Mr. Smith) had invited Helen to her first football game and she had no thoughts for anything but that. I doubt that she answered Charles' letter for a long time. As his three letters are the only ones still in existance, we shall never know what the "favor" he spoke of might have been.]

Oct. 21. My dearest Muddie—

Yesterday was a hard day. I was absolutely out of handkerchiefs, so, after breakfast, I went down stairs to the laundry and did some washing. Had quite an exciting adventure. I left the steam arrangement to boil the clothes turned on so long that it was so hot nobody could touch it; then I let cold water overflow the tub and make a puddle on the floor. I'll be wiser, next time.

For English, we met to select a subject for a debate and are undecided over the question of child labor, or that of the intercollegiate athletic contests as between Harvard and Yale.

I put in the rest of the day studying German and Phil. In the evening, the girls were up in my room discussing Philosophy, when the maid came up and said a gentleman wanted to see me. I asked if he sent a card or a name and she said "No." I demanded a description. She said he was short, quite "stout" and had a <u>mustache</u>! Well, of course, I thought it must be "Prof," so went down, fully expecting to see him and was confronted by—Arthur Brackett! *[an old schoolmate from Milton Mills.]* Perhaps I wasn't disappointed, happily(?) <u>of</u> <u>course</u>!

He had had a great time finding me, had wandered all over the grounds, as he had never seen the College. As there were several other young gentlemen callers in the little reception room, I took him over to see College Hall. He stayed until 9:30, which seemed perfect <u>ages</u> to me, I was so sleepy. I am afraid I was no end <u>dull</u>, but can't remember much of anything I said or did—it was like a nightmare, I did everything so mechanically. He has invited me to the theatre for a week from Saturday, so I guess I didn't quite disgrace myself. Funny he should be the first man to come out this Fall. Think I shall write Frankie <u>very</u> soon, incidentally mentioning the fact that Arthur Brackett came "out of the blue" one evening. "Prof" I shall let severely <u>alone</u>.

The laundry came today, everything in good condition. It was so thoughtful of you to send "the pink" and apples. The former is so sweet and the very first flower in my room this year. *[Helen is referring to the pink oxalis, which her mother had dug up and taken into the house for the winter—a yearly ritual. She divided it and sent Helen a root, which not only went to college with her, but was the ancester, one hundred years ago, of the pink oxalis plant which now sits in my sunny window sill, and of which I have divided and given sections to my daughter and granddaughter!]* We shall all feast on the apples without being obliged to hurt our consciences by "robbing" neighboring orchards.

There is a poor little homesick discouraged Freshman here from N.H. Bristol, I think. So I am trying to comfort and encourage her. Freshman year isn't so far in the past but what I can sympathize with her.

With stacks of love for all—Helen

Oct. 24. My dear Muddie—

We have about decided on the question of child labor in the East and the South for our subject. I don't know just how it will be stated, or which side I shall be on yet. When I know, I shall want Papa Fox to help me with some arguments, and ask him to keep his eyes open for anything relating to the subject as a whole.

Have you seen the comet? Last evening, quite a party of us girls went over to the Observatory and looked at it thro' the big telescope. However, it was not very plain, because of a mist—but still very interesting. I should like to have some Astronomy before I leave here. I like my Physics very much; it isn't hard at all, and explains so many common every day occurrences which I never understood before. The Philosophy is going to be very interesting, I think, tho' just now, a little dull.

Lots of love to you all—Helen

Oct. 26. My dear ones—

I am getting quite accustomed to spending my Sundays at Wellesley and I do love that day here, only it goes so quickly, even more so than last year, now that I'm with the other girls all the time. *[Her original group from Freshman year.]*

We went for a little walk this morning and got some lovely red leaves, then to church. President Hyde of Bowdoin preached on the Ten Commandments, and was very good. He must be considered very bright, I think, for they say that President Eliot of Harvard has spoken of him for his successor.

This afternoon, we had after dinner coffee in the parlor until about 3:00. Then Louise and I made chocolate peppermints. *[My father said, many years later, that the only thing Helen could cook when they were married was chocolate peppermints!]*

Later, we got together with Edith Fox and Mildred Franklin, the others on the debate, to decide how to state our question; also drew lots for sides. The question is —"Resolved: That the employment of children under the age of sixteen in the department stores and factories of the Eastern states should be prohibited by law." Louise and I are on the affirmative.

Please keep your eyes open for material and if you find any, let us have it as soon as possible. Our "brief," the outline of the thing, goes in this next Thursday, then the debate comes off <u>Nov. 13</u>. I hope it won't prove unlucky!

I must tell you about our visitor. One of the girls woke up about 6:30 this morning, hearing a queer noise and found a <u>screech owl</u> in her room. *[No screens on Stone windows, apparently.]* They caught him and he has been "holding reception" all day under a waste basket in the Botany Lecture room. He is such an odd little creature, I understand now what "solemn as an owl" means.

I expect to go in town tomorrow A.M. to read in the library there for my debate. *[This is the first reference to any library since Helen came to college. Perhaps the courses she took had not required long hours at the college library.]*

Much love to all—Helen

Oct. 30. My dear Mamma—

Got my brief in safely and feel <u>so</u> relieved. Shall just have time for a free breath and then it will be time to think of the debate itself.

Tomorrow night is Halloween. The Seniors have charge of affairs and we don't know yet what's planned. Our crowd is going to have a spread in one of the girl's rooms and end with a parade of sheets thro' the corridors.

A note from Arthur B. says he has seats for "Notre Dame" at the Colonial, so I shall see the inside of a theatre.

Oh, I forgot to answer your questions about the heat here at Stone. Part of the rooms have registers (mine does) others have radiators (steam). It is very nice and warm. I wish you would send some outing flannel petticoats, as I have left off my cotton.

With tons of love—Your own Helen

Nov. 2. My own dear ones—

I came very near missing the theatre, but it was not my fault! I planned to go in on the 1:07 with several other girls, and had decided to ride down to the station with them. Mary and I came out from lunch, waited outside the dining room for the others. Finally, when we went out to the door, we found the carriage had already gone, and they with it. It was then within twelve minutes of train time and it is a good <u>fifteen</u> minute walk (in long skirts) to the station. We finally half <u>ran</u> over to Fiske, and succeeded in getting there just as the last carriages drove past, so we were safe. The other girls thought we had walked on ahead—it was a mistake all around.

Arthur met me at the terminal, looking <u>very</u> spruce and we went directly to the Colonial, getting there just in time for the orchestra's opening number. The play was very good—Victor Hugo's "Notre Dame," dramatized in English. It was about the most thrilling I have ever seen.

After the play, Arthur proposed that we go to Marston's for supper. It was only about 5:00 o'clock— but I didn't want to; somehow, it seems to me as if supper, etc., puts one under more obligation to a man. So, I made the best excuse I could and he put me on the 5:30.

Oh, Papa, this will please you! On Halloween, we floated walnut shells with little candles in them. The one whose candle went out first was to be the "old maid;" the one whose candle burned the longest, would be married first. Well, mine went out <u>first</u> and Louise's last. So I am going to give up all attempts and settle down to a life of "single blessedness."

Love to all, your own "little girl"—Helen

P.S. Field Day tomorrow with basketball, hockey, tennis and running contests. Quite exciting. Look for an account in the paper.

Nov. 4. My dear Mamma—

I feel very smart tonight; I began on my German at 8:00 and had it all done, translations and questions, by 9:15. Our usual written work for Psych. for tomorrow is postponed till Friday, so I shall take it easy. It is so hard to work when it is so <u>lovely</u> out—and then get out after 4:15 when the sun is most down. I feel almost as if under a ban with the debate hanging over me, but once it's over, I'm going to celebrate.

The chrysanthemums (is that correct? Remember, I have <u>no</u> dictionary!) which you sent are as fresh as ever, so bright and pretty.

Love to all, Helen

Nov. 7. My dear Mamma,

I have made my first "floor speech" in Debates. I mounted the platform with my heart under my <u>tongue</u> and pronounced a few "well-chosen words" as "Prof" used to say. I really wasn't as scared as I might have been. Miss

McCauley said that she liked what I said very much. So I don't dread next Thurs. quite so much.

Don't worry about "Jack The Hugger." You needn't be the least bit alarmed. I don't believe I've been <u>out</u> an evening for months. We are not allowed to go—even from here to College Hall—alone after dark. *[Her parents had read in the Boston papers about attacks on young women in the city and wrote that she should not go out at Wellesley after dark.]*

Time to say goodnight—With stacks of love to all—Helen

Nov. 9. My dear ones—

Yesterday we had the pleasure of listening to a lecture by President Eliot of Harvard. It was scheduled to be on "Education in the lower schools" but was a complete surprise in being on "Woman's Work"—its great opportunities for her mental and spiritual development (just think of that when you wash dishes or sweep the floors) and of her greater reward in the love of her children, etc. He was really grand.

I had a very industrious fit last evening, perhaps brought on by Pres. Eliot's address; I mended, <u>darned</u> my gloves and a pair of stockings.

Tomorrow, I begin debate work, and don't expect to <u>breathe</u> <u>freely</u> again till after 3:00 P.M. Thursday. We shall go into town in the P.M., to work in the Boston Library *[which probably had a better collection of newspapers than the college library.]*

I have finally answered Charles Jones' letter of almost a month ago—just simply have had no time to do it.

Good night—Your own loving "Little Girl"

Nov. 13. My own dear Muddie—

Well, the "awful hour" has come and gone and if I weren't too tired to feel excited, I should be most hilarious that I have done so well! Not so well that I might be excused from all further work in Debates, or as to assure my being on the Wellesley-Vassar Debate, but quite well enough to satisfy myself and Miss McCauley, I guess, for my first trial. (At least she said nothing to the contrary.) She doesn't award any <u>decision</u>, which is disappointing, after the exciting ones Mr. Smith used to give at Nute. The debates here are not as <u>yet</u> public; only put on for our own division at present.

It was very interesting and exciting and I was so far from being terrified that I used up all the time allowed me and then would have given heaps to go on the stage again, (we have it in the Old Chapel) and say some things I forgot. *[The Old Chapel was in College Hall.]* We are both very glad to be through and intend to celebrate soon, tho' just what we will do, we have not yet decided. Perhaps go in town to some "Dime Museum!"

    With tons of love for all, Helen

[Visit to Aunt Abbie's in Needham.]

Nov. 22. My dear Muddie—

    I have written to Cousin Edna that I shall be glad to "take up" her invitation for Thanksgiving. I really think, much as I should love to, that it's best for me not to come home. I am coming home so soon for vacation that we can have that to look forward to—all the more.

    Ray came out Weds. evening bringing Helen L. *[a friend, who summered in N.H.]* We had such a good time, you could almost hear us laugh from home—or perhaps the echo! Ray is about the jolliest, best company I know—and Helen, too. Ray pretended to be heart broken when I told him I had been to the theatre with Arthur. I hope he will console himself with Helen.

    I had a letter from Charles Jones yesterday, which almost made me tear my hair. He said that had I only answered his previous letter sooner, he should have invited me to the Harvard-Penn game. That almost broke my heart. I'd give "worlds" to go to the Harvard-Yale game, tomorrow, if only—

    Much love to all—Helen

Nov. 24. My own dear ones—

    This has been such a busy day for Sunday! But before telling you about today, let me tell you I have been to the Harvard-Yale game! I imagine you have visions of "Prof" appearing at the last moment, etc.—but they are all wrong. Perhaps I ought to have said "to a H-Y game." That which I attended was played here at Wellesley by what are usually known as Wellesley girls, at 4:15 P.M. Friday. The score was 5-0 in favor of Harvard! It was the best fun I've had in a long time and almost as exciting as the real one last year. We all crowed lustily over Harvard's victory, but last evening the Yale people, hearing the news of the real game, crowed over us with true cause. Too bad, poor, poor "Johnny Harvard"!

    Last evening, we had a cute little play at the Barn, then toasted marshmallows, made lemonade, etc. afterwards. This morning, I got up too late for breakfast, but after Louise, Ethel and I had been down to the "ville" to get the Sunday papers, Margaret made us some coffee and I contributed my crackers, so I didn't <u>starve</u>.

The President of Brown University preached this forenoon and I liked him better than almost anyone I've heard this year. After dinner we had after-dinner coffee in the parlor and "met" Miss Pendleton who was a dinner guest. After washing and drying my hair (which now looks very "poodle-doggy"), went to musical Vespers and a Somerset "Y" meeting afterwards.

Tomorrow, I expect to go over to Radcliffe. There is an advanced course in gym work offered this year which I mean to try for. Only 10 from each class are to be taken in and we are invited to go over to Radcliffe to an exhibition of <u>their</u> gym work.. (Perhaps I may run across Mr. S. or Charles J. while in Cambridge!)

So with a busy day ahead, I really must say goodnight.

With much love to all—Helen

Nov. 26. My own dear ones—

I wish you all a very happy Thanksgiving! I am writing very early this morning so that you may get <u>it</u> instead of <u>me</u> this evening. It seems queer not to be coming home and I wish I were; but perhaps it's just as well, for I have a slight cold—due to the changes in the weather, I guess, and I think this will be a cold, windy day.

We went to Radcliffe on the 9:55 and took a Harvard Sq. car to Cambridge, going right past Mr. S's rooms, both ways, but no luck—didn't see him, only a red sofa pillow in the bay window. The exercises at the gym, a fine, new building, were very interesting. That was the only building we saw and I'm still glad in spite of Radcliffe's close proximity to Harvard, that I am in <u>Wellesley</u>.

Time to get up—I'm writing this is bed—so I'll say "<u>Good</u> <u>day</u>"!

With tons of love, your own little girl—Helen

P.S. Ran in to say hello to Ray after lunch in town and we consoled each other about not going home for Thanksgiving. *[Ray was working at a bank in Boston.]*

Nov. 30. My dear ones—

I had a lovely time at Edna's, and a fine, regular Thanksgiving dinner, but it didn't <u>seem</u> a mite like Thanksgiving, and I thought of you all at home. But wasn't it nice we could talk on the telephone? Surely the next best thing to seeing one another.

Yesterday, I worked all day writing up my debate. Then Miss Bliss invited some of us to meet a friend who was visiting her, and have something to eat. We had an awfully good time, she is so jolly and not a bit like "faculty."

I slept till 10:25 this morning and had to hustle to get ready for church at 11:00. Mr. Stokes, a Trustee of the college and on the Faculty at Yale, preached and he was <u>fine</u>.

I have been up in Ethel Moody's room, reading Ernest Thompson Seton's "Wild Animals I Have Known," and writing letters.

Goodnight—Your own "little girl Helen

Dec. 2. My dear Mamma—

I met Aunt Ada in town early yesterday to begin the hunt for my new winter coat. We went <u>everywhere</u> and I believe I tried on over <u>thirty</u> coats, if I did one. I saved Jordan Marsh for last. I had about given up. Well, I found my fate at Jordan's! I like it <u>very</u> <u>much</u> and think you will, too. It is long—three quarters— and loose, with a "plaited" full back (new style) and very becoming. It has a little triple cape, worn very much this year, over the shoulders. It is a medium castor *[yellowish?]* shading to drab, rather than yellowish-brown, of Melton cloth with a satiny finish and a "Skimmer" satin lining. It was marked $26.50. I said I didn't want to go over $25.00, so the sales woman had a consultation with a man, Mr. Strong, and he said that as it was the only one of that style (it was a "pattern coat"), I might have it for $25.00. They will send the coat out as soon as the sleeves are shortened. I wanted to get gloves to match, and forgetting that your order was limited to "<u>coat</u>," said to put them on it, too. Mr. Strong called my attention to that, but said if <u>I</u> were sure it would be all right, he would fix it. The only gloves I could find to match were $1.50.

I was so tired last night that I <u>dreamed</u> coats. I am so glad it's over and hope you'll be satisfied as I am. I shall be well supplied with a good coat and nice dress for next year.

With a heart full of love—Helen

Dec 8. My own dear ones—

This has been a cold, bleak day and my room has been cold for the first time, but I've been in it so little that I haven't minded. I got up late and went down to the parlor, where there was an open fire, then Mary, Louise and I had hot chocolate and crackers in Louise's room.

As it was snowing hard again, I didn't wear my coat to church, but my walking skirt, jacket and fur, as it's only a step from Stone. The minister was Pres. Hopkins of Williams and he was <u>very</u> good. We had communion and Miss Hazard and Miss Pendleton passed the plates, as they always do. I think it is quite symbolic that <u>they</u> should serve <u>us</u>.

I had an ambitious "<u>fit</u>" last Weds. and moved <u>all</u> my furniture around and hung my net of photos and posters. It is really quite an improvement. Yesterday, the snow was so glorious, I was wild to go sleighing in the P.M. and we <u>were</u> going, some of us, but couldn't get a team. However, we had a double-runner and slid down the hill by College Hall, which was full as good, while it lasted. Longfellow Pond has been frozen over for a week or more and yesterday, the lake was skimmed. I <u>may</u> wish I had my skates here if this cold weather continues.

Next Monday, there is to be a fine organ recital in the Chapel. I have almost decided to ask Frank out. I hesitate between that and Christmas Vespers next Sunday, but they are extra strict now about us entertaining <u>men</u> on Sundays. I suppose I can fall back on "Artie" Brackett if worst comes to worst, but don't really want to just before I come home. *[He would be home for vacation, too.]*

I need a new hat to match my coat; one of those "fur-felts" they are wearing so much, need very little trimming and can be bent in any becoming shape. I think a castor one, trimmed with that black ostrich feather and castor ribbon to match will be lovely. Should be about $4.00 plus the trimming. So, Mamma, as my "cashier" will you please send me $8.00 of my own money. (The extra will go for Christmas presents.)

With heaps of love, your "Girl Goldie"

[An overnight visit to Melrose.]
Dec. 12. My dear Mamma—

Thanks so much for sending the feather, but it didn't come in very good shape. I think someone's curiosity must have been aroused, for the box was torn almost to pieces, but the feather was safe. It is very pretty.

I found a hat—a lovely soft, black, silky "beaver," up on one side and down some in the back; with the feather and some black velvet on top, and some lovely pink panne velvet under the brim, next to my hair—a regular picture hat! It cost $6.50.

My new dress came today and I tried it on before "an admiring throng" (Mary and Louise) this evening. They agreed in declaring it really "swell!" I am very proud of all my new things.

[Two letters in one] Dec. 14.

My last Sunday before vacation. I began well (?) by missing breakfast (my clock was ten minutes slow), but one of the girls made me coffee and another contributed crackers and an orange, so I made out very well.

Louise, Miss Bliss and I went to church and I christened my new coat. I decided to keep the hat and dress until after Xmas, as that is when all the girls will come back with their new things.

The preacher today was Pres. Angell of Michigan U., and he was very interesting. We went again this P.M. to hear him speak on Missionary work. Then, this evening we had the Christmas Vespers and they were truly fine. I wish I could have had Mr. S. out as he would have enjoyed them so much.

Tomorrow I am going in town to do my Xmas shopping in the A.M. The Junior Play is in the P.M. and the organ recital in the evening. Frank, whom I invited, hasn't been heard from yet. I don't understand and feel decidedly cross. I do seem to have bad luck, don't I?

Never mind, I'm coming home Thursday and that seems a panacea for every woe! I shall send my trunk Weds. P.M., so it will get there as soon as I do.

With a heart full of love—Helen

Dec. 16. My dear Papa—

Frank didn't come, but I heard from him the last moment; he had thought the invitation was for next Monday, so hadn't hurried about accepting it and couldn't come this Monday. Stupid thing! However, as I've been so busy and was pretty tired, I was rather glad not to have a man to entertain. Louise and I went, as Mr. Lemare is considered the best organist of the day, and we enjoyed him so much.

We had our Christmas party tonight instead of tomorrow. Will tell you all about it when I get home. So—Goodbye, till Thursday at 8:00 P.M.!

Tons of love—Helen

CHRISTMAS VACATION

Jan. 8, 1903. My dear ones—

It has been a hard day, not getting to Stone until 9:30 P.M., but I had company all day, and Louise got on at Beverly. I unpacked my case, had some hot lemonade in Ethel's room, made my bed and got into it. This A.M. we went over to College Hall and registered, then came back and read some for the debate. I found plenty in "The Outlook," "Harper's," etc. and made a floor speech this P.M. Miss McCauley said that my <u>material</u> was excellent, but that I spoke so hurriedly as to make it rather indistinct. So, I'm very glad I have one more speech off. We have to choose a subject for our second ("<u>real</u>") debate before next Thursday. If you think of any, let me know.

My trunk finally came, and I've been unpacking and putting away things ever since. I am glad I haven't any more things, as I shouldn't know what to do with them; everything is <u>full</u> now. But I am beginning to feel settled again.

With a heart full of love and kisses for all—Helen.

Jan. 11. My own dear ones—

Bishop Lawrence preached today, so of course church was crowded— he is such a grand man. I like him especially because he looks like you, Papa. He wore the funniest robe today, with big balloon sleeves of some thin white material (all I could think of was <u>cheese cloth</u>) over silk.

This evening, we have just come back from a Memorial Service for Prof. Nenchlebach. The report that Louise saw of her death was true *[over vacation.]* She died Dec. 29th at College Hall. I don't know exactly what the trouble was. The funeral was held in the "Old Chapel" and she was buried in the college cemetery which Mr. Durant established for "life faculty," etc. I never knew of its existence before, but believe it is somewhere in the village. She was the Head of the German Department; a very intellectual woman, well known outside and will be greatly missed there, as well as here. It will seem so queer not to see her. She was a funny little woman with short hair, trotting thro' the corridors.

The Shakespeare Society is having an "At Home" tomorrow which I plan to go to, so I shall not be going into town, but will look for a dressing sacque for you, Mamma Fox, when I do.

With all the love in the world, Helen.

Jan. 18. My own dear Muddie—

Last evening, we went to a little play at the Barn—a take-off of Shakespeare, introducing several of his heroines together. As cute and laughable as it could be. Our college orchestra, new this year, played and reminded me of our high school orchestra; only Mr. Smith wasn't directing.

This morning, Margaret had invited me down to her room to have breakfast with her. We had quite a feast—bacon, fried in her chafing-dish (you see, they really are useful), bread and butter, some of my olives, coffee with real cream and oranges! It took so long, I had to hustle to get my room picked up and myself dressed for church.

Robert Speer, the Secretary of some Missionary Society, etc. was the preacher. He comes every year and all the girls simply worship him. He is the grandest man, about 40, but much younger looking. He talks very simply and directly, with great earnestness and has a wonderfully magnetic manner. He spoke again, informally, this afternoon in the "Old Chapel." His subject was the opportunities of college life and their importance and was just what I needed.

The exam list was posted yesterday and I was "happily" disappointed in my lot. They begin Weds. the 28th, but I have nothing till Sat. P.M. when I have German; then nothing more till the next Weds. P.M.—Physics. My other two, Bible and Philosophy, come Thurs. and Fri. P.M.s, so, you see, I shall have ample time to prepare for them all. I do have a paper in Latin due the last Sat. and a debate brief due this last Thurs. So, I guess I shan't get any time to go away. You know how I dreaded to come back to work; well, I am so happy, I have been just so interested and glad to. I guess it is because I am rested.

I must speak about shoes. If I don't have some soon, Papa, I must go barefoot, and that would be rather uncomfortable in this weather. My emulsion, Mamma, is nearly gone. What comes next, more of the same, or iron tablets?

With a heart full of love—Helen

Jan. 25. My dear ones—

I got up for breakfast this morning and then almost wished I hadn't, for they didn't have my favorite sugared doughnuts! However, I made do with an orange, shredded wheat, beans, brown bread and a glass of milk. Then we went in the parlor for prayers and stayed awhile around the open fire.

We had a Presbyterian minister from New York today, who was very good. His text was "Be Kind;" I wonder if he chose it because he knows college girls sometimes gossip rather unkindly about one another. This afternoon, we had the pleasure of hearing a little Filipino girl play the piano. She is a "special," lives in the village and was up with one of the girls for dinner. She plays very prettily.

I forgave Frankie and invited him out to the Ice Carnival, when we have it. The skating has been fine the last few days, and there was some talk of next Sat. evening, but today's snow has spoiled it for a time, at least.

My shoes came and are <u>O.K.</u>, very pretty and fit finely. Thank you, Daddy.

With a heart brimful of love for all, Your own Helen

Jan. 27. Dear Mamma—

I seem to be wholly out of medicines, and as midyears begin tomorrow, feel as I ought to have some on hand as a "preventative." Could you send me by mail some "sedlits" powders, some liver pills, some Hill's cold tablets, and some pepsin tablets. And you might get a few iron pills from Dr. Gross. One would think I were in the "last stages," but don't be alarmed, I just discovered that I was out of everything.

Exams start tomorrow and tho' I haven't anything till Saturday, I shall be very busy preparing for them all.

I helped serve chocolate frappé, etc. at a reception given by the Latin Department for Prof. Warren of Harvard, who lectured here.

Think of me often.

With a heart full of love—Your own Helen.

Feb. 1. My dear ones—

I have been writing Carnival invitations all day! I have invited so many people during rash moments during the year, and they will feel hurt and mad if I don't second the invitation now. So, after realizing it is about the only <u>wholly free</u> thing (and we even give voluntary contributions to this) during the year, I've decided to "do it up brown." So, I've invited Winnie and Walter, Willa and Ernest, Frank and his sweetheart and Burt *[Ricker cousins]*, Ray, and Mott *[Buck cousins]*, Helen L., and her sisters, Frankie, Artie B. and Charles Jones! Only 15 but they probably won't all come—at least, I <u>hope</u> not! It is to be Sat., Feb. 7, if there <u>is</u> skating, and I do hope there will be, to get it over with. It won't be so bad tho', they are mostly couples, so I shan't have to look after them much and some of the girls will help me with the odd men and all I shall have to do is distribute myself a little among them all. Just the same, I shall guard against such rash moments in the future!

All the medicines came O.K. Thank you very much and I'm sorry if I gave you such a scare, Mamma. My new laundry case came, too, and is fine. I eat, sleep and <u>study</u> right now, and that's about all. My German exam yesterday was a pleasant surprise; if they are all as easy, I ought to come out with flying colors.

I've taken it easy today—didn't get up till after 10:00—just in time to go hear Mr. Henry Van Dyke (the author) preach. He was grand, so simple and interesting. He spoke of the hymn, "I want to be an angel" and said he thought it was a wrong, morbid view, that <u>he</u> <u>didn't</u> want to be an angel! It sounded so funny.

With a heart full of love for all—Helen

Feb. 3. My dear Mamma—

I received a letter from Frankie, saying he would be pleased to come out for the Carnival, and Helen L. wrote that they would, also. I'm afraid there won't be any for them to come to, as it has been like Spring today, and the ice is "rotting" dreadfully.

Now, don't be surprised—I have written to Mr. S.! A purely and decidedly business letter. The subject we have chosen for our side in Debate is a hard one on which we want all legal opinion possible. "Resolved: That in criminal cases, a majority vote of the jury constitute a verdict.." We are on the negative, but nearly all the articles we have found are on the affirmative. The girls on that side are working hard and have stacks of letters from different men—lawyers. So in sheer desperation, I put my pride in my pocket and wrote to Mr. S., as he is the only lawyer I know. I don't consider it a "great unbending," or I shouldn't have done so. Now, Papa Fox, we want <u>your</u> help. "<u>Why</u> should the verdict remain unanimous?"

With tons of love to all—Helen

Feb. 8. My own dear ones—

Hurrah! Exams are over at last! And tho' it's too early to brag yet, I think I passed them all. It does seem so good to get thro' work, for I have worked harder these last two weeks than anytime since I've been in college.

It hasn't hurt me any, tho'—only a little tired, but I'm getting rested now.

We didn't have the Carnival after all, as the ice wasn't safe enough, so I had to send cards to all my people. Artie B. invited me to go to the theatre the 23rd, when he answered my invitation; said he was just on the point of doing so. Of course, I accepted with pleasure.

Margaret, Ethel and I went in town yesterday to see "Beauty and the Beast," a very pretty light opera. The staging is the best I ever saw—all one <u>gorgeous</u> color display. Just the thing after midyears!

Now—don't you want to hear what Mr. S. said? He gave me an elaborate resumé of the subject, which will help immensely. He then went on to ask how I was getting on, etc. Said he had been on the point of coming out to see me several times, but had been prevented by "unforseen circumstances;" that he had intended asking me to the Harvard-Dartmouth game, had bought the tickets, but was called out of town on business for several days. He said "There will be plenty of good ball games in the Spring, however." I hope I shall see <u>all</u> of them <u>this</u> Spring! Guess I'll have to write that there's Float Night and all the Commencement things coming in June. He wrote from the Hotel Touraine and hoped I would excuse the hastiness of the note as he was stealing time from his lunch there! Isn't he extravagant? Perhaps he had only crackers and water. It was awfully nice of him to give me so many points for the debate tho', and I'm very glad I wrote.

I somewhat expect Charles Jones in the P.M., as I told him to come out then, as perhaps there <u>might</u> be some skating, but there won't be. My debate doesn't come till the 19th, but I shall have to get to work on it soon.

With a heart <u>very</u> full of love—Your own "little girl." Helen

SECOND SEMESTER

Feb. 10. My dear Muddie—

My check came this P.M., after causing me quite a little trouble. I thought I <u>had</u> made it clear to Papa that I had to have it today. (And the mails seem to have been late getting here several times recently) We are not supposed to go to recitations until our 2nd semester's bills are paid. As I was very anxious not to miss my first recitations today, I had to go to the cashier and ask permission. He was very nice about it and let me go, but it was considerable trouble, as all the "red tape" here is. I suppose, however, it was my fault in not making it clear <u>when</u> I had to pay.

The "flunk notes" are out today and I was "slighted," so passed.

Helen L. wrote asking me out for the 22nd, but I don't want to miss the Glee Club Concert here; then Artie B. invited me to the theatre the 23rd.

With stacks of love—Helen

Feb. 13. My dear Muddie—

I am down in Mary's room, assisting her in making chocolate "peps" for a Valentine party at her table tomorrow evening.

My laundry came, emulsion and all, and I have promptly started in on that and with a glass of malted milk before bed every night, I ought to get fat very soon!

Weds. was Louise's birthday and Margaret, Ethel, Mary and I had planned to take her out to ride. It looked like rain, and began at 3:00 P.M., about 10 minutes after the carriage came. It was a covered one, so we decided to go just the same. It was heaps of fun, tho' everyone looked at us as tho' they thought we had gone crazy. We had hot chocolate and some of Louise's birthday cake from home afterwards and didn't get any cold at all. It is so Spring-like and the lake-ice is breaking up, so I guess no Carnival this year.

Everyone's mind is now on Glee Club Concert. There was such a rush for tickets I couldn't get any for Sat. and had to go over at 7:00 this morning to get a number in the line for getting the tickets for Mon. evening. However I succeeded in getting fine ones. You have hinted that you think it my duty to invite Mr. S., so I am thinking about it, (only to please you, of course.)

Must stop now. Lots and lots of love—Helen

Feb. 15. My own dear ones—

I had dinner with Edna Taylor at Wilder this noon and had such a nice time! Everything there is so pretty and new and they have such nice dainty things to eat. Alice *[Dalrymple]* was out to dinner somewhere, so I didn't see her.

Vespers this evening were so queer—the organ gave out today and they had a piano instead, and as it happened, this was a hymn-singing service. The girls have been in my room since we got back, helping me finish your cake. Mamma. I'm afraid their praises might turn your head!

What do you think—they are taking a "trial order" of our caps and gowns to get a rough estimate of the numbers, grades, etc. There are two grades; one for $16.75, the other, which nearly everyone gets, for $14.75. There is very little difference in the material and they say the $14.75 wears fully as well, so I think I shall get that. What do you think? I've signed for that, tho' the choice is not final, of course.

You keep telling me to look out for colds, etc., Mamma and now I'm going to tell you to! It's just "grippe" season now and you must be careful about getting all tired out!

Tons of love to you all—Your own Helen

Feb. 18. My dear Muddie—

It snowed so hard, with wind and drifting, that I dreaded to go into town yesterday, which I had to do to read for the coming debate. I waited until the P.M., however, and it almost cleared off, so I got along nicely. I feel quite at home in the Boston Library now, and enjoy working there.

I had a note from Artie B saying he has tickets for "Beauty and the Beast," which I saw with the girls a week ago. It is so pretty I shan't mind seeing it again. Well, I have written inviting Mr. S. to the Concert. I could get tickets only for Monday and am much afraid he can't come then.

Feb. 19. Report cards are out! I was pleasantly surprised at the monotony of mine (all CREDIT). I felt a little shaky over Psych. and Phil., so I am more than proud of my card. Lots of girls got only "Passed" on that and quite a few for Eng. 15 "Debates," too.

My debate came off this P.M. and was a great success. The other girl on my side was taken ill with a bad cold last night and couldn't come, so one of her friends read her speech. Of course, that made it harder for me and upset me a little, so that I really thought I was doing badly and expected a poor criticism. I was happily surprised when Miss Mc said we won on it!

With a heart full of love—Helen

Feb. 21. My Dear Mamma—

Well, I heard from Mr. S. and he will be very glad to come to the concert; said the Glee Club would just suit his taste. So, if it is only pleasant weather (no blizzard), I anticipate a good time. Let's hope it will be.

I don't want to brag, but I've been very lucky in not getting any cold so far this winter, (I'll knock under the table now), and hope I may escape. So many of the Glee Club girls have bad ones.

Now, I must write Mr. S. again and let him know what time to arrive.
So—goodnight and thanks for the stamps!
Your own "little girl" Helen

Feb. 22. My own dear ones—

We are living in very exciting times now! Last evening—Sat.—was the first concert, you know. We had a "collation" here, to which quite a few of the girls had guests and everyone dressed up for it. We have been "kept short" for about a week, that is, had fruit, nuts, etc. for dessert every night—which I suppose was really good for us—to economize for the "collation" last evening. It was very good; salads, oyster patties, rolls, lettuce sandwiches, cake, ice cream, hot chocolate and coffee. Afterwards, everyone went into the parlor; then, after the <u>men</u> were out of the way, we "old maids" danced.

Today has been very festive, too. We were allowed to have men callers, even to Sunday dinner! And there were several men at dinner! Then, this evening, there has been a special Musical Vesper service, from which I have just returned, and there were lots of men there, too. It seems to be men, men everywhere and not a one for me! But never mind, I'm looking for mine tomorrow night.

Ethel Moody and I had quite a "thrilling" adventure on our walk this afternoon. On our way back, we passed three little boys; two of them were teasing the third and smallest boy. One, especially, was a real <u>bully</u>, who kept pushing the little boy down in the snow till he was almost in tears. We stood it as long as we could and then Ethel and I determined to interfere. So I spoke to the bully and told him to stop being so hateful. He answered very saucily and Ethel and I took him and sat <u>him</u> down in the snow and pushed his face into it. He was greatly surprised and mad. Meanwhile, the little boy had made good his escape. As we were right at the College gate, we left the young bully to brush off the snow and call us some bad names, for which, I should like to have ducked him again. I imagine the other little fellow told his Mamma a wonderful story of how two beautiful (?), <u>strong</u> college girls rescued him!

Tomorrow will be quite a giddy day, with the theatre <u>and</u> concert, won't it?

With mountains of love and kisses for all—Helen

Feb. 24. My dear Mamma—

My "giddy" day passed all right and I'm alive to tell the tale. I spent the A.M. getting clothes laid out for both afternoon theatre and evening concert, mended my gloves and studied a very little.

Artie B. met my train at Huntington Ave. I decided that I wouldn't tell him I had seen the play before, as it might make him feel embarrassed to be taking me a second time, so I had to be very enthusiastic and surprised at it all. I came very near giving it all away once, when one of the actors said something different from before, but I stopped just in time. I really enjoyed seeing it again, as it is so lovely and spectacular. Again, he wanted me to stay for dinner, but I told him I was sorry I couldn't, as I had an engagement at college and must get back. I missed the 5:10 train, so had to hustle with my change of clothes. All the girls helped me, however, so I didn't have to keep Mr. S. waiting but a few minutes.

I wore my new dress for the first time and the girls say I never had one so becoming. He didn't say anything, but he must have liked it, I know, for he does anything green—for Dartmouth, you know! He is looking very well, has grown "fat" tho' I forgot to tell him so. *[Slimness was not admired in the early 1900s—in either men or women.]* He proceeded to enquire about my health—said I was looking just the same, only had grown a little, he thought. He asked after all of you, and as always, particularly for Papa Fox.

At the concert, we talked debates, etc., between numbers. Do you know, he has been working on the Richardson murder case, helping her counsel. He also said something about being in N.Y. next year; said he had had "several splendid" chances offered him in Boston, but they "paled before the great metropolis of N.Y." I don't know whether that means he graduates *[from Harvard Law]* this year, or not. I was so overcome, I didn't ask.

The concert was fine and he enjoyed it very much. It was so long, however, that there was no time to talk or show him much of Stone Hall or introduce any of the girls afterward. We didn't have more than 15 minutes here before the house closed at 10:30, and he had to leave. He thanked me very much for inviting him and said he had enjoyed it immensely. I told him I hoped he would come again now that he had found his way to Stone. There, I guess that will do for what S. said and what I said—I should have taken notes while he was "saying."

Your own loving "little girl"—Helen

March 1. My own dear ones—

I was ambitious and got up in time for breakfast this morning. Then Mary and I took a little walk, leaving Louise, Ethel and Margaret in my room "roosting" on my unmade bed. I was just about to make it when they came in and for some reason, decided not to let me. When I came back they had torn it all to pieces, draped all the chairs with blankets, piled my pillows with bed slippers on top in the window seat, etc.! I had to hustle to get things to rights before church!

I had Alice Dal. over for dinner today and had such a nice time with her. We see each other so little this year, as we are both busy, and Wilder and Stone seem so far apart. She got the proofs of her Senior pictures in cap and gown and they are <u>fine</u>. I am to have one, so you will see it. Nina just gave me a little "snap" her father took of her last fall.

This P.M. Louise, Miss Bliss and I went for a long walk and nearly blew away in the March wind. It was glorious!

We have had our first lecture by Prof. Warren of Harvard in Latin, and I think we shall like him immensely. It seems <u>great</u> to have a <u>man</u> in the classroom once more. He is a funny little man, about fifty, I should say, who makes a great many of the same gestures that Mr. S. did.

Then I went to a Domestic Science lecture and got lots of valuable hints about ventilation, etc., which I have promptly proceeded to put into effect. The speaker, Miss Davis, said that we were too much used to <u>very</u> much overheated rooms; that they ought to be from 65°–70° at the uttermost.

A letter from Frankie yesterday says he wants to come out some Sunday soon. <u>Now</u>, I wonder—where is <u>Charles Jones</u>?

And now—I'll say goodnight

With a heart full of love for all—Helen

March 3. My dear Mamma—

I have just come up from dinner and a house meeting for business in the parlor, have read some in "Othello" with the girls, have done my Latin, and had a few minutes call from Alice Dal. and Julia Ham *[another girl from N.H.]* and., it is only 9:30 now—don't you think I'm smart? Julia snatched up Mr. S.'s photo, exclaiming, "Where did you get this?" She says she has always known him, that is, known who he is, but never met him: wants to, if he comes out again!

Helen L. wrote about meeting me, when I go there to visit Sunday.

Said she meant to invite "Mr. Buck"—Ray—and offered to invite Artie, too. I'm quite eager to see Ray with his beard, tho' I <u>know</u> I won't like it.

Well, it's now nearly 9:45, so I'll say goodnight.

Your own "little girl"—Helen

March 16. My dear ones—

I am at Helen L.'s in Roxbury. She was so busy, I told her not to meet me, but I got out here all right. In the evening Helen had invited about 16 men and girls. They were awfully jolly—two of the men were at Harvard and two were at Tech. We played ping-pong and other games until almost Sunday morning! Helen and I got up just in time for church, and I met heaps of nice people.

Ray *[Buck, cousin]* came before dinner. And I <u>did</u> know him, and think his <u>beard</u> rather becoming—or would be, if he were older. Helen, Ray and I went in town to the Lenten service at the Emanuel Church, which was fine. Mott met us at the car and we came back here together. In the evening, we four <u>did dishes</u>! Then sat around the open fire, ate Helen's homemade candy, talked and "fooled." Ray is just as full of fun as ever and had a grand time teasing me about Artie!

I am going home early today to get started on my Bible paper. Wish I didn't have to. With love to all—Helen

March 19. My dear Mamma—

Well, I feel somewhat better to have that old Bible paper done and <u>in</u>. And I'm not feeling <u>nearly</u> so tired, in spite of working late on it, as I did before Xmas vacation. Guess the emulsion and Dr. Gross's iron pills are helping me.

Yesterday, stopping in town only long enough to buy me an umbrella, I went out to Melrose, staying at Winnie's last night for the first time since she and Walter were married. Helped her get supper, wash dishes, etc. We were both sleepy and went to bed about 9:15, leaving Walter type-writing. Guess he followed soon after. I went in town when Walter did in the morning and got out here at 9:15. Have been hustling ever since.

The birds are all here now and the flies, spiders and <u>moths</u>—one of the latter has just paid me a visit—and I heard the frogs tonight.

I had a note from Artie B. saying he was to be out this way Mon. and would call, if I were to be at home in the evening. I shan't be however, for

I'm going over to Cambridge to the Harvard-Yale debate! Not with Mr. S. or Charles, but with lots of other girls from here. Our table is nearly all going at Miss Hart's proposal. I think it will be great fun and very instructive as I am having debate work myself. Hope Harvard will win.

One week from tonight, I shall be home!

With tons of love—Your own "girl Goldie"

March 23. My dear ones—

Sat. P.M. I went to a little "tea" which Nina and Helen gave for a girl visitor of Helen's. In the evening there was a very cute little play at the Barn. Went to church with Louise and had Edna Taylor here for dinner, after which, we made fudge in Louise's room and she stayed until quite late. Then I wrote letters and in the evening, Mott and Frankie came. They were so late I'd almost given them up, but Frank had to go 'round by Norumbega to get his "bearings," he said.

Harriet Foss was in the choir (for Musical Vespers), so Louise helped me "take care" of them during the service; then we four and Harriet came back to the parlor here. We had <u>heaps</u> of fun. I shall never call either of them <u>bashful</u> again! Louise had kept some fudge and that made us all acquainted. We told stories, jokes, etc. It is so much nicer having <u>two</u> men and other girls than just <u>one</u> man, that I've decided to always have them by "couples" after this. They didn't leave until almost 9:45. I wish Ray could have come, too, but perhaps he will later with Helen L.

This afternoon we're going to the Shakespeare Masquerade—only <u>without</u> masks, I expect. Then, this evening, to Harvard, in a special electric car. Wonder if I shall run across Charles or Mr. S. at the big debate? Probably not—it would be like finding a needle in a haystack!

With heaps of love to all—Helen

March 25. My dear Mamma—

I <u>did</u> go to Harvard, even in that pouring rain, and it was a <u>glorious</u> debate! Harvard just "wiped the floor" with Yale and it was decidedly exciting. I thought once that I saw Mr. S. there, but decided on second thought, that it was a taller, <u>better-looking</u> man!

I found an express box, about the size of a shoe box at my door yesterday. I wondered if Papa had sent me some more shoes, then thought it must be a mistake. When I looked at the address, I saw that it was from

Artie B., and on opening it discovered a box of candy! "To help pass away the time till vacation," his card said. I suppose he had intended to bring it out if he had come to call, so sent it instead. Very acceptable, I'm sure.

Will get my trunk checked tomorrow. Then, day after, I'll see you all.

With a heart full of love—Your own Helen

SPRING VACATION

April 12. My dear ones—

Well doesn't it seem as if I'd been back for ages? I can't get reconciled to <u>write</u> everything again; talking is <u>so</u> much more satisfactory.

We arrived in a pouring rain, but all of "us girls" were back on time except Mary, who has a bad cold. I got all nicely settled yesterday, so begin to feel at home again—it always takes a few days.

I wish you all a Happy Easter! It has been a lovely "holiday-day" here. Prayers in the parlor after breakfast, after which Louise, Ethel, Miss Bliss and I went for a walk. It is just perfect here now—the grass <u>so</u> green, the trees coming out fast. It hardly seems possible that one week ago today at home, we were walking in <u>mud</u> and over <u>snow</u> with our heavy coats and furs on.

I looked quite "swell," dressed for church today, in my old light suit, my <u>new</u> hat, white waist, pink ribbon and a little turn over [?] and ribbon belt I bought yesterday. Lyman Abbot preached today—a fine Easter sermon. "Now is Christ risen from the dead and become the first fruits of them that sleep." He is such a grand old man. The Chapel was not over-decorated—just two beautiful large azaleas, one on either side of the pulpit and some low green plants on the communion table. There were some very pretty gowns worn and this P.M., everyone has been out walking in their finery.

I went over to Wilder for dinner with Edna Taylor. She is homesick and worried to death over a forensic subject for Debates—or rather, the <u>lack</u> of one!

I am glad I took Debates. I have ten out of twelve floor speeches made and don't expect to have another debate till June 11th.

Louise and I walked all the way to Natick yesterday, for the first time—about three miles. We rode back on the car.

Had a note from Frank inviting me to go to the theatre with him the 25th. Guess he got my wish by "mental telepathy."

Easter Vespers were <u>fine</u>—makes me cross to think Ray and Mott, whom I had asked, could not share them with me.

I'm getting sleepy so—

With much love to you all—Helen

April 16. My dear Mamma—

I went in town yesterday and bought me—at last!—my little tea kettle, a little beauty for $1.50. Haven't used it yet, as I have to get a permit. Went to Bible lecture in the evening and reception afterward. Tomorrow, I am invited by Miss Hart (the English Head) to meet Longfellow's daughter, Mrs. Thorpe, who is going to speak of her visit to the Ojibways and read selections from "Hiawatha."

I've just finished a long evening of study, and want to go to bed, but want you to know my mayflowers came and are <u>so</u> sweet. Thank you for them.

With a heart full of love—Helen

April 19. My own dear ones—

Dean Hodges preached this morning, an Easter sermon, so we have had <u>two</u> this year.

We have been out all afternoon. Peggy, *[Margaret?]*, Ethel, Louise and I have been reading "Othello," so we took the book and our capes to sit on. We walked down by the Charles River and came to an old boat half drawn up on the shore and moored, so we sat in it and read aloud awhile, then walked <u>up</u> the river. Several canoes passed us. It has been such a perfect, beautiful day, and has gone so quickly.

The supper bell has rung—

<u>After supper.</u> Mary, Louise and I have been out for another little walk— it is <u>so</u> lovely out now. I am up in Louise's room and she is writing <u>her</u> home letter, too.

Yesterday was <u>very</u> windy and the lake was covered with white caps and over by Hunnewell's, they were like real salt water waves. We walked over to see them and nearly blew away!

Harvard vacation began yesterday, so I suppose Charles went home, and very likely Mr. S. will go up to Milton, too. Oh— I had another letter from Frank, settling the theatre question. He suggested going in the evening and my staying with the Lancasters in Roxbury. I hated to ask to stay Sat. night, as that would be practically inviting myself for over Sunday, especially as I had been there so recently. I wrote him so He then arranged for the afternoon performance and hoped I would pardon him for being so <u>dense</u>!

I have learned that I can play field hockey if I buy some <u>special hockey shoes</u> to brace my ankles—for $5.00! As I probably shouldn't use them for much else, I don't think I shall play. But, I want to do something, so am going to join the golf club, otherwise, I'll have to pay 25¢ every time I play. So, will you please send me an order for clubs, Papa? I shall want three at $1.00 or $1.50 each and the balls, 25$ or 35¢, I believe. I will repay you out of my own money, so you needn't be afraid to trust me!

I am going to make myself a shirt-waist, Mamma. Peggy is going to show me how. She makes all her own clothes and has a sewing machine here—rented. So, you may expect me to come home a full-fledged dressmaker!

Must stop now and get to work on a Philosophy paper due Tuesday. With much love to all—Helen

April 22. My dear Mamma—

If I don't write coherently, it is because Louise and Ethel are here, talking debates. Thanks for all "the groceries" in my laundry bag; the girls were here for the "ceremony" of opening it, and we had great excitement opening the various things. The apples and oranges I like so much better than olives; they are <u>so good</u>.

For the last two mornings I have been all dressed for breakfast at 7:15 and have taken a little walk before breakfast! If only I can keep it up! And I mean to; unless I am an invalid, I shall rise earlier this summer than I have in past years.

It was Mary's birthday today, so we all clubbed together and bought her some flowers of the woman who sells them here every morning. Our housekeeper, whose room is opposite Mary's, came along as we were buying them and in learning for whom they were, began to praise Mary, and us for getting the flowers for her. Then, this P.M., she praised us to Mary, saying "Oh, I just love Miss Fox, she is such a nice girl!" So we all laughed and swapped compliments.

Saturday evening the Wellesley-Vassar return debate comes off <u>at Vassar</u>. I expect there will be much excitement here when we get the news—probably that night. Wish I were going. However, I shall be at the theatre with Frankie, which is <u>some</u> consolation.

With loads of love—Helen

April 26. My own dear ones—

We have lost the debate again—and yet not really again as everybody thought we really won last Fall and the judges were biased. They telegraphed the news about 10:30 last evening. But, as there was no account of the debate in the papers, that's all we know—that we lost.

We sent the debaters off Friday morning at 8:30 A.M. and nearly the whole college was at the train to see them off. We cheered and waved till the train went round the curve. Then Saturday morning, the other girls—about 100—went. I didn't go down to the station then, as I had a Physics Quiz, but we saw all the girls from Stone off with much cheering.

I have hated myself ever since, to think I didn't plan to go, or at least ask you if I might. It is such a grand opportunity to see Vassar—another college, as a college girl. But, today I'm glad I'm not there, as it must be dreadfully hard for the poor girls to keep their spirits up.

Here, as we waited for the news, about all the 700 girls who didn't go were at College Hall, talking, singing and playing games, to pass the time we even "went through Harriet," that is, crawled underneath the chair on which Harriet Marteneau's statue sits. *[Harriet Martineau (1802-1876) was an English intellectual, who, in her writings, popularized classical economics, favoring a Utopian system. She espoused the Abolition Movement in 1897 after traveling in the United States.—Encyclopedia Britannica Online.]* Finally, Kate Lord, the Student Government Pres. came out from the telegraph office and you could have heard a pin drop. She merely said, "Well girls, Vassar won." And everyone gasped. Then she said, "Let's cheer for Vassar!" And we did, a good generous cheer, tho' it almost choked us. Then we cheered for Wellesley and the different debaters. Then everyone waited, and Kate said, "Well girls, do you want to cheer any more?" And no one did. I guess we were all too stunned. It didn't seem as if we could lose this time. I felt cross at first, it seemed so unjust. But, in a way, I think it will be a good thing for us; it will just make us more loyal to each other and to the college. Outsiders won't understand that we have not had the practice in debating that Vassar has had, and it may lower their opinion of Wellesley. That's what's the hardest. We'll just have to work all the harder next year to make up for this year and last by a wide margin!

It seems ages since I went in town on the 1:07 yesterday. Frank met me at the station and we went directly to the theatre. It was a pretty, bright play which I enjoyed very much. As he wanted me to stay in for supper, I did. We did not go to the Touraine, but to the Essex, just across the street from the station, so I wouldn't miss my train. *[The Essex also was then one of the better hotels in town.]* Papa, next Friday, our $10.00 registration fee for next year is due, so please be <u>sure</u> to send it in time. (I came very near forgetting it!) Then, a week from Thurs., we draw for rooms again. I hope we all get good numbers and can get to Wilder or Norumbega. I'd rather come back here than go on the Hill alone. I really like Stone very much, even better, since vacation. The fare has been better, I have a new bed spring, and it <u>is</u> lovely here by the lake in the Spring.

Goodnight to you all—and much love—Helen

April 29. My precious Muddie—

I've been afflicted with that horrible sore throat (like what you said everyone at home is having, I guess.) It came on Sat. and at first, I thought it was only the effects of all that cheering. I dosed well that night and Sunday and Monday and now it is nearly all gone. Tell Papa they ought to get *[for the store]* some Hydrogen Peroxide, or Dioxogen, it's called, put up by the Oakland Chem. Co., N.Y. It's great for sore throats.

There is to be a party at the table tonight; Miss Hart entertains some of the other English faculty, so I must stop now and dress in my <u>challis</u>.

Well, the party's over. Went into the reception room a few minutes afterward to see Nina's Howard who was spending the afternoon and evening with her. (You remember him from Freshman year.)

Oh, our defeat in the debate wasn't as bad after all. When the girls got back Monday eve. they said it was <u>very</u> close; the judges were out a half hour and our girls did <u>grandly</u>, so we're all happy once more!

Yesterday was election of Student Gov. President, and very exciting. We have a dandy girl, our own last year's class president. Friday is May Day, then, in the evening, President Hazard gives a reception for the Juniors. Everything seems to come at once.

It is so <u>hot</u>, I think I'll make some lemonade to cool off, then go to bed.

With stacks of love to all—Helen

May 1. My dear Muddie—

Have just come in from the May Party. It was so cold that I didn't wear my little dress after all, but was a boy again in my gym suit, with a shirt waist under it for warmth. *[Sweaters seem not worn much in the early 1900's as they have never been mentioned in three years of letters. They seemed, rather, to keep warm by adding layers of warm clothing <u>under</u> thin ones, as* *needed.]* It was just as pretty a party as ever, Lots of the girls wore low neck and short sleeved dresses. I should think they would have frozen! They had ice cream, candy, etc. to sell, a hurdy-gurdy, jump-ropes, etc., so it was like a real play ground. This morning all the Seniors rolled their hoops down the hill from College Hall to Chapel. It was quite exciting to watch them and realize that <u>next</u> year <u>we</u> will be doing that.

I hate to think of it, in some ways. We are so happy now and I even think, <u>carefree</u>, as you say, tho' sometimes it seems as if we had <u>cares</u> enough. I just try to appreciate and make the most of it all while I'm here and just think of what it will be to look back on!

Well, I have had dinner, went down in my little boy suit, danced with the other "children" in the parlour and been to Miss Hazard's "informal" evening! We had such a nice time at her house, looking at her pretty and interesting things, and she has <u>so</u> many; eating and singing and hearing her play. She remembered me, said it seemed nice to see some familiar faces.

Well, this has been a lovely, long day, and having been several different persons, I feel pretty tired, so think I'll say goodnight.

With <u>stacks</u> of love for you all—Helen

May 7. My dear Mamma—

Our class meeting yesterday was the most exciting one I ever knew. Two of the different societies had banded together to "<u>run</u>" college next year. They got control of Student Gov. thro' the elections and attempted to elect one of their number as Senior Class President. It was a <u>fight</u>, I tell you, but we finally won and elected this year's Pres. again.

Today I have drawn for my "room number" and it seems as if Fate is against me, for I got 163! Louise has <u>39</u> and Mary <u>48</u>. Mine has dropped to 129, however, and that is really not too bad for a Senior. We may all come back here. If so, I shall not feel badly, as I have liked it here—much better since Easter, so I'm going to make the best of it.

With a heartfull of love for all—Helen

May 10. My dear ones—

At last I have some good news—grand! I have the honor to announce that <u>Helen G. Fox</u> is on the <u>Honor List</u> as a <u>Wellesley College Scholar</u>! It is a higher honor than that of Freshman year—in fact, there is only one higher, the <u>Durant Scholar</u>, which only the <u>very</u> brightest, really "geniuses" get. There are only three in the class of 1903 and six in our class. I am really very proud and glad to get <u>Wellesley</u>. I had hoped I might, but hadn't really worked for it and was much afraid my work wasn't good enough. Even now, I think it almost a matter of luck. I know lots of girls who didn't get it. Mr. Smith, I think, is something of a prophet. He said I would be among the first twenty in my class and there are just twenty-one on the Durant and Wellesley College lists together! Isn't it a queer coincidence?

Louise and Edna Taylor are <u>Wellesley</u>, too, and <u>Mary</u> is <u>Durant</u>! How it even happened, I don't know; she doesn't study hard at all! I always knew she was very bright, but now I know she is a **genius**! We are all so proud of her, even more than of ourselves.

I have been appointed proctor; have to hush people, in other words, for the rest of the year, which I don't consider a particular honor! It hasn't been very bad or disagreeable, however.

Our honors were announced yesterday morning, with great "pomp" at Chapel. In the P.M. we celebrated by going in town to see Viola Allen in "<u>The Eternal City</u>," and had very good seats for 25¢. She was perfectly grand! Afterwards, we went thro' the public gardens where the tulips are just one blaze of color. Then, last evening, the Sophomores gave a little Japanese play, which was pretty as could be.

Today, Dr. Albert D. Lyman of Brooklyn preached a fine sermon on "self knowledge, self control and self denial." This afternoon we went for a walk and picked some lovely violets. This evening, Mrs. Ballington Booth of the Salvation Army spoke at Chapel of the work they are doing in prisons.

Tomorrow, we choose rooms. I think Mary, Louise and I will try for Wilder or Norumbega, They will be able to go to either all right, I think, and I can probably get there on application. I will let you know, as I know you will be anxious to hear.

Tomorrow evening I have invited Arthur Brackett to a concert by the Elocution Dept., Then I must have Frankie out, and my "debts" will be paid. Charles Jones, I guess, has entirely forgotten me, And I'm wondering when those baseball games Mr. S. spoke of begin!

With a great deal of love for you all—Helen

May 12. My dear Mamma—

Artie B. came out last evening —about 8:30—missed the 6:20 train so had to take the car. I was getting a little cross, but we managed to get seats in the gallery and the concert lasted until 9:45, so we heard quite a bit of it. But, he didn't have any time to stay afterwards before the closing bell. He has shaved off his mustache and looks "queer," but really better, I think.

I have chosen my room—22 Norumbega, a very pleasant west room on the third floor almost opposite my last year's room. I shall apply for a change to Wilder, as both Mary and Louise are to be there. I shan't feel so awfully bad, even if I don't get changed, as Norumbega will seem so homelike and there are to be some very nice girls there..

With stacks of love for all—Helen

May 14. My dear Muddie—

We are having our first real thunderstorm and it is a hard one. Louise and I turned the lights off just now, to watch the lightning. It is so vivid that it shows up even the green of the grass, and strange to say, now that there's no one to keep me up, it doesn't make me feel sleepy as usual. *[This remark refers to the ritual at home; when a thunder storm occurred at night, even if all were in bed, the whole family dressed, came downstairs and sat it out in the sitting room, until it was over. In case of a strike, they could then <u>perhaps</u> help save some of the contents of the store, the P.O. and Papa Fox's office. Saving <u>anything</u> from fires in country areas at that time was nearly impossible. And buildings were totally lost. But they wished to be ready "in case."]*

Well, yesterday, I was a "widow in deep mourning"! The last forensics for the year went in then. All the girls who took them went to Chapel with powdered hair (to show how hard they had worked) and in <u>white</u> to celebrate. All we debaters wore black, as our work is not over yet. I borrowed a black waist and wore it with my black skirt. They tell me I should always wear black, as it becomes me!

Well, my proctor duties are over for tonight, as the 9:45 bell has rung. So I'll get to bed early. With tons of love—"girl Goldie"

[A visit to Aunt Abbie's.]
May 24. My own dear ones—

Well, I did a little shopping in town and got the material for my white dress—8 yards (very wide) of very fine India lawn at 50¢ and 5 yds. at 17¢ for a drop skirt. I shall have it made at home. I also got me a very pretty sailor hat for common. They are being worn quite a lot this year.

The exams were posted Thurs. I have only two the last Tues. and Weds., June 16 and 17, so I shall have from the 11th to study, rest, etc. I can't decide whether to stay for Commencement, may have to "toss up." As you say, it would be well for me to stay and see what I shall have to do next year, etc. I'm glad you won't mind my going to Nina's. I think it will make a nice "vacation."

With a heartfull of love for all——Helen

May 28. My dear Muddie—

Nina and I are planning to start about 5:00 tomorrow P.M. There is to be a little party tomorrow evening, so I shall have a chance to meet some of her friends. Then Sat. (and Sunday, perhaps) we shall go driving with her father and be generally lazy! I shall wear my light suit and sailor hat, take my blue dimity for tomorrow evening, a white shirt-waist for Sunday with my suit and my blue shirtwaist dress to wear "around the house." I hope it will be pleasant, so we can have a good time out doors.

We have to make out our schedules for next year by June 6. Is there anything you would especially like me to take? I intend to take some more Latin and German, but am undecided about other things. I think some of Geology 1, or 2 and 3 of Economics, and of Lit 1 or 14. You can look them up in the catalogue, and give me your advice. I don't think I'll take over 13 or 14 hours. Don't worry about my going to Ayer with Nina. I'll be very careful about "electric cars and things" as I always am.

Goodnight——Your own little girl——Helen

[Visit to Nina's Home in Ayer.]
May 31. My own dear ones—

Well, I feel as if college were closed and we were off on a prolonged vacation! I have had the <u>best</u> <u>time</u> and my brain feels quite rested! We got here about 7:00 P.M., hungry as two bears. Mrs. Hill didn't know just when to expect us, but had supper all ready. Then, we dressed, I in my blue dimity, to go to the party. It was a little dance gotten up by the young people in Nina's set. Howard called for us, then Mr. and Mrs. Hill came up later. I met nearly all the boys and girls and like them very much. You should have seen me dance! I really got on very well. Two of the boys I had met when I was here before and at the beach Freshman summer, so we all felt quite well acquainted, and I had a <u>fine</u> time.

Yesterday Nina's father took me out for a little drive while she went to see her aunts. Later Phil Wilder, a Worcester boy, came over on his wheel to spend the day. Then Mr. Hill drove us over to Shirley where we watched a baseball game and I got quite enlightened on the game, with Mr. H. and Phil as coaches. Last evening Howard came over and Phil (who is a cousin to Nina) decided he could stay all night if he left at 6:00 A.M. this morning.

This morning, instead of church, we went up to Mr. Hill's farm— Nina, her grandmother, her father and myself. It was <u>lovely</u>. we wandered about—even found a few wild strawberries—in <u>May</u>! Then, this afternoon, we drove down by the river to another farm on which Mr. H. has a mortgage. After leaving the horses there, we walked farther down the river banks.

Nina is majoring in Botany, and her father knows quite a little about it, also about animals. We found plenty to interest us in the trees, flowers, several turtles and a muskrat!

This evening, we have been to Meeting and then Nina played and sang for awhile. Now, she and Howard are "cooing" in the next room. They have all been so nice to me and made me feel perfectly at home. And I have enjoyed <u>so</u> much all the drives with their horses. Tomorrow, we will be driving some more, about the town, as Nina has to draw a map of the town and locate the different trees on the streets for Botany. We shall go back to Wellesley about 4:30.

Nina has just asked me if I'm writing a novel, and says to tell you she has tried to take good care of me, but one of the boys whom I met before appears to be much "crushed," came home with us Fri. night, and is going to see us on the train tomorrow; he is an express agent, so will be <u>on</u> the train! The joke of it is, he is quite a noted flirt, so I imagine he thinks he has made an impression !

Good night now— "Your own "little girl" Helen

June 3. My dear Muddie—

Well, "the child is born" as Papa Fox says! I have just finished my article for the Nute paper on "Wellesley in General," and feel quite proud. I shall go over it tomorrow and copy it to send to Miss Berry. *[Her English teacher at Nute.]* Considering the vagueness of the subject, I feel it is quite decent.

A letter from Eunice came with the news of Alice's graduation and that they had both learned to dance and hoped I wouldn't be shocked if I <u>didn't</u>. Funny, wasn't it, when I had just made <u>my</u> dancing debut? *[Eunice and Alice, sisters, were Buck cousins living in Washington, D.C. Many years later, Alice's daughter, Janet Bragaw was in <u>my</u> class 1935 at Wellesley, but* *transferred and graduated from Radcliffe.]* She says they expect to come North again this summer.

I also had a very short letter from Charles Jones. He thought I had owed him one. He said he had been ill about all Spring—neuritis, I think, tho' he said "it hurts as badly as if they called it something else!" He doesn't get thro' at Harvard till the 17th. Mr. S. still remains to be heard from. I suppose he is very busy now, studying for his law exams. I'm afraid those "fine ball-games" won't materialize—at least for me!

Tomorrow comes the chief excitement of Junior year; the burning of our forensics and debates, or rather, the useless notes etc. We are to burn them on a somewhat open space by the Charles River accompanied by Mr. Perkins, the <u>one man</u> about college and several policemen to guard against the fires spreading, at about 8:00 P.M. The time and place are kept secret, if possible, from those prying Sophs, who follow to see if they can. Afterward, we march back in sheets and pillow cases, carrying candles and singing a Latin dirge written for the occasion. It is a weird sight, as you may imagine. Then Friday is Tree Day—all the excitement comes in a lump!

You didn't give me any advice about my next year's courses, so I take it that you have no special suggestions. I talked with Miss Walton, my Latin teacher, and she advised me. She said my work in Latin had been excellent, that I ought to continue with it <u>after</u> graduating, and that she would like to see me going to some Roman School!

The 9:45 bell just rang, so I'll say goodnight to you all,
  With heaps of love—Helen

June 4. Dear Papa Fox—

This is a "business letter." I'm awfully ashamed to write it for fear you'll think me <u>dreadfully</u> careless, but I don't see <u>how</u> it happened. I want you to stop payment on that $6.00 check you sent me a week ago. Don't be too alarmed, for I think it is burned up. I put it in one corner of my desk drawer under some papers until my new hat should come, to pay for it. I intended to put it in my money bag, when I went to Nina's and thought I did, but couldn't have, as I wore it and didn't open it while I was there, but the check isn't in it now. I have looked everywhere in my room for it. Today, when I wanted to send it for my hat, I first discovered its loss. I don't think anyone would take it unendorsed.

I <u>never</u> have lost anything. I think I must have torn it up with some papers—it is blue, the same color as this stationery—and thrown it in my waste basket, which I empty almost every day. I can't think of any other explanation unless I hid it in my sleep!

So, if you will stop payment and send me another check, I'll not let it out of my sight! Please don't think me so <u>dreadfully</u> careless!

With love to all, Helen

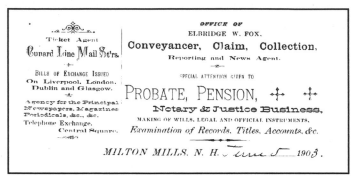

<OFFICE OF>
ELBRIDGE W. FOX,
Conveyancer, Claim, Collection,
Reporting and News Agent.

Ticket Agent
Cunard Line Mail St'rs

BILLS OF EXCHANGE ISSUED
On Liverpool, London,
Dublin and Glasgow.

Agency for the Principal
Newspapers, Magazines
Periodicals, &c., &c.
Telephone Exchange,
Central Square.

SPECIAL ATTENTION GIVEN TO
PROBATE, PENSION,
Notary & Justice Business,
MAKING OF WILLS, LEGAL AND OFFICIAL INSTRUMENTS,
Examination of Records, Titles, Accounts, &c.

MILTON MILLS, N. H. June 5 190*3*.

Papa Fox's Letterhead

June 5, 1903.

My dear Helen Gertrude,

I am sending you enclosed a <u>duplicate</u> check for $6—in place of the one you think has been lost. If the <u>original</u> one comes to light please return it to me without delay. Be a little more careful in handling checks as a careless use of them might cause some needless trouble and great inconvenience.

All well at home.—

With heaps of love I continue as ever, Elbridge

June 8. My own dear ones—

I want to thank <u>you</u>, Papa Fox, for sending me the other check, which is safe in my money bag, and for not scolding me. I <u>will</u> be more careful. The first check hasn't ever turned up; I feel sure I tore it up when it got in the trash, so it's safe.

I feel as bright as a pin! Lucky, for I have a busy day before me—a debate to write out, German to get, <u>hair</u> and <u>stockings</u> to wash. Then there is a Crew contest at 10:00 and a reception from 4-6 that I want to take in.

Tree Day was one of the loveliest ever. First in the procession came the Seniors in cap and gown, then we Juniors in white with big bunches of violets and white or violet parasols. (I got a white one.) The Sophs., dressed to represent all the old fairy tales and lastly, the Freshmen all in different shades of blue with gauze veils of all colors to represent clouds, and their dancers in white, as stars. Their dance was one of the loveliest I ever saw! The Seniors' was much more elaborate, but no lovelier. Alice Dalrymple was one of the Senior dancers, and very cute in a little short, low-necked yellow dress. After it was over, there was cheering, singing class songs, etc. plus a collation—lots of good things to eat.

Then in the evening, our class planted the ivy, which only the <u>even</u> Junior classes plant, and the Seniors serenaded. It was a lovely day and I'm glad I have one more to look forward to.

Well, I've passed in my next year's schedule of courses. I shall keep on with Latin and German, but everything else is new; Art 3, Elocution (I'm going in for <u>some</u> <u>culture</u>, you see). Then for some practical things, Economics and Geology 3 (Phys., Geography) I think it will be a very interesting, helpful course and not a hard one—not as many hours as this year.

Tomorrow is our last recitation day. And Friday, Nina and I are going to Melrose for the day—our long-planned visit to Winnie.

I shall keep my new hat to wear for Garden Party, if I get an invitation. Alice D. is going to invite me to something, but doesn't know what just yet. I think I shall stay over the 21st for the Bac. sermon; that will give me plenty of time to see things and to pack-up.

With a great deal of love to you all. Your "Girl Goldie"

June 11. My dear Mamma—

I intended to write last night, but one of the girls came in and stayed until after 10:00 P.M. telling me of her love affairs, etc., and I really couldn't send her home; then such things are always quite interesting!

My debate work is all done and sent in yesterday. Tues. was our last day of recitations as Juniors, just think! Yesterday Louise and I went in town for about 2 hours and I finally found a tea table for Winnie. Bamboo, like mine, for $1.25. The stores are full of lovely things now—it makes one long for a fortune! Still, it's fun to pretend and pick out what you'd like.

I wrote Frank Lee yesterday and invited him out to Float. Shall invite Winnie and Walter, too.

Miss Berry was much pleased with my paper about Wellesley for the Nute paper, but didn't say when it was to be published. *[I checked with Nute, but they have no records before 1916.]*

Must stop now and get this in the 10:10 A.M. mail, so you'll have it this evening. Heaps of love—Helen

June 14. My dear Papa Fox—

We took a walk yesterday and found some <u>pink</u> sweet clover and wild roses. I never saw so much sweet clover, which grows by the road-side nearly all the way to Natick.

The preacher at church Sunday was Dr. Palmer of Andover, a brother of Alice Freeman Palmer's husband. However, I thought him not as interesting as Professor Palmer.

I went over to Alice D.'s for a little while. She, too, is thro' work now and is busy arranging things for next week. Her aunt comes tomorrow and her father and brother are coming for Commencement. She invited me to Garden Party, Glee Club Concert and the Senior Play, which I think is awfully good of her. I shall make her let me pay for the play ticket, at least, as she has <u>so</u> <u>many</u> expenses. I think I shall wear <u>burlap</u> all next year to save up for Commencement!

Tons of love for all—Helen

June 19. My dear Mamma—

Senior Play this evening.

I have made my plans for coming home at last, and don't plan to change. I am going to pack things up to Mon. evening, so shan't leave here till Tues., sending my trunk Tues. morning. Then, Louise and I are going into town together right after lunch. I have a little shopping left to do (Mamma Fox's gloves, etc.) Then Louise is leaving for home and I shall go to Winnie's for overnight; then come up on the 4:00 P.M. train Weds.

I shall need travel money plus a little more for storage, which must be paid in advance—$1.00 or more, and 75¢ or $1.00 to get my trunk home.

You don't know how glad I shall be to get <u>home</u>! It seems perfect ages since I've seen you all, and I shall have so much to tell you. Am going to talk a <u>week</u>, then <u>sleep</u> and <u>eat</u> a month!

With a heartfull of love for all—Your own "little girl," Helen

END OF JUNIOR YEAR

SENIOR YEAR, 1903-1904

FIRST SEMESTER

Sept. 20, 1903. My dear ones—

Well, here I am back once more in Norumbega, for I wasn't changed after all. It is horrid to be separated from Louise and Mary, but it seems delightfully homelike here, and I am already beginning to feel acquainted with and like the girls here. And it seems so good to see all the "old" girls again.

Norumbega, Senior Year Dorm

Went direct to College Hall when I got here, to register and "learn my fate" as to my room. Miss Tufts *[from Dover, NH—had a niece in my class—1935]* remembered me and was perfectly lovely—as sweet as the old registrar was cold. She said she was sorry that she had been unable to make all the changes. I told her that as I hadn't had much hope, I wasn't much disappointed. I met Louise there and we came over to the Hill together.

Mrs. Newman was very glad to see me back and sent up some egg and milk, so with the malted milk I had in Boston, I didn't go hungry. My room is the one I chose, a very pleasant west room with one window on the third floor, near the stairs and bathroom. The wardrobe is built into the wall, closet style. The bureau is plain-topped, and the bed is very comfortable, with a woven wire spring.

We went over to the reception a little while last evening, but I was pretty tired, so came back early and was in bed by 9:30. My cake hasn't been cut yet and Louise gave me a box of candy, which I haven't opened. *[Helen's birthday was September 19.]*

I woke up at 7:30 this morning and breakfasted on hot water, cream of wheat, graham bread and milk. My trunks were brought up this morning and I have taken out skirts, waists and pillows. My chair and box are here, too, so I can get quite nicely settled tomorrow.

Went to church this morning with Louise and Mary, heard a fine sermon and wore my new dress, which they thought very pretty and my pearl chain.

I am not going over to College Hall to telephone you tonight, as it's 8:00 P.M. and I might not be able to get through to you then. Oh—I have just thought—I have forgotten to bring <u>Mr.</u> <u>Smith's</u> <u>picture</u>! What <u>shall</u> I do? Please send immediately!

Well—I hope you are all not too tired, are all resting and have written me today.

Goodnight—With a heart full of love for all,

Your own "little girl" Helen

Sept. 22. My dear "Muddie Dee"

It is 8:30 and I am seated in kimono and slippers under the electric light in the center of my room, as cozy as you please. There has been a vast change in my room since yesterday—everything put away and done but for putting up curtains and pictures.

Louise came over just as I was finishing dressing at 7:30 this morning on her way to College Hall for cap and gown. We all were much afraid that they wouldn't come in time for our first appearance in them at Chapel this morning. For once, we were lucky and they came all right. We went over for them before breakfast, then got ourselves "rigged up" in them. They are really quite becoming to most everybody. Made me feel very dignified at first, but I declare, the longer I wear them, the more "Freshmany and dressed up in Mamma's clothes" I feel. My white pique skirt and white waist with embroidery down the front looked quite "swell" under the gown.

Louise and I were the last in line, as we were late, which tickled Helen Peck almost to death (she knows my tendency to lateness), for I was ready first.

Miss Hazard spoke beautifully to us of our duty and honor, service and loyalty to Wellesley. I saw her afterwards and she stopped to shake hands and called me by name, so I felt quite honored.

The rest of the day, I've spent getting books, fixing schedules and going to classes. I think I shall like my work very much and don't think it will be dreadfully hard, tho' more is expected of Seniors. I don't intend to <u>overwork</u>, however.

With stacks of love to you all—Your own "Girl Goldie"

Sept. 24. My dear Mamma—

I've been back almost a week! It's beginning to seem almost natural to study again. I haven't been overburdened, yet it really takes about a week to get ready to start in.

I feel very grand indeed in my cap and gown, quite as if I were favoring my instructors to go to class at all, and as for lessons, why it seems as if they ought to be content with a Senior's <u>looks</u> and not ask her embarrassing questions!

My appetite is back and I am hungry all the time. We get really <u>good</u> things to eat. I wish Mamma Fox could have some of our chocolate ice cream. They still put out the milk in the evening before bedtime, so I can get my four glasses a day.

I heard from "Frankie-Dee" today. His vacation begins Oct. 3 and he wants to come out here that evening as he expects to go to New York the next day. Guess I'll have to let him; he's pretty good and doesn't bother me much. "Artie" hasn't shown up yet. I'm going to mail this and get my glass of milk.

With much love to you all—Helen

Sept. 28. My dear ones—

Louise and I and two other girls went to church. I couldn't see the minister because of <u>hats</u>—the girls have taken a fancy to wear them to church this year. As the sermon wasn't particularly interesting, I found my mind wandering in a shocking manner to <u>clothes</u>!

It's so funny in this half-way season; the girls wear everything from white dresses, very thin and chiffon hats, to heavy suits and felt hats! I even saw a feather boa today! I wore my new linen dress again, as my white one had no dress shields.

I took dinner at Wilder with Louise and enjoyed it immensely. You see, we do manage to be together most of the time, even if we do live in different houses. This P.M. we went down to the ville to call on a Freshman she knows, who lives in the new village dormitory, the "<u>Noanett</u>" which is very swell.

Last evening was the Barn Swallow Reception. I took Grace Mosely, the Needham Freshman who was *[cousin]* Beulah's chum. She is a very nice little girl indeed and we quite enjoyed the evening in spite of the dreadful crowd.

We had the funniest experience last evening. While I was undressing about 9:45, the electric lights suddenly went off—the whole house! Leaving us all in the same predicament and there were various laughs and screams. Soon, I thought of my candle and, as luck would have it, I had a box of matches. So, I lighted it and then dispensed matches to all who were lucky enough to have candles. After flashing on and off again several times the lights <u>finally</u> came on again and everybody went to bed.

Now, we are having a thunderstorm which I hope will make it cooler! My room is going to be a warm one, as the afternoon sun comes in beautifully and so does the <u>heat</u>, even with the register <u>closed</u>! So you needn't worry about my taking cold!

With a heartful of love, Helen

Sept. 30. My own Muddie—

Went into town with Mary and Louise yesterday and had great fun shopping. They were getting curtains and things for their rooms. I got a very pretty kimono, blue bound with ribbon, for $1.30 and a pretty little corset cover.

Last evening was the Freshman Concert, the Albion Quartette and Hoffman, violinist. It was grand. Today, I had my first "declamation" in Elocution, tho' that's a rather dignified name for it—a one minute description which we had to get up and say before the class. I chose Addie

Day's little boy, the "Yellow Kid" and made them all laugh, and Miss Chamberlain, the teacher, said, "good, <u>very</u> good." Feel as if I were "speaking pieces" in school once more.

I continue to like the girls here very much. The girl right across the hall from me, Katharine Macy, is especially nice. She is a new Senior from Iowa, whose father is instructor of Economics at Iowa College. He and her mother are staying in Boston right now and tonight Miss Hazard had them out here to dinner at her home and Katharine went over, too. Isn't that great?

I shall have to let her know when <u>you</u> come down, Mamma. Don't forget that you <u>are</u> coming now, will you?

Lots of love to all—Helen

Oct. 4. My own dear ones—

Today has seemed short, as do most Sundays here. After breakfast and prayers, Mary, Louise, Carrie (one of the Seniors here—a dear little Vermont girl) and I went for a walk before church. As it was really warm, I wore my white dress for the first time and didn't even need my little blue shawl. Dr. Hall of Union Theological preached today. He was very interesting and I had no trouble keeping my mind on what he was saying, tho' I couldn't see him for all the <u>hats</u>.

Well, Frankie came out last evening and we had a very good time. He said something about this being Mr. Smith's last year at Harvard, so I guess he must still be in Cambridge. Frank wants me to come in to the theatre some evening this month. I told him perhaps I could arrange to stay overnight with Helen Lancaster. It would be quite a dissipation to go to the theatre in the evening!

Between books, ticket-books, etc., my money is swallowed up. And please send enough so I can go in town this week to get my Fall hat. I ought to be able to get one for about $3.00 or $4.00.

A heartfull of love to all—Helen

P.S. Did Herm *[a Buck cousin]* tell you that I had taken up the study of farming? I wrote him for some information about it for Economics. It's a fine study and I'm learning lots from it.

Oh dear, a horrid "beast" has flown in my window and is swooping around my electric light. I'm going to turn it off, leave my hall door open, while I put this in the mail and see if I can lose him.

Oct. 6. My own dear Mamma—

Since I last wrote, I have been to the beach! The geology class went on an excursion to Winthrop yesterday—only 10¢ for the round trip. We left here at 8:13 *[either by train or trolley]*, then by ferry across Boston Harbor, and a cute little narrow gauge railway train arriving at Winthrop about 9:30. We "camped" awhile on "Great Head" getting a grand view of Shirley Point, Deer Island and Marblehead, and enjoyed the glorious sea breeze. Then we went down on the beach and walked along the base of the cliff. I took it all in—breeze, view and lecture and enjoyed it immensely. Got back here about 2:45 and spent the rest of the P.M. studying. In the evening, went to an Astronomy lecture, which everyone expected to be short and interesting. But it proved to be long and boresome and I nearly died of sleepiness.

So—goodnight, with heaps of love—Helen

Oct. 11. My own dear ones—

Prof. Palmer of Harvard, Alice Freeman Palmer's husband, preached. I liked him very much. His text was "And Jesus increased in wisdom and in stature and in favor with God and man." He spoke of the three purposes of college life; the gaining of wisdom, of physical development and of the making of friends.

This P.M. Mary came by, I changed to my walking skirt and we went for a short walk in spite of the rain, which came on worse than ever. There are musical Vespers tonight But I didn't care enough about going to change my skirt for the fifth time today!

Don't worry, Mamma, about doing the little petticoats I sent home in my laundry, for I have put on a flannel one.

I hope you have good luck in getting a hat. I shan't be able to get into town to look for mine this week, as I have no end of work. Saturday, I have my first real "piece" in Elocution (pity me)! I have taken it from "The Land of the Lingering Snow," which I have had out of the library ever since I came back. I shall feel a little like a school girl once more. Do you remember how I always used to have to learn my pieces the last minute?

I had a funny little letter from Charles Jones telling me how he is located at Harvard and saying he wants me to go to a game later on with him—actually, he said "he hoped to have the pleasure of my company!" Isn't Charles improving. I also had a letter from Helen L., planning a party she is giving.

Louise is over and we have just finished studying Economics. Don't you hope I'll learn to be more economical, if such a thing is possible? Had Art, Lab. work today and am getting on very well. You'd be surprised to see the fine hand I drew.

With heaps of love for all—

Your own "Girl Goldie"

Oct. 18. My own dear ones—

I didn't get up until 10:00 this morning! And missed church for the first time this year. I didn't have any hat to wear—haven't had time to go in town to buy a new Fall one, and was ashamed to wear a straw one so late. So I stayed home and watched it <u>pour</u>! Yesterday it poured harder than I ever saw it and I got completely drenched, just going over to College Hall for my 1:30 class. I went into one of the girls' rooms and she fitted me out with dry stockings, shoes, petticoat and skirt.

I went over to Wilder to dinner with Edna Taylor and then to a play at the Barn. It was a cute little thing, written by one of the 1903 girls. I feel quite as if I had <u>two</u> <u>homes</u> here at college this year—this, and Wilder.

Went for a walk to the ville with Mary, and we stopped at Miss White's, where she called on a girl she knew, and I visited with Miss White. She looks just the same and was very glad to see me, but is as hard to say <u>goodbye</u> to as ever. Then Edna came over to have supper with me. Haven't had much time to miss Louise, who was home for the week-end.

I've had two souvenir postals from Frank Lee; the Brooklyn Bridge and Central Park. He wrote again about going to the theatre. Artie B. still hasn't shown up, but will be coming to Helen L.'s Halloween party.

If you haven't sent laundry—I forgot to say—please send a <u>big</u> bottle of <u>grain</u> alcohol as we aren't allowed to burn <u>wood</u> alcohol this year.

A goodnight and love to all—Helen

Oct. 25. My own dear ones—

I have just come back from Musical Vespers. It was so restful to listen with the lights all turned off in the Chapel proper, just a little light way up in the gallery by the organ.

After breakfast today, we went into Mrs. Newman's room and she showed us literally <u>stacks</u> of beautiful pictures which her brother took, mostly in the western part of the state; some of the Mohawk Valley, and some here.

Edna & I went out walking this P.M. and came back just after sunset. The reflections on the lake were lovely. We came back to hot chocolate and your good cake, Mamma—the first time I've used my little kettle this year.

This weather is getting pretty cold for a little jacket and I should freeze, getting home for my coat, so you'll simply <u>have</u> to <u>bring</u> it down! Can't you plan to come this week or next? You promised to come this Fall.

With a heart full of love—Your own "Girl Goldie"

Oct. 27. My dear Muddie Dee—

I have just finished writing to <u>Mr. Smith</u>! Now, aren't you curious? Well, the unexpected has happened at last, and "Prof. A.T." has reported. I had a nice little note from him yesterday, inviting me to the Dartmouth-Harvard game Nov. 14th. He wrote this early, he said, to be sure to get ahead of any other engagement I might make! You can imagine how surprised I was after such a long silence. He is still in Cambridge. Of course, as I have <u>no</u> previous engagement, I shall be most delighted to go, and have just written a note to that effect, also inviting him to call, as I suppose was the proper thing for me to do. *[To "call" does not refer to the telephone—an instrument rarely used, but to come out to Wellesley to pay a call].*

I certainly seem to be in great demand just now; had a note from Frank inviting me in to the theatre some evening this week or next. (I shan't go till next). Then Sat. A.M. is the Carlisle game, to which Charles Jones partially invited me. I didn't write to accept until Sunday, not knowing it was so soon, so maybe he's huffy and won't take me. If he does, I shall have to go out to Helen L.'s for the Halloween party directly afterwards. Wish they weren't on the same day. Expect Artie will put in a plea when I see him at the party, from what I hear thro' Helen Thomas here, who knows a man who knows him, he is not seriously offended. Oh, it's hard to be so "popular"!

Should you think I could <u>study</u> <u>at</u> <u>all</u> with so much gaiety? I have managed to keep my head so far, even to the extent of learning another short piece for Elocution, washing about a dozen handkerchiefs and changing the location of things in my room, since I received Mr. Smith's note.

Oh—I went to the first concert of the Elocution Series—a recital by Beatrice Hereford—fine, wish you could have heard her. Don't know when I've laughed so much.

Tons of love to you all, Your own Helen

Oh, Papa Fox, will you please send some more stamps. It takes so many to answer so many notes!

Oct. 30. My dear Mamma—

Thank you for sending my coat, which came yesterday, not a bit wrinkled. And for check and stamps. It doesn't seem as if I'd need my coat, fur, or long drawers in a hurry with today's warm weather, but it may snow by tomorrow.

I've just been interrupted by various squeals and giggles out in the hall and on going out, found two men! Don't be alarmed, they were only girls dressed up for the rehearsal of tomorrow night's play. I'll be sorry to miss it, but shall be at Helen's. They do make such funny men—such little hands and feet. Have just written a note to Frank, asking him to call and meet the Lancasters Sunday evening. Wonder if he will dare alone?

Oh—about Charles and the game—as I didn't answer in time, not realizing it was so soon, he had given me up and asked another girl, and she had accepted, too. He wrote to know what to do, saying she is having such a hard time at her school that he hated to disappoint her, and would take me to the Yale or Dartmouth game instead. Of course, I let him off as it was mostly my fault. I'd much rather see the Yale game anyway. So I may see the two "big" ones, after all.

With a heart full of love—Your own "Girl Goldie"

[Halloween party at Helen L.'s home in Roxbury.]
Nov. 8. My own dear ones—

I've been quite busy, with a written lesson and my "piece" to speak besides my usual work, so this week has just flown. Got a fine criticism on my piece; Miss Bennett, our teacher, said she was proud of us all, that our work was admirable! Mine was a bit from Kate Douglas Wiggin's "Penelope's Progress," which you ought to read, if the library has it, Mamma—it's such a cute story.

I wore my heavy coat and new hat which goes well with it, to church today. The preacher was Mr. Mott, a YMCA man and he was fine; very earnest and simple and convincing. The Chapel was packed.

Haven't heard any more from Mr. Smith. I do hope Sat. will be pleasant for the game, but if not, I can wear my raincoat.

Tons of love for all—Your "Girl Goldie"

Nov. 11. My dear Mamma—

I've been busy every moment this week so far—had one little written lesson and one paper due, which accounts for part of it, tho' I'm always very busy the first of the week. I found time for a nice walk after 5:00 P.M. and enjoyed it so much after being shut up in the library. *[This is the first real mention of the library since she came to Wellesley! Perhaps she did not have much work to do there because of her subject choices.]*

Thanks for the new orders, Papa. Can't wait to get my raincoat and boots.

Heaps of love—Helen

Nov. 15. My own dear ones—

I have such oceans to tell you tonight that I'm perfectly at sea as to where to begin! And here I started with a <u>pun</u>!

I'll begin with Friday—my shopping trip with Aunt Ada. After looking at raincoats and raincoats till my head spun, I decided on one in R.H. White's. It is a peculiar shade of olivy-browny-grey, with fitted back, belt, full front, triple capes and a black velvet collar. It is cravenette, which will not wet thro', they say, medium weight, so I can wear it all year, by wearing a jacket under it in winter. I had it fitted over my jacket, to be sure. I will take it to the dressmaker who shortened our Senior gowns, which will cost 50¢ or $1.00.

I also got a perfect beauty of a walking skirt at R.H. White's—black cheviot, very light weight, but close and firm, made with close habit back, straps set on to form a yoke with little black cloth buttons and a few straps running all the way down to the flaring bottom. Length is fine, and it fits <u>perfectly</u>. The price was $8.95. Aunt Ada approved.

My boots came Friday and are beauties and a fine fit. With all these, plus a new pair of grey woolen gloves and a new black neck ribbon, I feel all new.

Now, for Saturday!

You must have seen in the paper what a glorious victory it was for Dartmouth and how surprised everyone was.

Well, to begin. I arranged myself in my fine clothes; long undervest and pants for warmth, new black walking skirt, green silk waist for Dartmouth's color, new black neck ribbon, Louise's white golf jacket, my long heavy coat, my fur, hat, new gloves and Katharine's muff. (Oh my, wasn't I <u>hot</u>!)—and waited for "Prof," who appeared about 1:30 and we set out.

He was as nervous as ever, kept looking at his watch all the way over, to see if we would get there on time. The car *[electric]* did seem to <u>crawl</u>. He asked about all you people, especially Papa Fox, as usual, *[he was one of the trustees of Nute]* and had a long conversation about the school and the new principal, and I told him all the Milton news I knew. He asked about my college work.

Well, we got there just in time for the game. The new Harvard stadium is great, built all of stone, with seats only of wood, so there is very slight fire danger. It is not completed yet and this was the first game to be played in it. It was the most exciting thing I ever saw, even more than the Harvard-Yale game two years ago. Mr. S. almost went off his feet and punched me in the ribs madly, he was so excited. The cheering and singing were fine, and the playing <u>grand</u>. I was so glad Dartmouth won, but I couldn't help pitying poor Harvard! To be defeated for the first time by Dartmouth at the first game in the new stadium must have been a dreadful blow. The Dartmouth men, old and present, of course, went wild with joy.

As we were leaving, we met Mr. Chandler, Mr. S.'s roommate, whom I'd met two years ago. Mr. S. said they'd all met last night for "a jubilee" and if he ever <u>drank</u>, he thought he should have done so last night! We walked around some more, then went to the café where he takes his meals and had a fine dinner, then started for Wellesley, getting there about 7:30. Whatever we talked about on the way back—and we talked about almost everything, Mr. S. would keep going back to the game. He was simply tickled to death over it.

He came in when we got back, and stayed until about 8:15. We had an open fire in the parlor, and it was very pleasant. Then one of the other girls came in with a Harvard man, whose name happened to be Smith (and hers is Helen, too—isn't that queer!) so they discussed the game.

He finally left and I told him what a good time I'd had and asked him to call. He said he would and said I'd been an excellent mascot and he would recommend me!

Today I've been lazy—didn't get up till 10:00 A.M., so no church. Took a short walk and since, have been writing letters. Wrote to Frank Lee—oh, Mr. S. asked if I had seen Frank lately!

A heart full of love for you all—Your "Little girl"—Helen

Nov. 22. My dear Mamma—

It has been so cold here that my window was frosted over this morning and Longfellow Pond by the library was frozen! However, I guess I shan't need my skates before Christmas. We have taken long walks the last two days.

Oh, will you please direct all my letters to 30 Norumbega from now on, as we are to have free delivery beginning tomorrow. No more running over to College Hall to get my mail!

I have lost my fountain pen. I left it in the entry here, where we do our books when we come in for lunch, and it disappeared. I need another one "muchly." Will you send me one of those in the store, Papa, or shall I buy one here? About $1.00 here, I think.

Dr. Henry Van Dyke who wrote "The Blue Flower," a lovely book, preached a fine sermon today on faithfulness in little things. He is the man who said last year, "I don't want to be an angel, but a <u>man</u> and <u>live!</u>" And he was just as practical today.

What do you think—we had a <u>man</u> to dinner at Wilder, where I went with Louise. He is a brother of one of the girls there—an "old" Harvard man, who had come up to go to the game. He was very nice, and didn't seem at all embarrassed by so many girls.

After dinner, several of the girls played the piano and sang and we stayed and talked awhile, then walked till nearly supper time.

Well, my pencil is getting blunt so I'll say goodnight.

With a heartful of love—Helen

P.S. Thanks so much for the check to keep me from getting "stranded," Papa.

THANKSGIVING RECESS WITH THE LANCASTERS IN ROXBURY

Dec. 4. My dear Muddie—*[Using for the first time, note paper with the official Wellesley seal.]*

Today has been my "off" day for classes, but I've kept busy getting my room ready for sweeping, etc. this P.M. *[No vacuum cleaners then.]* Dec. 6. My own dear ones—

How do you like my new paper? Isn't it pretty! And only 25¢ for a big block.

I got up this morning, but made it down to breakfast just before the doors closed. By the way, we're having a run on a new breakfast food just now—"Ready Bits," which looks a good deal like "Force" but tastes more like "Corny." You ought to get some to try. After breakfast, Louise and I went down to the ville to get the *Sunday Herald,* which has an illustrated article on Wellesley, its history, etc. Have you seen it?

President Hyde of Bowdoin preached a fine sermon on "Perfection," and it was communion Sunday. This evening, there is to be a Memorial

Service for Alice Freeman Palmer, as today is the first anniversary of her death. Prof. Palmer is to be here and speak.

When I came back from the village, I found a letter from Mr. Smith saying he would be very glad to come out to Vespers next week. He really did very well, to let me know so soon! I wrote him that I had had a chance to inform people quite a little about Dartmouth since her grand victories, and he said he was very glad I'd had the chance to tell people about "the grandest college in the U.S.!"

Goodnight with a heartful of love—Your own Helen

Dec. 13. My own dear ones—

I have just come in from a glorious walk and it is as cold as Greenland—real winter weather at last!

I did go to Aunt Abbie's and it seemed so good to visit them all again and get all the family news, which I'll share with you when I get home.

Alice Dalrymple *[her good friend from N.H. who graduated in 1903]* dropped in to see me Friday afternoon, after doing some Xmas shopping in Boston. She looked very well and happy and has a "beauty" ring. I made her confess and she will try to get up while I am home and tell me all about it.

I had to hustle after she left, to get some Art work done to get it "in" by 5:30, then spent the evening on a paper and studying for an exam Saturday.

Ray and Helen *[Lancaster]* came out last evening—late—8:30—but we had a fine time—an open fire in the parlor, where we toasted marshmallows. And Ray brought me a fine box of candy. Katharine came down and joined us and liked them both very much.

As I told you, I'd been out earlier walking, so was in my short skirt *[about 2 or 3 inches off the ground]* for supper. I came right up afterwards to change, but before I finished dressing; "<u>Prof</u> <u>arove</u>!" I hustled and got down as quick as I could, prepared to apologize for keeping him waiting so long and found him chatting away with the other Mr. Smith from Harvard and one of the girls he met when he was out before!

We went to Chapel very soon and got fine seats. The music was beautiful and he said he enjoyed it very much. We came back to the house afterwards, had a nice open fire and "gossiped," looked at some "College News," etc. Katharine had a Harvard man out, too, so we introduced them and my, how they did talk! I thought <u>we</u> would never get a chance to speak a word again! Mr. S. enquired for you all and wished to be remembered especially to Papa Fox, as usual. Oh—he also informed me that he should settle in N.Y. next year.

Well, it is after 10 and I must get to bed as I've got to shop early tomorrow. Wish me luck. Please don't forget my allowance, as I must have it to get home on as all the money I have now must go for Xmas presents.

With a heart full of love—Helen

CHRISTMAS VACATION

Jan. 7, 1904. My own dear Mamma—

I'm "tuckered-out" unpacking and settling, so—only a short note.

I reached the Lancasters' in Roxbury all right, but the train ride down to Boston never seemed so long as it did yesterday. I studied my "piece" for Saturday, however and kept my clock out to count the time it would take me to speak it.

Helen had quite a surprise party for me when I arrived. Ray and Mott, Frank Lee and some of the girls from the Halloween party. Artie was invited, but was away. We made fudge, popped corn, played games and had a general good time.

With a heart full of love to all—Helen

P.S. My cold and my hands are much better. I slept <u>warm</u> even without my hot water bottle, which got left at Helen's.

Jan. 10. My own dear ones—

We had a fine stormy day yesterday, the fourth stormy Sat. in a row. I had Elocution in the morning and was so glad when it was over. Miss Bennett gave me mostly praise on my "piece" (was glad I had "practised" it on the train coming back). She said it was beautifully direct and showed my appreciation of it, tho' I didn't give as much of the real <u>spirit</u> of it as I might have. Anyway, she said, "Fine work!" I was quite "puffed up."

It was so stormy that both our Latin and Art teachers, who come from out of town, didn't get here, so we had "cuts." However, it cleared enough in the P.M. so we went for a little walk and I gave my hair a partial shampoo *[Probably just her "front" hair around her face. With no hair dryers to speed the process, women with their heavy, long hair, frequently did such a "partial".]*

After prayers today and a half hour walk, we went to hear Bishop Lawrence at Chapel. He preached a fine sermon on "There was a man sent out from God"— on the influence of a strong personality, and what went to make it. He is so simple, direct and quiet.

I thought of you at dinner, Mamma Fox, for we had vanilla ice-cream with hot fudge sauce and it was "lappin' good" as Ray says!

I enclose some questions for material for my Economics paper, which I need you to answer, please, Papa. It is to be on rent, to show that the rent of a house depends on its location, and also on the demand for tenements *[apartments]* being higher when business is good and almost all are occupied, etc. *[Helen's father owned several houses in the village, which he rented, and the family firm held mortgages on many others over the years.]* It is due Saturday. Anything you think would be helpful will be appreciated.

Hug Little Yellow Tail for me and a heartful of love to you all—

Your own "little girl" Helen

Jan. 12. My own dear Muddie—

I wish you could look into my room tonight—you wouldn't know it! No, I haven't had a fire or bought new furniture, etc. I have had a <u>Xmas</u> present of a <u>couch</u> from Norumbega and have hung my pictures! I'm so glad I didn't spend $2.00 to have my bed made over into a couch! They are changing them all gradually and mine came today. It looks very nice and I think will sleep well, as it has the same woven wire spring and mattress as my bed.

My pictures do look fine, especially the Hermes—it is a beauty. *[No color photos, then, even of famous paintings or statues.]* The girls have been coming in to see, so I've had quite a little "reception." What a difference a few pictures will make in a room.

We've had so much snow here—a real old fashioned winter that I'm afraid our Carnival will have to be a <u>sledding</u> one instead of skating.

With a heart full of love for all—Your own "sweet Girl Goldie"

[A Long Postponed Visit to all the Melrose Relatives.]
Jan. 20. My dear Muddie—

Two weeks more and I'll be through midyears. Well, I've worked hard for two days and expect to do so the rest of the week. These last weeks before midyear exams are tedious, I tell you. I wish you could see all the fine drawings I finished in Art yesterday. I'm very proud of them.

Frank is to come out Sat. evening and, according to Helen Thomas, the girl whose man knows Artie, <u>they</u> are coming out to Vespers Sun. evening. They had planned on Monday evening, but there is an Elocution entertainment which I want and am expected to attend. I'm not sure I'll know Artie, I haven't seen him in so long. So—I shall be quite gay for a few days, shan't I?

Stacks of love to all—Helen

Jan. 24. My own dear ones—

Midyears begin Weds. and my first one is Thurs. afternoon.

Louise and I went to Chapel to hear Dr. Brown of Union Theolog. School, who is a brother of one of the teachers here at Norumbega. He preached a fine sermon on "Consecration." Then Louise stayed for dinner, we went for a walk, after which the girls carried me off to Wilder for supper. It seemed like old times, when we were all in Stone Hall.

Frank couldn't come Sat., so I went to the "Barn" play, given by the Sophs., and written by one of them. It was cute as could be, full of hits and take-offs.

Oh, remember my new chain, and that I didn't know what it was made of? <u>Macaroni</u>! The kind that comes ready for soups! That's what Edna said. So, when it goes out of style or breaks, I can make soup!

A heart full of love to all—"Girl Goldie"

Jan. 26. My dear Muddie—

Another nice snow storm and I would have loved to get out and walk in it, but as I was busy writing a paper for Art and also have a wee bit of a cold today, and knew I'd get <u>wet</u>. I decided to stay in. One of the girls here, a Senior, too, is shut in the "pest house" with chicken pox. Imagine—just at midyears, too!

I have had a caller since I wrote the above—Artie! Helen T. told me this afternoon they were going to attempt to come out tonight, and they did. I really had a very nice call from him—hadn't seen him in so long that we had plenty of things to talk about. Then Helen and her man came over, so we had a very pleasant evening. Artie doesn't seem to have changed any by absence and seems to have forgotten his "mad" at me.

You say yes, I may come home after exams. I can get home at 5:00

P.M. Weds. and needn't leave till Tues. as I have only two recitations that day, which won't amount to much right after midyears and there's no "law" against cutting them. I shall bring my laundry with me.

Please put <u>30</u> Norumbega on your letters, as they are distributed by box number, not by name, and if there is no number, are sometimes delayed.

Thanks for the stamps and loads of love—Helen

Jan. 29. My dear Mamma—

Hope you got my post card all right. After getting two papers in and an exam yesterday, I couldn't seem to write a letter. The exam was Elocution and very easy, but quite long and my hand got <u>so</u> tired.

Went to Chapel this A.M. and then devoted the rest of the morning to cleaning house and dusting. This afternoon, the girls from Wilder were over to review our Economics and we studied until 5:30—even omitted our usual walk, as it was still so stormy. The reviewing was so much easier than I thought it would be that I feel quite relieved. I was sort of "scairt" of that exam.

I want heaps to eat when I get home, for I am just hungry all the time lately. Can it be those <u>iron</u> <u>tablets</u> you sent, or maybe just because I've been studying so hard?

Don't worry—I shan't have to cut any exam short, for they are over at 11:30, so I can get the 11:45 train for town as neat as a pin!

Goodnight for now and much love—Helen

Jan. 31. My own dear ones—

This has been an even shorter Sunday than usual as I didn't get up until <u>10:00</u> this morning!

We were over in Louise's room making chocolate "peps" last evening, so didn't get to bed very early. We were all so tired that Mrs. Newman said she wouldn't ring any bells this morning and that although breakfast would be at the usual time—8:00 A.M., she would keep fruit, cereal, milk and coffee out for us until 11:00. So nearly all of us took advantage of her kindness. I had two glasses of milk, dressed & made my bed, etc. in time to go to church at 11:00. Didn't I do well?

Bishop McVickers was the preacher and gave us a grand sermon. He is such a <u>big</u> man in all ways, very tall and large with a great big, soft, very impressive voice, very simple and sincere.

Ethel McTaggart invited me over to Stone for dinner, so I went right there from church. I had such a nice time, sitting at my old table and going up to the parlor as we used to after dinner. It all seemed very home like and nice, still I'd rather be here at Norumbega this year than back there.

Yesterday, it was <u>so</u> snowy and lovely, we were out about all day. If only we could get some skating, too. I shall be cross if they should have it while I'm home, tho' I suppose I <u>could</u> come back for the <u>Carnival</u>.

Well, the bell in South Natick is just ringing—9:00 o'clock and I'd better go to bed so as to feel like studying hard tomorrow. We aren't to have breakfast until 8:00 tomorrow, too. Isn't Mrs. Newman a dear?

A heartful of love for you all—Your own "Girl Goldie"

MIDYEAR BREAK

Feb. 11. My dear Mamma—

Here I am, back at work again and I don't like it! As the little boy said in yesterday's *Globe,* when his uncle asked him if he liked going to school. "Yes, I like <u>going</u> and coming all right, but not the time between!" However, when I really get "curled down" to it again, it will be different.

I had a very cold ride over to Union. *[Four miles in the "stage" which, in the winter was an open sleigh with three hard cold wooden seats.]* However with the heavy fur robes you tucked around me and my <u>tam</u>, which luckily I had with me, pulled down over my ears. I was really very comfortable, except for my feet. Did you discover that I forgot my <u>hat</u> and left it at home? I hope you find something to send it in by express. My tam wasn't exactly what I should have chosen to travel to Boston in and I expected to see everyone I knew on the train, but nobody remarked on it—at least to me.

I got out to Wellesley on the 1:15 and spent the afternoon getting settled and <u>eating</u>, as I had not had a chance to do so since my <u>early</u> breakfast at home and was pretty faint. Ethel McTaggart came over from Stone after dinner to do Latin together, so I didn't get to bed early. Mrs. Newman got my note all right and nothing was said about my coming back late. Wish I'd stayed another week! I paid my check, this A.M. and went to class as usual. This P.M., I've been studying a "piece" for Elocution.

They say our report cards are to be out sometime this week. We don't have to present them at the first recitations after all, merely get the Cashier's signature and drop them into the Dean's office. The "flunk notes" are said to be all out and I wasn't favored, so conclude that I must have passed everything.

Time to go to the village with Katharine now, so I'll stop,

With stacks of love—Your own Helen

Feb. 14. My own dear ones—

You've probably read the enclosed report card <u>first</u>. Isn't it fine that I got all <u>credit</u>? I wasn't certain of it in Economics or German, tho' I thought I <u>ought</u> to have it. Louise, Mary and Edna got all credits, too, and Katharine all except one. There was great excitement yesterday when the cards came out, as you can imagine.

Dr. Van Dyke gave a reading of his own poems here yesterday P.M., which was fine. Katharine had her aunt and cousin out to hear him and have dinner. I saw quite a little of them and they are very pleasant. They are traveling here in the East this winter and were in Washington when she was there at Xmas, then came to N.Y. and now to Boston and Cambridge, where her cousin is in Harvard Law School. She is going to invite them to the Glee Club Concert. Louise and I have decided to go together. I shall probably wish at the last minute that I had a man, but I tell Louise in that case, she can sell me her ticket!

Ethel Moody took me off to Stone for dinner today and I stayed "gossiping" afterward until 4:00, when Mary and I took a walk until Suppertime.

Tomorrow is going to be a busy day. In the P.M. there is a Class Social at one of the society houses; then, in the evening, a lecture under the auspices of the Latin department and a reception afterwards, at which I am to help feed the people. (Probably shan't get time to get any good things myself!)

Well, my <u>hat</u> came yesterday and I was truly rejoiced to see it again! Think of where I'd have been, without that <u>tam</u>, though. I shall <u>never</u> part from it, now. Thanks for sending it, Mamma.

With a heart full of love—Your own "Girl Goldie"

Feb. 16. My dear Mamma—

Well, I have been "domestic." Yesterday A.M. I fixed up my room, did a little mending and <u>polished</u> my <u>silver</u>! Then in the P.M., we went to the Class Social and had a fine time talking, eating, etc. Most of the girls took sewing, but as I'd done mine, I didn't seem to have anything I could take. In the evening, we went to the Lecture on Excavations in Corinth, which was <u>very</u> interesting, and then to the reception where we had nice "eats"—chocolate, coffee, cakes, etc.

We had a Valentine party at the table last night, with cunning little heart-shaped place cards and little imitation nutshells with things inside. Mine had a tiny kettle, and one of the others, a bell, etc.

Will you tell Papa I shall have to have some more money, please? I have had to spend some $2.50 for books, besides paying for my glasses, which has drained my purse pretty low. If you should give me a dollar for each one of my "<u>credits</u>," it would fill it up again nicely!

Give little Kim kitty a hug for me. I dreamed last night he was trying to get out of the coal bin window to chase another cat!

With heaps of love for all—Helen

Feb. 18. My dear Mamma—

Are you all snowed in up country? It has been <u>so</u> <u>cold</u> here, that I nearly <u>froze</u> two nights running, in spite of all the blankets I piled on my bed. Last night, although it was just about as cold, the wind had changed and didn't strike my side of the house, so I slept warm again. But I really wish Spring would come.

I've been busy as usual this week—more so, perhaps, as I'm preparing a piece for Elocution Saturday. It is a very tragic account of Jason's death— much too tragic for me to attempt, probably, but I must try.

Not another speck of "news" tonight, so I'll say "goodnight"—
With heaps of love to all, Helen

Feb. 24. My dear Mamma—

We had pantomimes in Elocution yesterday morning, which was great fun. I was a man calling on a girl here at college and made them laugh by hitching up my trousers so they wouldn't bag at the knees, curling my moustache, etc. The teacher said we did well.

Today we got back our midyear's Art papers and I got a fine criticism, so feel quite "puffed up." (Wonder if I'll get some sort of a "fall"?)

It's time for studying, but I wrote this first, tonight to be sure to get it in the post.

With heaps of love for all—Your own "girl Goldie"

Feb. 26. My dear Muddie—

I had a note from Criss *[Criss Mathews, an R.N., former teacher and old family friend from N.H., then working and living in Boston.]*

She wants me to come over this Sunday. Luckily, I can all right. She writes that the Italian man who posed for the Holy Grail painting in the Boston Public Library *[by John Singer Sargent]* lives near her and she got acquainted with him through one of the lodgers. He has invited her and any of her friends to see his collection of pictures, curios, etc., so she is going to take me and I am anticipating a great treat.

With heaps of love for all—Helen

Feb. 29. My own dear ones—

Criss introduced me to a little Syrian girl who lodges here and she took us over to see Antonio Corsi. He is fully as interesting as his things—a rather small but quick, wiry man, with a clean-shaven face, regular Italian eyes and teeth and a perfect "<u>mop</u>" of curly black hair. You would know he was <u>something</u> to look at him. His collection of things was very interesting; pictures of all kinds for which he has posed and the suits, etc. which he wore for them, completely covering the walls of a good-sized room. I was bewildered by <u>so</u> <u>many</u> and would like a <u>day</u> to look at them.

In the evening, we went up to the little Syrian girl's room and she showed us all the lovely things she has to sell—hundreds of dollars' worth! I contented myself with buying some medallions—little beauties at 12 for 50¢—and <u>wishing</u> that I had about another $2.00 to spend.

Yesterday morning, we went to Trinity Church. I had not been there since it was renovated, and never for morning service and I enjoyed it very much. We heard a splendid sermon on the advantages of difficulties. Every hindrance or difficulty is an opportunity, the minister said. Which reminded me of Ray's "sermons" to me when I rebelled against going anywhere with Artie. (Don't get a chance to, now, do I?)

In the afternoon, we went to see the Whistler exhibition of paintings, which I found rather disappointing, then into the library to see the Holy Grail paintings. They are simply <u>wonderful</u>; the most beautiful I ever saw! I do wish you could all see them.

In the evening, Miss Pratt, the head fitter in Hollander's, came down and Criss got her to give me lots of suggestions for my Commencement gowns. She gave me lots of ideas, sketched things for me and is going to "take me off" patterns of things. Hollander's, you know is about the "swellest" store in town, <u>very</u> expensive. Any dressmaker I have, can follow her directions, she says. I shall feel pretty well fitted out. I am going to write for samples right away, and think I'd better speak to Tal right away, as it is getting pretty well along in the season and I don't want to have to hurry and worry the last few weeks. Miss Pratt's taste is excellent; simple but fine, and she didn't suggest expensive things.

Well—I know Papa and Papa Fox must be tired of dressmaking, but they'll have to yawn in silence, as they're apt to hear more before June.

With heaps of love for you all.

Your own "Girl Goldie"

March 3. My own dear Muddie—

You don't know how busy I've been! Have had scarcely time to eat and sleep. Had a written lesson in Latin today which took lots of studying and when we went in today, she calmly announced that it would be continued Sat., which means some more studying, of course, and that the whole thing will be almost like another midyear exam! I could shake her, I'm so cross, for I have another "piece" for Elocution Sat. and an Art paper due, too. Well, I shall get thro' some way, as usual and have about all day tomorrow to work.

I wrote for some samples this P.M., also to Tal. I should think this would be early enough to get her. I hope so, as we are so well used to each other.

Oh, I got my cards *[engraved "calling cards," which everyone had in those days. I even had some in 1935!]* I think they're very pretty, don't you?

With a heart full of love for you all—Helen

March 6. My own dear ones—

I am still alive and at the end of this hard week. I got thro' it very well indeed; got my paper done all right, the written lesson in Latin was easy and Miss Bennett was much pleased with my Elocution piece. She said, "Fine, fine!" and didn't even keep me for any criticism at all. So—I am much relieved.

Yesterday, I walked to the ville with Louise to meet her sister who came out for the P.M., then sewed awhile on a collar I am making. I went over to Wilder for dinner and stayed until about 9:00. Wilder seems about as much like home as here, I'm there so much.

After early breakfast and prayers this morning, we went out for a walk over by where the new dormitories are to be. They already have the stakes up and the foundation for one laid. It is going to be quite large. *[The Quad, Pomeroy first, built in 1904. I lived there for three years.]*

Our division began practicing for the Tree Day dances last Weds., and I think it's going to be good fun. Will tell you about it when I come home.

I guess I'm never going to see Ray and Mott or Artie or Frank, for that matter. Well, I can stand it—haven't shed any tears yet.

Shall look for your letter tomorrow.

> Your own "little girl"—Helen

March 8. My dear Muddie—

I heard from Tal yesterday and she can't do the work for me for my Commencement gowns; I am really disappointed. Oh dear, aren't clothes a nuisance!

I'm tired. Washed 29 handkerchiefs yesterday, then went to a concert in the evening and didn't sleep well last night as it was so warm. Today have washed my hair and ironed.

Winter's spell is broken, and Spring <u>must</u> come before long!

I'm a little sleepy now so will say goodnight—

> With tons of love—Helen

March 13. My own dear ones—

Weds. I was busy with lessons all day and preparing for a debate at the Debating Club Thurs. evening. The Club is entirely independent of class work and is made up—my division—of Seniors and Sophs. The other division is Juniors and Freshmen. We want to gain practice so that Wellesley can whip Vassar next time. And the next time depends on the success of the Club. The faculty will not let us debate Vassar this year. They say we are not prepared, but we may do so next year, if the Club is a success this year. So, we're all anxious that it should be so—and it is going to be, I think. The subject was "Resolved that the methods employed by Labor Unions are unjustifiable." We had the Affirmative. It was very interesting and I really enjoyed the work.

Friday I was busy fixing my room, dusting and sweeping, then studied awhile and then in the afternoon, <u>we went skating</u>! The meadow *[now the parking area for Green Hall]* opposite the Chapel has overflowed and the skating that afternoon was grand. We had a splendid time and stayed out until time for dinner.

In the evening the first meeting of our new German Club—the "Deutsche Verein," was held at the Shakespeare House. I went with fear and trembling, wondering how on earth I could speak German for a whole evening. I shan't fear any more, for we had a perfectly lovely time, nothing stiff or formal about it at all. We were asked to bring our sewing, but didn't do any after all. Instead, we spent the whole evening playing games in German, <u>eating</u> delicious German pancakes—like great thick doughnuts with raspberry jam filling—then winding up by singing German songs. I got on very well talking German. Didn't realize that I could do as well, and learned several new words. I wish we could meet more often than once a month.

Sat. evening, we went to a mock Republican Convention for the nomination for President given by the Agora Society, which is the regular debating and political society. It was interesting and bright. They nominated Roosevelt [*"Teddy"*] for President and Fairbanks for Vice Pres. Afterwards were dancing and refreshments.

I have heard from Frankie at last and he wants to come out soon; he goes rather by fits and starts. I guess I'll let him wait awhile.

I think I'll hie me to my little bed and say goodnight.

With a heart full of love—Your own "Girl Goldie"

March 21. My own dear ones—

A day late, I know, but I was so busy yesterday it seems to me I didn't have a moment to <u>breathe</u> from the time I got up! Tho' I didn't do that till nearly 11:00!

Saturday we went to a lecture by Jane Addams, the President of a settlement house, called Hull House, in Chicago, which was very interesting. Then, in the evening the Stone Hall Seniors gave a dramatization, "Lady Rose's Daughter," which one of them had written. It was very good and the little farce which preceded it was too funny for words, taking off some of the silly new rules lately passed by the faculty.

I did not get to church yesterday. Nina came over here to dinner with me and stayed late. Then I had to write out a report which took me until supper-time. Didn't even get our customary walk.

Right after supper, Artie and Helen's man arrived. Artie looked wonderfully "spruce," with a pink carnation (the shade I particularly abhor) in his button hole. We went to Chapel early, but not too early, for the doors weren't open and there was a <u>crowd</u> waiting to get in.

Did you see the <u>grand</u> comet or shooting star about 6:45 P.M.? It came while we were all waiting there on the Chapel steps. I never saw a grander one and it lasted so long.

Vespers were good, as usual, besides having a larger choir, there were four men and a lady out from town to sing. She had a beautiful voice. They gave some selections from Gounod's Redemption and it was grand.

I have been staying over at Wilder about half the time lately. Edna Taylor went home early, all tired out, on Saturday. Helen had her place; so, after Vespers Artie and I came over here and got my suitcase to take over to Wilder, as I was going to stay over there all night. I expected Mrs. Newman would hold up her hands in holy horror to see me, at that time of evening with a <u>man</u> and a <u>suitcase</u>! She didn't see us however, so Artie was spared the embarrassment.

The men stayed until about 9:30, eating fudge and talking and said they had a good time, but Helen and I were too sleepy to be very entertaining. I slept in Edna's room and it made me "homesick," with everything picked up and put away, so I had bad dreams. But now, I attribute them to the <u>earthquake</u>. Did you have it at home? It passed here about 1:00 A.M. and was really quite heavy. The walls and furniture all shook and Katharine thought her wardrobe was going to fall over. In some of the rooms at Wilder, the vases tumbled off stands, or whatever they were on. It seemed to have been strongest at the other end of the house. Helen and I and the people at our end, didn't hear it at all. I am rather glad, as everyone who did was dreadfully frightened. But, I feel a little cheated, too, now it is all over.

I have an 11:45 class on Friday, so I can't make the early train up, so don't look for me till night.

Until then—Heaps of love—Helen

March 22. My dear Mamma—

Today came the excitement of the year; honors were read in Chapel this morning! No one really expected it, tho' there was a rumor that they would be the last moment. Only a few people were there— it was nasty and wet.

I suppose you will be disappointed that I am still only "Wellesley." I was, a little, myself, for while I hadn't really worked for that, I have worked a great deal harder this year and thought that I might make "Durant."

But I didn't, which will perhaps save me from conceit! Louise is a

"Durant" Scholar and we are all <u>so</u> proud of her. And she was so surprised, too. And so was Edna, and I'm gladder for her than for anyone I can think of, even Louise, for if ever a girl "suffered and bled" for it, Edna has. She is the most conscientious worker I ever saw—always worrying, an actual slave to her work. I really wouldn't want to be like her, for all the world—even for the "Durant," for she is not happy. Louise, Katharine and I telegraphed her this forenoon (you remember I told you she was ill and went home early) to let her know and contratulate her. And, Mamma, I am happy, too, for at least I haven't gone <u>back</u> perceptibly.

We are all so sorry about Mary, who was a "Durant" last year, but this year, only "Wellesley." Isn't that a shame? I haven't seen her yet, but altho' she has said all along that it would be this way, still she must be very disappointed, and think how disppointed her family will be. After all, it is only for you, our families, that we care about it, anyway.

With very much love, Your own "little girl."

SPRING VACATION

April 14. My dear Mamma—

Well, I had a fine time at Miss Hazard's. I wore my green dress and a pretty yellow jonquil that Mary gave me and looked quite "swell." I didn't have much to say, for there were three other Seniors there, one who talked enough for us all. We had a very fine dinner—too long to tell you what. Then Miss Hazard showed us her curios. She has many very interesting ones. Then some other Seniors called and we served them with coffee, cookies, candy and nuts, then had some music. First, one of the girls played the piano and another sang, and then Miss Hazard played. She is a very clever woman who both plays and paints with considerable skill. I missed our German Club meeting, which came the same evening and was so sorry because there will be only one or two more—but then, one doesn't get invited to Miss Hazard's for dinner every day.

My veil came this morning, Muddie, and I had time to just peek at it before class. It will be lovely with my hat. Thank you ever so much. I also got my Wellesley seal pin and feel so proud of it.

Must get this in the mail. Shall look for a letter tomorrow.

Lots of love—Your own Helen

April 17. Dear Papa——

Just think, a week ago today you were here. Don't you wish you were again? Oh, I forgot to tell you and perhaps I ought not to now for fear it will make you vain—the girls all thought you were <u>fine</u> and one of them quite fell in love with you! There, Mamma, you'd better come along with him next time!

Some of us walked down to Natick to the greenhouse the other day and saw some of the loveliest roses—some were $<u>4.00</u> or even more a dozen!

Yesterday, Mary and I went to Grand Opera in town and heard Calvé in Carmen. My, but she was grand! We got very good seats, too, for $1.00. Both the singing and acting were fine, We had to go in before lunch, so got it at that little restaurant where we went before—and for 20¢. I don't see how they can do it.

I am going to write to "my woman" in Melrose who said she would do my work for me, and try to get there May 15th to get it started. She said that I would need <u>14 yds.</u> of lawn and <u>12</u> of linen, which is all nonsense, I believe. I shall ask the nice clerk, when I get it and go by his directions, for I don't want yards and yards left over. As I've said before, aren't clothes a nuisance!

Must get this down for the postman.

Good <u>afternoon</u>. With lots of love for all, Helen

April 21. My dear Mamma—

Went into town with Louise this A.M. and got the material for your dress, at Chandler's first of all. I think it is perfectly beautiful and will make up beautifully and be just what I want my Muddie to have. You must have a big black hat to go with it and then you will be just lovely. And don't you want the ostrich plume on my beaver hat for your hat? Oh, you didn't say how <u>much</u> material for your dress, so I asked the clerk, a lovely old man, and he said 15 yards. Then I got my own Persian lawn and he said 12 yds. Got my linen there, too—10 yds., he thought. They are so nice there—act as if <u>you</u> were doing them a favor instead of the other way around, as they do at Jordan's and White's. (Oh, I tore up the order for White's, so no one else could use it if I should lose it.) Then I looked for my hat and went to a little place way up Washington St., Katharine told me about. They don't keep much of a store, but trim nicely and are very reasonable.

Well, I lighted on a sort of modified turban I liked—light, but not all on the yellow—just right for my jacket. The clerk trimmed it very simply for me with wide brown ribbon—for only $2.75 for the whole thing! So I made up the extra I spent on my jacket.

[Pencil] Now—my pen's run dry and I've hardly any room or time left in this letter to tell you about going to Winthrop on the 19th *[Patriot's Day in Massachusetts.]* We went early, stayed till about 11:00 A.M., had a fine time, tho' a quiet one; then, as there was no place to get lunch, we came back to town for it and then back to Wellesley on the 3:00 P.M. train.

I must study for Elocution, so goodnight.

Heaps of love—Helen

April 24. My own dear ones—

We are having quite a Norumbega reunion today. Katharine is away over Sunday, so I am having Edna over in her place and it's quite like the old times Soph. year. Last evening, the Freshmen gave an awfully cute play at the Barn, which we took in, and by cutting dessert (fruit & nuts, which take ages), we managed to get good seats. This morning, after breakfast and prayers, we took a little walk & went to church.

I wish I could make you see how perfectly beautiful it is here now, everything so fresh and green and the lake such a wonderful blue. It all makes me want to stay outdoors all the time. But, I resolved to be good and went to church. I wore my new hat and coat and looked quite fine. Dean Hodges of Cambridge Theological School gave us a fine sermon on gossip and slander, which I think particularly appropriate for college girls. I'm afraid we do get in the habit of gossiping about our neighbors.

After an afternoon of reading, writing and walking, we made a little call on Mrs. Newman. She told us stories about the "old days" of the college. I sometime wish I could have been here then, only I wouldn't want to give up <u>now</u>. I wonder if that is the way my great grandchildren will feel when I tell them about my college days! *[Helen did not have a chance to do this, as the only great-grands she ever knew—of her eventual fourteen, were two little boys, ages three years and six months.]*

I wonder if you have been to church today. Do tell me about the new minister's son who is in college. Where is he, and what color are his eyes? *[She favored brown eyes.]*

Forgot to say I spoke in Elocution yesterday, and got a fine criticism.

Edna sends her love to the whole family—

And lots and lots of love from me. Your own "little girl," Helen

April 26. My own dear Muddie—

I had quite a surprise call last evening. we went to a reading of "Lord Chumley," a very cute play, by Leland Powers. There was also a concert up at College Hall. When we were coming out, I said to Louise, seeing some girls with men, "I almost wish I'd a invited a man out," when just then, walking toward us, I saw someone who looked very much like "Artie" B., and on looking again, saw that it was he!

He came out about 8:00 P.M. to make me a call, and as the maid at Norumbega told him that I had gone to the concert at College Hall, he spent the evening walking about and waiting in the reception room there until 9:15 when it was over. I was sorry it happened that way and tried to persuade him to come in and stay until 9:45. However, he would then have had to wait until almost 11:00 for the next train, so he just walked back to Norumbega with me, then "scooted." I wager that he is another man who won't come out here to see me again without letting me know in advance. He has only himself to blame.

This P.M. we had the Student Government election of next year's president, and our caps and gowns seemed real "garments of woe" that the end of this year was so near and our time here so nearly over. It is only the beginning of the end, which I suppose will be even harder, when we see others take our place. Oh dear, wouldn't it be nice if there wasn't such a thing as change? Still, that would never do, would it? I'm sure you wouldn't have wanted me to stay a squally infant always, would you?

With love for you all—Your own "Girl Goldie"

May 2. My own dear ones—

We did not have our May Day celebration after all. It was far too wet to roll hoops or play on the campus so the affair was postponed until tomorrow, when it will probably rain again. So—I spent Saturday washing my hair and in the evening we went to a little society dance at the Barn and had a very good time.

Yesterday morning, Louise and I took a walk and inspected the new dormitory which is coming along very fast. It is going to be quite swell, but too near the railroad tracks and car [electric] tracks to be very quiet. They intend to have the plan ready for selecting rooms this spring, I believe. The notice for drawing numbers is already posted and it seems so queer to think that we shall be out of it. I'm glad, on the whole, for I should probably get 200+ this year, with my usual bad luck.

The postman has come up the hill so I must catch him on the way down—so Good morning.

With loads of love—Helen

May 6 My dear Mamma—

Last evening I went down to a little reunion of Norumbega girls which Mrs. Newman gave, so did not get off my letter to you. These last two mornings I have been getting up at 6:00 A.M. to practice Tree Day dancing and let me tell you, I now know how to pity you and Papa, getting up so early every day! Our division only has to do so once or twice more, while the others may have to more often. There are advantages in having an unimportant part! I have enjoyed it very much, however, when once up, as it is so lovely early in the morning. In fact so much so, that we mean to get out by 7:00 A.M. some mornings of our own accord.

Miss McAllister has asked me down to spend Sunday with her and I plan to go—take the 3:20 from Boston, and she will meet me at the Gloucester station. I may stay until Tuesday. I will write to you while Miss "Mac" is in school Mon. *[Miss McAllister was a former teacher of Helen's at Nute High School with whom she had kept in touch.]*

With a heartfull of love—Helen

[A weekend trip to Gloucester to visit Miss McAllister.]
May 10. My own dear Mamma—

Another letter night and if I didn't write tonight, I suppose you'd picture all sorts of dreadful things befalling me on my way back from Gloucester. (Hope you got the letter I wrote from there).

I left there at 4:00 P.M. yesterday and got back here at 6:00. Miss Mac was very busy and as I had a lot to do here and it was rainy so we couldn't walk anyway, I thought I'd better not stay another night. But I did visit her school, sat in on her French classes, met the other teachers and saw some boys doing military drilling. She is afraid she cannot come to Commencement, but will come Sat. P.M. of that week. So you will see her if nothing happens. I think I will write Mr. Smith and Frank for the same time.

I had a note from Frank saying he would be out Sat. evening. And oh—the little Syrian girl I met at Criss' was out here this P.M. to see Mary, whom she knew in Washington, thru' an uncle (of Mary's) who knew her lover in Syria. She wants to exhibit her goods here, so we took her around and are going to try to arrange it.

Now I must study for a quiz tomorrow, so "Goodnight."

With lots of love for all—Helen

May 13. My dear Mamma—

The campus is perfectly beautiful now—just like emerald velvet and the trees have just burst out these last few warm days. I do hope we have this kind of weather for Commencement.

Yesterday, I sallied forth into town in search of shoes and was not very successful. They hadn't a thing in tan, which I'd set my heart on, except samples which they wouldn't sell me, and they didn't know when they would have, for they can't get them in fast enough to fill back orders. So I shall have to go barefoot, for all of them. They were not half as nice at this place as that place on Congress St.—Lambkin and Foster, wasn't it?

I hope you won't faint when you see all the clothes I've sent home, mostly things I'll not be needing here anymore, so you can just put them away. Some don't need washing. There'll be less to pack and send in June. I took my hoop down, too. What about bringing home my Morris chair, screen and tea table? I'm sure the freight charge will be high; shall I enquire here? I'd like to keep them and I know I can't get anywhere near what they are worth here.

I've made arrangements to sit for my picture Weds. and I'd rather go to the Dr. a dozen times! However, Partridge is a very good photographer and willing to give you an infinite number of sittings, a fact which I shall probably take advantage of. I shall sit for some in my cap and gown and the rest in either my fagoted yoke dress, or my white one, probably the latter. Please write any directions or advice you may have. I shall have to pay $2.00 down, then the rest depends on the kind and number of pictures finished; 50 for $9.00, $10.00, or $12.00. I'll find out exactly and let you know, but that doesn't have to be decided until later.

Well—time to stop and get my "beauty sleep"—I'll need all I can get before the sitting. So goodnight.

Your own loving "little girl," Helen

May 15. My own dear ones—

Well, here I am in my own little room tonight and Louise is here, writing to her family. We have just come over from Wilder, where I took supper with her. They <u>do</u> have the nicest Sunday suppers at Wilder. And afterward, we had a little "sing."

This morning after breakfast, I tidied my room and fixed my flowers, and as I have every vase full, that took quite a long time. Then to Chapel to hear President Eaton of Beloit College, who gave us a very good sermon on "Christ the Mediator."

Ethel McTaggart came over to dinner with me and stayed a good part of the afternoon. We had a good time gossiping—harmlessly of course, until I went over to Louise's.

I've managed to write a letter to Little Linnie, thanking her for picking the mayflowers for me, which reached me yesterday in very good condition and just perfume my room with their sweetness.

I've heard nothing from the dressmaker in Melrose whom Winnie recommended and who said she would make my dresses for Commencement, so I think I had better go see her, as she should be ready for me by now—if she's ever going to be. I think she must be the most ill-mannered, unbusinesslike little creature I ever heard of! If she <u>ever</u> <u>does</u> get my work done on time, I think I shall enclose an expression of my opinion when I pay her bill.

Thanks for laundering the little collar, Mamma. I've had handkerchiefs out bleaching in the sun since Friday. *[No Kleenex then!]* I hope they haven't mildewed instead.

Frank came out last evening in spite of the drizzle and we called on his friend, Mrs. Coolidge in the village, who gave us several lovely branches of apple blossoms. Mine adorn my room, with my mayflowers, and his were to go to his mother, but I'm wondering if they ever got there, as most men don't care to carry such things on a crowded train.

With heaps of love for all—Helen

May 19. My dear Mamma—

I worked all day Tues. on Art plates which were due today. Then, Weds. morning, Louise and I went to Newtonville at 8:30 to get our pictures taken and didn't get home until 11:30. The man was very nice and took great pains to make me feel comfortable, for I told him, and he could see for himself that I was a difficult subject. He tried to keep me smiling to prevent a strained look, and I feel as tho' I grinned broadly in all poses. However, we'll see tomorrow when the proofs ought to come. I dread to see them, tho' I think I ought to get at least one decent one out of the lot. I wore my white dress. I will send you the proofs as soon as they come.

Yesterday and today, that little Syrian girl, Miss Aramanoosie, was here to display her goods and I had her over to dinner. I'm afraid she didn't do as well as she'd hoped, but her things are pretty expensive and college girls don't have much spare money to spend on such things.

After dinner, and she had left, I went with the other Seniors from here and Wilder, over to Miss Hazard's, who had invited all our class for an informal talk and evening. We had a fine time, She talked to us about what our four years here ought to mean to us in our lives, etc. We didn't get home until 9:45, and I tumbled into bed.

Oh, I had a letter from Mrs. Mosher, the dressmaker, saying she'd been very busy, and had had "such a lame back that she couldn't walk without pain." What on earth that had to do with writing me a note, I can't explain, but maybe she can. So, if nothing more happens, I shall interview her Saturday.

With much love to all—Helen

May 20. My dear Mamma—

The proofs have come and I enclose them. I don't consider them a howling success, but they might be worse. Let me know what you think and whether I should have another sitting. Louise feels the same about hers, so I feel better, as "misery loves company." I've marked the worst ones, and I have practically no choice of the others.

I also enclose my trial announcement list for your additions, and return it as soon as possible, please.

I just got back from our "Deutscher Verein" meeting, so it is getting late and I must close.

Love to all, Helen

May 23. My dear Mamma—

I am very pleasantly surprised with the dressmaker, Mrs. Mosher. She is a small, plump, trim, dark little lady. I just can't reconcile her smart, capable air with her long delay in writing to me. But, she does all her own work and has no girls to sew for her, and does heaps of dressmaking, so I can forgive her. She showed me her books and talked and very soon I saw that she knew what she was about, so was glad to leave details with her.

The lawn dress is to have tucks around the bottom, then a wide ruffle tucked some more, with a panel down the front edged with fine lawn insertion; the waist is to have a square yoke, of the insertion, then a bertha *[collar]* making it very broad, long shouldered and full. The sleeves and details, she will do to suit herself. She is going to get the lawn, etc. and a corset cover to wear underneath the insertion. The linen dress, I've left almost entirely up to her. The skirt is to have two flounces, with some design worked in French knot. I believe the waist will have plaits, medallions scattered here and there, and more French knots.

I don't dare to boast yet, but I think I shall like her. I told her I must have them by June 10th for sure. I am to go out over next Sunday to be fitted.

All the Melrose relatives are looking forward to your visit in June, Mamma, when you both come down for Commencement.

Thank Papa very much for the check. I'll try to be prudent with it, Daddie. With tons of love—

Your own "Girl Goldie"

May 26. My dear Mamma—

You don't get very long or frequent letters from me any more, do you? But if you could know how busy I am, you would forgive me. Your letter came this P.M. while I was drying my hair, an operation which took almost three hours, as the sun played its usual trick on me and went in just as soon as I wet my head.

Louise and I went down to Newtonville by trolley yesterday to order her photos and to see about another sitting for me. We started in plenty of time to get back for dinner, but the cars were cranky; we had to change and wait at every possible place both ways and as a result, did not get back to Wellesley Square till about 6:45. As it was too late for dinner, we went to the Inn and had a sumptuous repast of sandwiches and wished we had a man along to pay for a regular dinner! The other girls had forgotten to register, so didn't have to hurry back to cancel, but I had to before 7:30, so I left them eating ice cream about 7:10 and started up to College, getting caught in a heavy rain storm on the way.

I shall have to make the same trip to Newtonville tomorrow, as I am to sit for my picture again. This time, I'll wear my fagoted dress and I think I'll try the cap and gown again, too.

I'll continue tomorrow—

With much love to all—Helen

P.S. Many thanks for the oranges in my laundry—they are delicious!

May 27. My dear Mamma—

A short continuation of last evening's popular serial story. Well, I went down to Newtonville again today—all alone this time, wasn't I brave!? I wore my fagoted yoke dress, this time without ruching. It ought to be plain and old maidish enough! Both Katharine and Mary thought it would "take" better that way. The photographer was very nice and gave me several more sittings and also two more in cap and gown. I'll send the proofs when they come. I do hope they'll be good, for I've no more time to spend on this project.

This afternoon, we had our Class Social. Some of the girls "took off" the faculty and it was great. I laughed until I ached. This evening, I have been down to the "sing" on the Chapel steps. Tomorrow A.M. Mary and I go into town (if pleasant) to call on Little Miss Aramanoosie; then I go to Melrose for my fitting and will stay over at Winnie's returning Tues. as Monday is a holiday.

No more news for now.

With heaps of love for all—Helen

May 29. My own dear ones—

You'll be surprised to hear that I'm here in Wellesley, instead of Melrose, as planned. A note yesterday from Mrs. Mosher said she wouldn't want me until Monday, as she had not been able to get the materials until Friday. So, not wanting to be away two Sundays, I'll wait and go next week to stay over and just go early tomorrow for a fitting.

Mary and I had a delightful visit with Little Miss Aramanoosie. She is such a dear little thing and so anxious to do everything for us. She took us to see Mr. Corsi and Mary was greatly interested and fascinated by him and his collection. He told us some very entertaining stories about his experiences in posing. Then Miss A. made us tea in her room and the afternoon went quickly until we went back to Wellesley.

That evening, Edna came over and we had a good old-time talk. She says that her father, Dr. Taylor, whom I met Soph. year, is already planning and looking forward to my visit to her next year!

I visited with Mrs. Newman this morning out on her piazza, until time for church. We had a very good sermon by Rev. Herbert Jump of Bowdoin. And this afternoon, I read out under the trees by the Art building and fought mosquitoes and hosts of little green bugs. Then we had a picnic supper outdoors and ate about three times as much a usual. Then

Katharine and I went for a walk and picked flowers—lovely <u>sweet</u> clover.

I hate to think of how few Sundays are left to enjoy here; yet I'm looking forward so much to being at home without having to hurry back. I know I shall enjoy a good rest and being with you all, but it makes me feel rather lazy when I hear some of the other girls talk about teaching. Louise has had correspondence about a position in Middletown, Conn., Bennington, Vt. and Plymouth, N.H. But she doesn't want to go out of Mass.

I must get out of bed early tomorrow, holiday or not, to go to Mrs. Mosher's for my first fitting.

With stacks of love for you all—Helen

June 1. My dear Mamma—

I had to get up at 6:00 this morning and out for our last Tree Day rehearsal—at least the last at that hour, I'm glad to say. I think it will go off well.

I went to Melrose again and to Mrs. Mosher's for my fitting which took from 10:15 to after 12:00. She had only the drop skirt and corset cover ready to try, but will cut the rest greatly by those, as those are all right, and she can do the rest quickly. They are going to be very pretty; the skirt with a broad ruffle, with tucks and insertion and val. edge to match, and the corset cover full with ruffles across the bust to give a fluffy effect and hold out the waist. I shall have to go out once more at least, to be fitted again.

You should have my new proofs by now, I think they are even worse than the first ones, which are really quite presentable now they've darkened by exposure. What do you think?

I shall look for your letter tomorrow.

With heaps of love for you all—Girl Goldie

June 5. My own dear ones—

Friday night was the Senior Serenade. We started at 9:00 P.M. and didn't get back till 12:45! We wore our caps and gowns, the latter turned up for protection against the dust, and I was happy I'd worn a sweater underneath before I got back.

We went to Miss Hazard's, Mrs. Durant's, all the houses on campus and the principal ones in the village. We had treats in three places along the way; punch and cookies at one place, hot chocolate and sandwiches at another and lemonade at the third. Then, the Freshmen showered us with peanuts, sweet chocolates and flowers!

You can imagine how tired we all were Sat. morning. My first recitation wasn't until 10:00 so I didn't have to get up till 9:00, and didn't want to then. I felt better by afternoon, however, and quite ready for Tree Day. It began at 3:30 with the long procession of all four classes, we in our caps and gowns, the Juniors in white, with a long, green chain of laurel, the Sophs. as "Kate Greenaways" and the Freshmen in all shades of yellow, from pale lemon to a rich old gold. It was perfectly lovely. And our dance, they said, was beautiful, and the Freshman dance was fine, but so elaborate that one couldn't take it all in at once.

Our class took supper over in a little natural amphitheatre by Miss Hazard's as her guests and had lots of good things to eat.

Today, after prayers here at the house, we went over to a preparatory service for communion, which Miss Hazard had requested all the Seniors to attend. Then we went to Chapel and heard a fine sermon by Rev. Artemas Haines of N.Y. (I think)

Ethel Moody came over to dinner with me. She has a teaching position for the next year in the Academy at Gilmanton, N.H. We are planning all sorts of visits back and forth. It is quite near, isn't it? *[Though Gilmanton, "as the crow flies," was indeed fairly near Milton Mills, as nearly all railroads and roads ran North and South, it was very difficult and a very long day's journey to try to go anywhere East or West, especially if Lake Winnipesaukee was in between. It probably would have taken a whole day, with several changes by train, and perhaps nearly two days by horse and buggy.]* Ethel is a very sweet girl and I know you will like her immensely. She is so simple and childlike and so pretty. I shall be glad to have her so near next year! And I do hope Louise can be, too. Tell me, Papa Fox, do you know of any vacancies at any of the schools in our area?

I'm really getting quite enthusiastic about teaching, myself and beginning to want a little to do so. Guess I'll have to organize a private school at home.

The Commencement invitations and announcements have come, also the tickets for the various things. I shall need $5.00 for those expenses.

Mrs. Mosher asked me to come Sat. for another fitting, but the Shakespeare Play comes that evening, so I shall try to arrange to go earlier. I have only one more recitation and possibly a Lab. period. Then, I expect, my class work at Wellesley will be over. Oh dear, I hate to think so; yet I am glad, too. And I'm sure you are.

Now, Muddie, when are you and Papa planning to come down? You, of course will come before he can, for I do want you to see college more as it normally is, before all the bustle of Commencement. I know Papa can't get away for that long, so I'll excuse him, tho' <u>very</u> unwillingly. I do wish you could be here for Float Night, a week from Tues. Won't you please try? It is so lovely. Just let me know when you will come and I will go in town to meet your train, Mamma. And Papa, can't you come Sat. the 15th for Baccalaureate Sunday? Please try to.

With stacks of love, Helen

June 8. My dear Mamma—

Yesterday morning I went to my last recitation here (if I don't get flunked out)! but I haven't realized it yet that it is such. In the afternoon, Mary and I went into town and I was at last successful in getting shoes—at Lambkin and Foster. They are tagged $1.75 and are very neat and pretty—a rather vivid yellow now, but all they had, and they darken very quickly. I also got ribbon for my lawn dress girdle, soft white Liberty satin.

After trotting around this A.M. trying to get my check cashed and spending it (that didn't take long) I got off announcements until I ran out of stamps. If I run out of announcements I can get more and it is all right to send them like wedding ones on the very day. So, please do send me more stamps for them. Everyone is using 2¢ stamps on them, as they are sealed.

Now what do you think the College has done to us—cut us down to <u>3</u> invitations to Commencement proper. This is for lack of room, as we are such a big class and so many alumnae are coming back! I think it is dirty mean! Of course you and Papa will have your two, but if Annie *[her best friend and schoolmate from home]* is planning to come down, I can't disappoint her at this late date so I shall have to offer Criss something else as a substitute. I hate to horribly, but as she wasn't certain she could come, she can't blame me too much. I shall suggest Bac. Sunday service, as that is almost like Commencement.

Oh, I'm so rushed and have so many things to think of, I feel as if I were standing on my head most of the time!

Your own "Little girl," Helen

June 10. My dear Mamma—

I'm at Melrose again. Winnie will have to charge me board! This time I came all the way on the electrics, leaving Wellesley at 11:30 A.M. and getting here about 2:00 P.M.! Enough car riding for one day. I had to wait as much as a half hour at different places.

I went to Mrs. Mosher's who wasn't expecting me until tomorrow, as my postal didn't reach her. However, I did try on my lawn, which will be very pretty and dainty.

Mamma, I'm so sorry you can't come for Float Night. It is so hard, when the other girls have their mothers here to think I must wait so late for mine! But, I do appreciate how hard it is for you both to get away, so I'll try not to fret.

I think, if you can come Saturday, A.M., you'd have plenty of time to rest before the Glee Club Concert at 4:00 P.M. Then go to Uncle James and Aunt Ada's, as you usually do and where you are most at home. They want you to make your headquarters there. Then you can rest and visit there with them Sunday, and come here for Vespers, rather than Bac. which is much like Commencement anyway. I think you'll enjoy Vespers more, and so would Uncle James and Aunt Ada.

Please let me know when and where to meet you.

With lots of love—Helen

June 12 . My own dear ones—

My last Sunday letter to you all this year. Of course I shall have to let Papa and Mama Fox know how things go, as they can't be here. How I wish you <u>all</u> could be!

I went to Melrose again and got to Mrs. M.'s about 2:00 P.M. My dresses are going to be very sweet, I think. I am to go out this Fri. for a final fitting, and will have them then.

Last evening was the "invitation" performance of the Shakespeare play. They are giving "Romeo and Juliet" this year. It was lovely; well acted and so effective with the rhododendrons in full bloom now and grand old oaks for a background. The calcium lighting of the set and the actors was very skillfully done.

Our sermon this morning at church was by a Rev. Mr. Dewarton on the holiness of what we call "common things."

Tues. evening is Float and I plan to have a "hen party" this year and invite Helen Lancaster and two of her friends. We are going to have a picnic supper, for which they are going to bring sandwiches and home-put-up grape juice and I shall provide olives, nuts and fruit.

For now—goodnight and heaps of love—Your own Helen

June 15 My dear Mamma—

I go Fri. A.M. for my last "try" at Mrs. M.'s and to get my dresses. I had planned to stay there overnight, at Winnie's, to go in town from there Sat. to meet you and bring you back to Wellesley with me. But—I learned today that I shall have to be <u>here</u> directly after Chapel Sat. morning to practice for Commencement so I shall have to come back Fri. night. As I don't know how long the practice will take, I think I'd better not plan to go into town, but meet you right at the station here. Papa will be along, and he knows his way. And bring Annie right along with you. There's a 1:15 train from So. Station. I enclose some train tickets for you.

Can't think of much else of importance, but will you please bring a small bottle of Listerine, a cake of Pear's soap and some of <u>my</u> <u>own</u> <u>money</u>.

Float Night was lovely, my people came, we had our picnic and a grand time.

I shall look for a note Fri. telling me of your final plans.

With tons of love—Helen

June 16. *[Postal]* Dear Papa—

Both the rest of the announcements and my pictures came today, so I am much relieved. The latter are quite a little better than the proofs. Shall look for news tomorrow as to exactly when to expect you.

Love to all—Helen

The Class of Nineteen hundred and four

Wellesley College

announces the exercises

of

Commencement Week

June eighteenth to twenty-first

Wellesley, Massachusetts

[Included: A card showing dates, times and places of events and speakers for the Baccalaureate Service and the Commencement Exercises and the card of Miss Helen Gertrude Fox.

Letters to Helen from home from May 23 on are missing (as are those from March 23 until May 23), so we have no record from this source regarding the back-and-forth discussion of just when her parents did eventually come down for the occasion or where they stayed and for how long. However, a look in her grandfather's diary for June 18, 1904, notes "Everett and Carrie left for Wellesley." So we do know that they did go to Commencement, at least. "Everett returned from Wellesley on the evening train—June 21st." Elbridge also records that "Helen Gertrude arrived home June 25, 1904."]

AND SO END
HELEN'S FOUR YEARS
AT WELLESLEY COLLEGE

AFTERWORD

After her graduation from Wellesley in June, 1904, Helen returned to the "blessed sameness," as her mother called it, of life in her home village and her place in the family circle. Not much had changed in the four years she had been away at college. Her father's tall "Dutch" windmill still cranked and creaked, pumping up water from the deep well for the household needs. Helen's hammock under the old apple tree still swung lazily in the breeze. Her mother's beloved flowers still brightened the yard. The old yellow cat was gone, but there was a new one—always a cat; her father loved them.

Papa was still very busy with the store and office, but Papa Fox, her grandfather, had been obliged to resign from the New Hampshire Senate, as his life-long asthma attacks continued to worsen and his health would no longer enable him to make the rigorous day-long trips to Concord, or board there during the weeks when the Senate was in session. Mama Fox, ten years older than her husband, was beginning "to fail" and was often confined to her bed. Helen's "precious Mamma" was overjoyed to have her daughter home again, both for companionship and for her help in "sweeping and dusting," as well as in keeping Mama Fox happy. They did not have full time help, only neighbors who came in when called, as Carrie still preferred to take care of her own household and to do her own cooking and baking on the old black iron range.

Soon after Helen's return, her father enlarged the house, adding a big, airy bedroom for Helen over the summer kitchen ell. And (thanks to the windmill, as the village still had no electricity), a fine new bathroom with a stained glass window over the tub. He also enlarged the bay window in the front parlor, put in a golden oak framed fireplace and bought a new piano for Helen to play. A long wrap-around piazza now crossed the front of the house, with a high, sit-on railing overlooking the Square. Here the family sat on hot summer afternoons, with a cold pitcher of fresh lemonade for any friends who stopped by to visit.

To be sure, the mill whistles still shrilled the start and the end of the village business days. Horses were tied up to hitching posts along the sidewalk; there were, as yet, no autos. No one was in a hurry.

Helen fell right back into place and probably wondered sometimes if she had dreamed Wellesley! However, her college friends came for visits and she visited them often. She went to Ayer when Nina married her Howard. She also spent much time with her various cousins and their families, even as far away as Washington, D.C., as her parents at last realized that she had become a young woman who could take care of herself. Helen also spent much time every summer at the Lancaster camp on Lovell Lake, with her "other Helen."

There was a large group of young people in the village, all old friends, who got together frequently for hay rides and picnics at the lake in the summer, and skating parties and sleigh rides in the winter. Skiing was still in Norway, but snowshoeing was easy, even with long skirts, and a fine way to explore winter woods. There were also plays, socials, musical evenings of various sorts and occasionally a "Ball."

There was no particular pairing off in the group. Helen's friends Charles Jones, home from Harvard, and Arthur Brackett, were still in the picture, along with several other young men. But not "Prof." Perhaps he had gone down to New York, as he had told Helen he planned to do. Not once in over two years does his name appear in Papa Fox's diary, either as calling at the house, or being present at any of the Nute affairs in Milton.

Then in the deep winter of 1906, there is a strange and cryptic entry: "Feb. 13, 1906. Mr. Arthur T. Smith, who has been living in Luther Roberts' Duck Farm building is reported to have left suddenly last night."

What was he doing there, alone, in such weather? Why in Milton Mills, when his family had lived in Milton? Why did he not call at the house? Did Helen know he was there? Did she see him? Why did he rush off?

The next entry in the diary is equally short and explicit: "Nov. 15, 1906. Helen Gertrude went to Milton this noon to attend the wedding of Arthur T. Smith and Orinda S. Dickey, returning about seven p.m."

Orinda was Helen's old schoolmate, Ora, and the daughter of Mr. Dickey, minister at Milton. Whatever happened between Helen and "Prof," if anything? We shall never know, but at least she went to the wedding.

One by one, Helen's friends and cousins were marrying. Even Charles Jones. Arthur Brackett still courted her determinedly but vainly. As the years went by, Helen told her father that if she wasn't married by the time she turned thirty, she would study Law (nearly an unknown field for women of that day.)

Then, in the summer of 1911, a man she had met previously, returned: George Carmichael, Bowdoin class of '97 and a fraternity brother of Jacob ("Jake") Wignot and a brother of Jake's wife, Lena. Mr. Wignot had been Principal of the Milton Mills School while Helen was in college, then moved on to another position. However, they had become fond of the village and had made many friends there. Now they were back to go camping at Lovell Lake, and George was with them. Lena had indeed tried hard to be a match-maker earlier, but to no avail; her brother's eyes were not dark brown like hers, but blue. "Not interested," Helen had said.

George Carmichael
at the time of his wedding

There was to be a big party at one of the lake cottages, and Helen went. This time, when they met, eyes, blue or brown, didn't seem to matter. Nothing mattered except that they must be together. But George, who was the founder and Headmaster of Brunswick School (for boys) in Greenwich, Connecticut, had to be back at his desk. Begun in 1902, it had grown fast. (Still growing in 2000, with over 700 boys, it is the second oldest country day school in the U.S.). He could not linger. Helen never told me, but I believe they were engaged before he left. He came up to New Hampshire for the long Labor Day weekend and stayed at the house, so they must have told her parents.

At Christmastime, he came for the whole vacation, and for the first time ever, they had a Christmas tree in the house! Mama Fox and Mamma adored him. Papa Fox and Papa approved highly and this time, they went to church together, making their engagement public.

However, in April of 1912, Papa Fox died, so they put off their wedding. But only until Christmas vacation, when George returned for his bride. They were married on Christmas Day of 1912 in the front parlor, and rode off to the train in an old truck strung with ringing cow bells to live happily ever after. That they did for 53 years, when George died in 1965 at the age of 89. Still in good health, Helen lived until 1971, when she slipped away at the age of 90.

I have been asked what did Helen "<u>do</u>" after graduation, before her marriage and after it? And for what organizations did she volunteer? College girls of that day were educated primarily to be wives. A few did some teaching before marriage; fewer still remained in that profession, virtually the only one always open to them. College women expected and were expected to marry well and most of them did, although not always necessarily for love.

Although she married late, Helen was fortunate; Her husband loved her deeply and called her his "Lady Golden Hair." The feeling was mutual. They were a perfectly matched pair. Helen was his consort and confidante, his behind-the-scenes partner in his concerns with his school. He valued her judgment and they always settled any problems together. They knew the value of compromise. Last, but far from least, they laughed together, often.

George was the <u>do-er</u>. Helen's part of the marriage was to supervise the smooth running of their warm, serene home—his haven. It didn't matter that she still had never learned to cook (anything other than the chocolate peppermints from college days); she always had plenty of household help, some of whom stayed on for many years, becoming almost like family.

Life in the Greenwich of that day, just before World War I, was as different from Helen's life in New Hampshire as that Greenwich was from the booming, crowded town it is today. It was, then, still a New England town, despite the homes of the wealthy ringing the shore-front of Long Island Sound. As the bride of George Carmichael, one of the leaders of the growing community, and as a graduate of Wellesley College, Helen was widely welcomed into society.

Friends and relatives were always welcome in their home. The big dining table at holiday time was always extended with all its extra leaves. Helen's mother usually made several trips down from the village of Milton Mills every year; Everett, her father, who hated going anywhere (unless he could drive in his big Chalmers touring car), usually could not be coaxed and was content at home with his cat.

When they were first married, Helen told me with amusement, they enjoyed dressing for dinner every night and spent many evenings making music together—she at the piano and George valiantly playing the violin, although he preferred his banjo and mandolin.

This idyll, however, came to an abrupt stop with my arrival and that of my brother. And with the United States entering World War I, a great many changes took place. Since George was over draft age, married and much needed in the community and the school, he was not called up, and carried on with all his civic projects, busier than ever. Among them was the burgeoning American Red Cross.

Like other wives, Helen joined the Red Cross too, and spent countless hours rolling bandages for the boys over in the trenches. At this time the majority of women were <u>not</u> <u>volunteers</u>. They were <u>joiners</u>—of various clubs and organizations according to their interests. Helen joined the Ladies Aid Society of the Congregational Church, where George appeared every Sunday as a Deacon in his swallow-tail black coat and pin-striped trousers. She also joined the D.A.R., the Y.W.C.A, the Travel Club and the College Club. I have no memory of any Garden Club until years later; in the future were the Friends of the Library, the Hospital or the Parent-Teachers groups. Those were spheres which were thought better left to the professionals who ran them. It would be years before women could vote, so they had little interest in politics. Few women knew how to drive automobiles, or change a tire—or wanted to know.

However, after getting together during that war, as often as they were needed for Red Cross work, women were never quite content just to stay at home again. Like "Rosie the Riveter" in World War II, They had given up their time to help greater needs than their own and found they could do it well, even without masculine supervision, and they liked it. The age of Volunteerism had begun, but it took another twelve to fifteen years to become widespread.

Helen, maturing in her new life, became the epitome of the typical Wellesley girl she had written about in her very first freshman theme. "There was a certain air about her of style, of good breeding, of charm and of graciousness and cordiality." And she was the kind of woman that L.B.R. Briggs, Dean of Harvard College, idealized in his graduation speech to the class of 1902; (see *Wellesley*, Fall, 1998).

"As the power, not on the throne, but behind it, as the leaven that lifts men to higher things, as the standard of unselfishness, devotion, purity and faith—" Those were the goals that Helen and her classmates strove for a hundred years ago.

George and Helen
in their 70s

APPENDIX

THE ELSIE AVERY STORY

Elsie Avery, Helen's classmate at Nute High School, was the only child of the Postmaster at Milton. The two girls had gone off to college on the same train in September of 1900; Elsie to Vassar and Helen to Wellesley. They had kept in touch, writing each other about their college experiences.

In January of 1902, some time after they returned to their respective schools from Christmas vacation at home, Elsie suddenly became extremely ill. After four days, the authorities at Vassar put her, alone, on the train for New Hampshire, via Boston.

This is the story as it unfolds through the letters of Helen and her parents about the event. It is a window into the health practices and beliefs of that day, and helps us to understand Helen's parents' constant worry and concern over sickness and their fear of "taking a cold." Like everyone else then, they believed a cold was caused by getting chilled or overexposed to cold or wet weather.

The theory of immunization, shots or vaccine, for contagious diseases, was just becoming known. People were advised to get vaccinated for smallpox. Diphtheria, typhoid, scarlet fever, measles, all the childhood diseases and consumption (tuberculosis) spread unchecked. No one really knew how, but thought it wise to avoid crowds and not to "take cold" or overwork.

Country areas did not have hospitals, and only a few overworked doctors. It took much time for country doctors to make their rounds by horse and buggy (or sleigh). It was said that Dr. Gross of Milton Mills had his old horse so well trained that after calling on all his patients, he could sleep all the way home and the horse would wake him when they were back in their own barn.

There was always much sickness in every village in the winter. Houses were overheated, shut up tight against fresh air, and full of dust and dirt brought in from unpaved streets, which had to be <u>swept</u> out. (There were good reasons for the annual "Spring Cleaning") There always seemed to be more accidents in the mills and in the woods, too. One of Helen's friends cut his leg badly; Dr. Gross sewed him up; he seemed to be getting better, but suddenly developed "consumption of the blood" and died. Two families lost children to diphtheria that winter.

After notifying her of Elsie's illness, Helen's parents refrained from mentioning it in their next few letters, realizing that she was beginning her midyear exams and the news would upset her badly. However, as Elsie's decline progressed, they felt they had to let her know.

Jan. 9, 02.

My dearest Helen: I'm not in the mood for writing and wish you could run in and we could talk instead. Mr. Wallace from Milton was in the store today. He says that Elsie Avery is very sick. She was taken sick on Thursday before she came home Monday. They have two nurses now and her father stays at the house most of the time. Her temperature is nearly 105° and she has hemorrhaged from the nose—lost about 2 quarts of blood at one time. I should think her quite seriously ill and they must feel very anxious about her. If she recovers, I guess it will be some time before she goes back to Vassar again.

I hope you will take warning and take extra care of yourself. We want to feel that we can trust you and not have to worry all the time.

Much love from us all, Mamma

Jan. 24, 1902. *[Postal]*

Nothing new—all well. Notice by the paper that Elsie Avery is home sick with typhoid fever.— Love, Papa

Jan. 26. My dear little girl,

Try to do your best on your coming exams, which we know you will do, but don't worry about it. I was to hear something about Elsie Avery today, but have not. I should doubt if she goes back to Vassar for some time, if at all, as this must be quite a drawback if she has to stay out long. I wonder if "Prof" *[Mr. Smith]* knows she is sick and if he will go to Milton to see her.

Write when you have time and postals when you don't.

With very much love—Mamma

Jan. 30, 02. *[Postal.]*

Just heard Elsie Avery is considered dangerously sick with chances against recovery. Her temperature holds at about 104° for the past 36 hours. Think it very doubtful if she gets up. Yours etc. E.F.F.

Jan. 30. *[Postal.]* Have you heard from Elsie recently? I really trembled when I went for my mail yesterday, for fear I should hear bad news— worse than the last time. I feel as though she will get well after all, and hope and pray so. Please let me know.

Stacks of love to you all. Your little girl, Helen

Feb. 1. My Precious Mamma—

I didn't get Papa's postal about Elsie until after my English exam, for which I'm glad, as it gave me such a shock. Poor Elsie, I can't tell you how I feel for her. It seems some way to strike dreadfully near home. Only a few weeks ago, we were both of us planning to come home, young and strong and with so much to look forward to. And now she is there <u>so</u> sick, while I am here well, strong and getting along well in my work, and happy. It doesn't seem quite fair, does it? When I think of her, as I do, many times a day, I just pray she may get well yet and thank God for all my blessings. Isn't there <u>any</u> chance for her? Of course, they must have all the doctors and nurses necessary, and it does seem so pitiful that it makes no difference.

Our lives have been so much alike this last year that it seems almost as if it were myself. *[Elsie was an only child, too.]* You may be sure, Mamma, that I will take extra care of myself in every way, so don't worry any more than you can help over it.

With worlds of love—Helen

Feb. 2. My dearest Helen:

Mr. Wallace was here from Milton yesterday and said that Elsie is even worse—her temperature being even higher, at 105 $^1/_2$ after a week or more of 104⁺. Papa arranged with the telephone operator at Milton to call him up today and he said she was about the same still. I hear *[her parents]* have depended only on their own doctor. I should think <u>he</u> would want to consult with some other physician, even if they don't.

[same evening] My dear Helen—

One thing I don't want you to do and that is to go on a 25¢ rush ticket to hear Paderewski. It simply is <u>unsafe</u> and don't do it. Wait until a better opportunity occurs. There is an element of danger to us in any trip you make to Boston and we really wish it was so far away that you would never see it, only as you go and come from home.

With tons of love, Papa

Feb. 4. My dear Helen:

Papa enquired of the Milton telephone operator this forenoon and he said there was no chance for Elsie to live. She is breathing and that is all. However, they <u>may</u> be mistaken, as we haven't heard since. Will let you know when there is any change. How terrible her parents must feel. And I should think Mr. Smith would feel badly, even if he didn't care for her <u>specially</u>, as she was one of his pupils. About one half of the people in town here are sick with the "grippe," Dr. Gross says, and he is sick himself, but can't take time to be. Papa Fox has been sick, too, but is better.

Much love from us all, Mamma

Feb. 4. *[Postal.]*

Learn there is no hope entertained for Elsie Avery's recovery. A very sad case. Think her trip home is largely responsible for her present condition.

Hurriedly, Papa

Feb. 5. *[Postal.]* Dear Papa—

Poor Elsie. I can hardly keep from thinking of her in the back of my mind. I <u>won't</u> lose hope even now. She must have a very strong constitution to bear such a high temperature for so long. I hope and pray it will carry her through.

Feb. 6. My dear, dearest Helen—

We heard this morning that Elsie was dead. No particulars yet, but she was still living late last evening, so she must have died during the night. I think her parents must have considered Elsie dangerously ill from the first, even if their daughter didn't realize it herself, as Annie said *[mutual school friend of Helen and Elsie.]* She said they'd had perfect confidence in their doctor and that the nurses thought he was treating her just as the eminent physicians in the city would treat the same disease. I expect her father and mother are heartbroken. Why don't you write them a little note.

I want you to take <u>extra</u> <u>care</u> of yourself. I worry when I think of you wearing only your suit jacket, fearing you may take cold. Dress extra warm underneath—put on an extra under-vest.

With very much love from us all—Mamma

Feb. 6. My dear "Muddie-Dee"—

For the last two evenings, I have reclined on my bed with the light hitched behind me, reading poetry—in the most deliciously lazy fashion imaginable. Yesterday, I laid in bed till 9:00 A.M., got up, dressed and took a walk over to College Hall. Then, when I tidied my room, I got my breakfast—hot cocoa, crackers and olives, and really feasted. Edna joined me, and the droll old Irish chamber-woman came in, so I made her sit down and have a cup of cocoa, too. She was highly tickled with the honor (and cocoa) and amused us with her funny talk.

Alice was studying Chem., and couldn't go for a walk, so I meandered over to Stone to see Bertha. I found the poor child laid up; she had cut her hand (right, of course) clear to the bone on a broken water pitcher. She was so nervous from the shock that she couldn't study for her Chem. which came this AM. Dr. Roberts was very good and let her dictate it to another girl, as she couldn't write, and she got on all right, as it was quite easy.

I rather hoped for a postal with news of Elsie today, but I hope no news is good news. She must have a good constitution to bear such a high temperature. I hope and pray it will carry her through.

With a heart full of love & a dozen kisses apiece—

Your own little girl, Helen.

Feb. 8. My Precious Mamma

You know, of course, that Elsie Avery is dead. When I came from my Latin exam this morning, I found a letter from Sue Haley waiting for me and thought it rather peculiar that she should be writing to me, but guessed it might be on Nute Alumni business. Sue says she died very peacefully—was unconscious at the last I should judge. She knew Mr. Smith when he came to see her. Oh, how sad it is and how terribly hard for them all. I cannot realize it.

When I woke yesterday morning about 6:00 A.M., I had a most peculiar feeling about Elsie, as though it would do no good to pray any longer for her recovery, but I thought it was merely because I was so tired.

I went down to the florist's and ordered some hyacinths and maidenhair ferns sent, this P.M. I thought Mr. and Mrs. Avery might be pleased to know I thought of them and was sorry, as I too, like Elsie, was away at college.

I had intended to go in town and see Maude Adams' play tomorrow, but somehow, it seems dreadful for me to be at the theatre at the time of Elsie's funeral. So I sold my ticket. The money will pay for the flowers. It is so little, but yet all I could do. I am glad I did not hear the news before my exam, as it has saddened me and must have unnerved me for that. I went over to see Alice [Dalrymple] and she took me out for a walk and through Mrs. Durant's greenhouse.

Miss Hazard came out of her rooms just as I came down the stairs to lunch today, so we went in together. She spoke of the weather for the last exam day and I said I was all through. "And did you get through comfortably, Miss Fox?" she said. She was so sweet about it that I thought it lovely of her. I told her, "Yes, I think so." And I think I did very comfortably, though I'll knock on wood under the table and not boast much until I get my card back.

With no end of love—Helen

Feb. 10. My dearest Helen,

They had a cold, bleak day for the funeral. We hear that Mrs. Avery is quite prostrated, and I am not surprised. They have put Elsie in the receiving tomb until Spring. I am very glad that you thought to send flowers. I heard that Mr. Smith was in Milton twice to see Elsie. I think he was there the night she died and presumably stayed to the funeral. Someone said they sent for him.

We don't like the idea of your going into Boston very often while small pox is still raging. We notice new cases spoken of nearly every day. You are not immune against the disease in a light form, even though you have been vaccinated, and would have to be quarantined, just as if you had the real thing. [Helen's mother had smallpox when very young and, I believe, lost at least one of her siblings from the disease.]

Be careful about taking cold and take care of your eyes.

Papa adds: Glad you sent flowers to the Averys and hope you will write to them, certainly a very proper thing for you to do.

Tons of love—Papa

Feb. 12. *[Letter from Miss McClary to Helen.]*
Mr. Dickey conducted Elsie's funeral and several times referred to Mr. Smith as her "lover;" indicating that he indirectly loved her a great deal more than people here have thought, and I am very glad of it. Ora, *[Dickey—Helen's school mate]* is having quite a hard time. She was vaccinated four weeks ago and isn't able to walk yet.

Feb. 19. Dear Mama Fox—
Winter is back—about eight inches of snow in all, someone said, and drifting. I did not go out until 4:30 to get my mail.

I received a note from Frank Lee, saying he'd be glad to come Saturday; a note from Mrs. Avery thanking me for the flowers I sent; an invitation to a Colonial Dance, March 3, and an advertisement. Plus Mamma's letter and the *Rochester Courier.*

I turned at once to the notice of Elsie's death. It is certainly a beautiful tribute. It does sound like Mr. Smith, but I hardly think he would feel like writing it if he cared so much for her.

I enclose a collar I made for you, which should look very sweet over black or white.

A dozen kisses apiece—Helen

Feb. 20. *[Excerpt from Mamma's letter to Helen.]* Mr. Coles, here to go over the Milton checklist of voters with Papa Fox, has been working with Mr. Avery in the Milton P.O. the last few weeks. He said Mr. Avery is not at all reconciled to Elsie's death and thinks she met with an untimely death. He blames the Vassar people for sending her home, instead of notifying them to go over to her. As I understood, they didn't know of her coming, until just as she was on the way. They must have had <u>some</u> word, or her father couldn't have met her part way. They kept her in bed with ice on her head for four days and their doctor here said it was almost sure to prove fatal to move a typhoid fever patient. (Our Dr. told us the same thing). I don't wonder they feel unreconciled. I sincerely hope that <u>you</u> won't fall ill, but if you should, have some one notify us at once.

Feb. 24. My dear ones—

I should have written last evening, had I not had company—<u>Mr. Smith</u>! I don't believe you are any more surprised than I was. Louise and I had gone for a walk over to Hunnewell's and didn't get back till supper time, She wanted me to stay to supper, but as I had a letter to write, I came directly home. Not being hungry, as we had been snacking earlier, I had just settled down at my desk when Edna came dashing up from the dining room, exclaiming "Oh, Helen, your <u>best</u> <u>beloved</u> is downstairs," I laughed and asked who, then she crossed her heart that he was, and had been there for an hour. Of course, I went down then, and could hardly believe my eyes when I found Mr. S. in the parlor.

He said he didn't think of coming himself, until about 15 minutes before he started, but had nothing to do (<u>better</u>, I suppose!), so thought he would come out. Well, it happened to be Musical Vespers, so I had no lack of entertainment. He enjoyed them very much, he said, Then we went to walk down past Mrs. Durant's (it was too lovely to come directly in), then came back and I showed him the Legenda and my exams! We talked of almost everything save Elsie's death. I just didn't know what to say about it to <u>him</u>, not knowing exactly how matters stood, so thought I'd let him begin and he didn't.

Frank says he doesn't think at all that they were engaged, and Mr. S. has been out there since last Sunday and, you know, always tells Mrs. Lee everything. He certainly didn't act last evening as though it were so. I am glad for his sake, for of course it will not be so hard for him. He is looking well and seems almost as jolly as ever. I was surprised and just a little grieved, for I think he <u>ought</u> to feel it, since she cared so much for him. But of course, he might not want to show it to everyone.

Well now, the funny part comes. He knew all about Frank's coming out (at least so Frank told me) and <u>pretended</u> not to. Frank walked up when he came out and I said, "How did you ever know the way?" He said, "Oh, Mr. Smith told me." Frank didn't wear a dress suit because Mr. S. said last evening, "I didn't know as I'd find you." I said, "<u>Last</u> night was the Glee Club Concert, I had Mr. Lee out." "Oh, Frank?" he said, very innocent. I am afraid he doesn't understand why I didn't ask him, and how can I tell him. I imagine he thinks it's because he didn't come Xmastime, so came to make his peace.

I am well and happy, but <u>perplexed</u>. Your own little girl, Helen